Lecture Notes of the Institute for Computer Sciences, Social Informatics and Telecommunications Engineering 203

More information about this series at http://www.springer.com/series/8197

Eng Tseng Lau · Michael K.K. Chai
Yue Chen · Oliver Jung
Victor C.M. Leung · Kun Yang
Sandford Bessler · Jonathan Loo
Tomonori Nakayama (Eds.)

Smart Grid Inspired Future Technologies

Second EAI International Conference, SmartGIFT 2017
London, UK, March 27–28, 2017
Proceedings

 Springer

Editors

Eng Tseng Lau
Queen Mary University of London
London
UK

Michael K.K. Chai
Queen Mary University of London
London
UK

Yue Chen
Queen Mary University of London
London
UK

Oliver Jung
Austrian Institute of Technology
Vienna
Austria

Victor C.M. Leung
University of British Columbia
Vancouver, BC
Canada

Kun Yang
University of Essex
Colchester
UK

Sandford Bessler
Austrian Institute of Technology
Vienna
Austria

Jonathan Loo
Middlesex University London
London
UK

Tomonori Nakayama
University of Tsukuba
Ibaraki
Japan

ISSN 1867-8211   ISSN 1867-822X (electronic)
Lecture Notes of the Institute for Computer Sciences, Social Informatics
and Telecommunications Engineering
ISBN 978-3-319-61812-8   ISBN 978-3-319-61813-5 (eBook)
DOI 10.1007/978-3-319-61813-5

Library of Congress Control Number: 2017945284

Printed on acid-free paper

This Springer imprint is published by Springer Nature
The registered company is Springer International Publishing AG
The registered company address is: Gewerbestrasse 11, 6330 Cham, Switzerland

Preface

We are delighted to present the proceedings of the second edition of the 2017 European Alliance for Innovation (EAI) International Conference on Smart Grid Inspired Future Technologies (SmartGIFT). This conference brought together researchers, developers, and practitioners around the world who are leveraging and developing smart grid technology for a smarter and more resilient grid. The theme of SmartGIFT 2017 was "Smart Grid Inspired Future Technologies: A Smarter and More Resilient Grid."

The technical program of SmartGIFT 2017 consisted of 27 full papers, including four invited papers in oral presentation sessions at the main conference tracks. The conference tracks were: Track 1—Communications, Networks and Architectures; Track 2—Smart Control and Operation; Track 3—Grid and Components; and Track 4—Data Management and Grid Analytics. Aside from the high-quality technical paper presentations, the technical program also featured two keynote speeches, one invited talk, and two technical workshops. The two keynote speeches were Dr. Barry Rawn from Brunel University of London, UK, and Dr. Ian Llewellyn from the Department for Business, Energy and Industrial Strategy, UK. The invited talk was presented by Prof. Anurag Srivastava from Washington State University, USA. The two workshops organized were the Improving the Robustness of Urban Electricity Network (IRENE) of a JPI Urban Europe and Wireless Communications and Networking Technologies for Connected Smart Grids (WCSG). The IRENE workshop aimed to address the new dimension of threats in critical infrastructures through demonstration of IRENE methodologies and approaches. The WCSG workshop aimed to gain insights into key challenges, understanding, and design criteria of employing wireless technologies to develop and implement future smart grids-related services and applications.

Coordination with the steering chairs, Imrich Chlamtac, Victor C.M. Leung, and Kun Yang, was essential for the success of the conference. We sincerely appreciate their constant support and guidance. It was also a great pleasure to work with such an excellent Organizing Committee team and we thank them for their hard work in organizing and supporting the conference. In particular, the Technical Program Committee, led by our TPC co-chairs, Dr. Jonathan Loo, Dr. Sandford Bessler, and Dr. Eng Tseng Lau, who completed the peer-review process of technical papers and created a high-quality technical program. We are also grateful to the conference managers, Barbara Fertalova for her support, and all the authors who submitted their papers to the SmartGIFT 2017 conference and workshops.

We strongly believe that the SmartGIFT conference provides a good forum for all researchers, developers, and practitioners to discuss all scientific and technology aspects that are relevant to smart grids. We also expect that the future SmartGIFT conference will be as successful and stimulating, as indicated by the contributions presented in this volume.

May 2017

Eng Tseng Lau
Michael Chai
Yue Chen

Conference Organization

Steering Committee

Imrich Chlamtac	CREATE-NET and University of Trento, Italy
Victor C.M. Leung	University of British Columbia, Canada
Kun Yang	University of Essex, UK

Organizing Committee

General Chair

Victor C.M Leung	University of British Columbia, Canada

General Co-chairs

Michael Chai	Queen Mary University of London, UK
Oliver Jung	Austrian Institute of Technology, Austria
Yue Chen	Queen Mary University of London, UK
Kun Yang	University of Essex, UK

Technical Program Committee Co-chairs

Eng Tseng Lau	Queen Mary University of London, UK
Sandford Bessler	Austrian Institute of Technology, Austria
Jonathan Loo	Middlesex University, UK

Workshop Chair

Alexandr Vasenev	University of Twente, The Netherlands

Publicity and Social Media Chair

Chunsheng Zhu	University of British Columbia, Canada

Sponsorship and Exhibits Chair

Valerie Livina	National Physical Laboratory (NPL), UK

Publications Chair

Tomonori Nakayama	University of Tsukuba, Japan

Posters and PhD Track Chair

Qingping Yang	Brunel University London, UK

Local Chair

Eng Tseng Lau   Queen Mary University of London, UK

Web Chair

Anhtuan Le   Lancaster University, UK

Conference Manager

Barbara Fertalova   European Alliance for Innovation (EAI)

Technical Program Committee

Khan Ferdous Wahid	Airbus Group, Germany
Islam Bayram	Qatar Environment and Energy Research Institute, Qatar
Hông-Ân Cao	ETH Zurich, Switzerland
Stephan Cejka	Siemens, Germany
Deepak G.C.	Lancaster University, UK
Amin Khodaei	University of Denver, USA
Peng-Yong Kong	Khalifa University of Science, Technology and Research, UAE
Shunbo Lei	University of Hong Kong, SAR China
Qinghua Li	University of Arkansas, USA
Hui Lin	Fujian Normal University, China
Hieu Nguyen	Iowa State University, USA
Prashant Pillai	University of Bradford, UK
Haile-Selassie Rajamani	University of Bradford, UK
Harold Chamorro	KTH Royal Institute of Technology, Sweden
Emanuele Lindo Secco	Liverpool Hope University, UK
Boon-Chong Seet	Auckland University of Technology, New Zealand
Haijun Zhang	BUCT, China
Haozhe Wang	University of Exeter, UK
Chunbo Luo	University of Exeter, UK
Christoph Ruland	University of Siegen, Germany
Daisuke Mashima	Advanced Digital Sciences Center, Singapore
Paul Smith	AIT, Austria
Sandford Bessler	AIT and University of Technology, Vienna, Austria
Rasmus Pedersen	Aalborg University, Denmark

Contents

IRENE Workshop

WCSG Workshop

Communications, Networks and Architectures

On the Impact of Using Public Network Communication Infrastructure for Voltage Control Coordination in Smart Grid Scenario

Kamal Shahid[1(✉)], Lennart Petersen[2], Florin Iov[2], and Rasmus L. Olsen[1]

[1] Department of Electronic Systems, Aalborg University, Aalborg, Denmark
{ksh,rlo}@es.aau.dk
[2] Department of Energy Technology, Aalborg University, Aalborg, Denmark
{lep,fi}@et.aau.dk

Abstract. This paper focuses on the impact of using the existing public network communication infrastructure for online voltage control support and coordination of renewable generation (ReGen) plants in medium voltage distribution systems. The communication network infrastructure and related communication protocols have introduced several test scenarios and cases that are evaluated with respect to the related latencies and validity of the signals being exchanged between a control center and the ReGen plants. An exemplary benchmark grid area in Denmark, including flexible ReGen plants, is used as a base case for evaluating the network performance in terms of latency. The main outcome of this study is to provide a generic overview of the aspects and their effects related to the use of existing public network communication infrastructure for online coordination of voltage control in a distributed system, considering the huge ReGen penetration, in order to ensure a resilient voltage controlled distributed systems.

Keywords: Communication · Public network · ReGen plants · Coordinated control

1 Introduction

The Danish Government has a target to use 50% of renewable energy by the end of 2020, while making this to be a 100% by 2050. This goal is anticipated to be accomplished by a large scale integration of wind power plants (WPPs) and solar photo-voltaic plants (PVPs) in the medium voltage (MV) distribution system. The high penetration of these ReGen plants into the distribution systems may cause a reverse power flow and depending on the amount of generation and consumption, this will lead to rise in voltage levels. In order to deal with such problems, there are several solutions proposed, for instance, reactive power control using capacitor banks and inductors [1], on-load tap changer (OLTC) transformers at substations [2] and advanced power electronic devices based solutions for voltage control [3]. These solutions either have issues with the power quality, cause a huge percentage of failures or are too expensive for a large scale deployment. However, a simple solution proposed in [4] is the provision of reactive power support from the existing ReGen plants in the distribution grid. This will not only make

© ICST Institute for Computer Sciences, Social Informatics and Telecommunications Engineering 2017
E.T. Lau et al. (Eds.): SmartGIFT 2017, LNICST 203, pp. 3–14, 2017.
DOI: 10.1007/978-3-319-61813-5_1

it possible to down-regulate the entire voltage profile in the distribution system, but also keep the voltage within the limits at the given nodes.

Grids connection requirements for ReGen plants also necessitate the provision of reactive power support, which is offered by today's ReGen plants. However, this capability is not utilized by Distribution System Operators (DSOs), mainly due to the lack of technical infrastructure to communicate and control these units. The DSOs in Denmark have already started to install and deploy SCADA systems [5], but, controlling the ReGen plants may not be feasible in long term due to lack of regulatory framework. It is foreseen that aggregators of these ReGen units may take the responsibility, in close cooperation with local DSOs, for hosting voltage control capabilities besides the energy trading. An ancillary market for the provision of voltage/reactive power provision is also expected in the near future [6]. Thus, the needs for coordination in providing reactive power support and hence controlling voltage locally on a distribution grid is required in respect of the increasing number of dispersed units. This service may be provided by the same aggregators which nowadays are trading renewable energy or may be in the responsibility of the DSOs. Therefore, at this stage, we consider that it is the Aggregator control unit that is responsible for providing reactive power support and controls the voltage locally on the distribution grid.

Nevertheless, the coordination between ReGen plants and the Aggregator imposes high responsibility on the ICT infrastructure. Although implementing a reliable, high speed connection, e.g. fiber optics, to all ReGen plants in the grid seems the best possible option, but this being very expensive considering the huge penetration of ReGen plants, is not feasible. There exist several other options too, as detailed in [7, 8], but the idea is to use an already existing infrastructure that offers low operating costs, faster deployment, high speeds, flexibility and provide full expertise and manning to operate the network. Nowadays, cellular networks (e.g. UMTS, LTE) are already widely deployed by the telecom operators in Europe with high coverage [9]. Therefore, this paper focuses on the use of the existing cellular network communication infrastructure, e.g. owned by Tele Denmark Communication (TDC), as a base case and outline its impact on the online voltage control and coordination functionalities for ReGen plants in distributed grids. The outcome of this study serves as a generic guidance on the use of existing public network infrastructure to coordinate the voltage-stability support capabilities of ReGen plants in a distribution system with large ReGen penetration in order to ensure a resilient voltage controlled distribution system.

The control of power systems over cellular networks has been addressed in several papers. In [10, 11], the authors focus on the latency requirements of delay-critical operations in medium voltage grid. They perform an assessment of latency and reliability for LTE technology under various load conditions. The work is based on conducted field trials using IEC-61850 standard. The authors conclude that LTE, in general, fulfills delay and reliability requirements of medium voltage grid applications. However, the authors in [10, 11] do not focus on the voltage control coordination in particular considering the high penetration of ReGen plants in the power grid. [12] provides a comprehensive survey investigating the challenges and propose architectural and protocol improvements of cellular technology to support NAN applications in a smart grid scenario. The authors propose a redesign of current LTE cellular networks to enable autonomous and automatic interactions for smart energy systems, with emphasis on enabling mission-critical applications.

The remainder of this paper is organized as follows: Sect. 2 explains the voltage control coordination scenario in power distribution systems, highlighting several ways and challenges to connect ReGen plants to the Aggregator control unit. The challenges related to the online voltage control coordination in the MV grid are outlined by exemplary test cases in Sect. 3. In Sect. 4, time domain analysis is performed to test the impact of using public network infrastructure for online voltage control coordination. The conclusion of this study and future work is given in Sect. 5.

2 Power System and ICT Challenges

2.1 Voltage Control Coordination in Power Distribution Systems

One of the challenges in power systems is to keep the voltage profile within the desired tolerance band margins, stipulated by the so-called Grid Code requirements that need to be fulfilled by any generation unit being connected to the power system. In MV distribution grids the voltage has to remain within ±10% of its nominal value [13]. If these limits are violated at certain points within the grid, affected generation and consumption units need to be disconnected, which can eventually lead to severe stability problems in the entire power system. One way for a single ReGen plant to contribute to voltage regulation is realized by a local voltage controller as shown in Fig. 1.

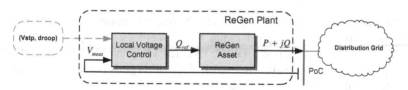

Fig. 1. Voltage control scheme of ReGen plant [4]

The ReGen plant has an inner control loop for regulating reactive power provision at the Point of Connection (PoC) and an outer voltage control loop for controlling the voltage in the PoC. A typical droop function is to be configured for the ReGen plant controller, i.e. a voltage reference point V_{stp} and a droop value needs to be specified. It has been ascertained in [4] that it is sufficient to introduce these settings once as an off-line initial system analysis in order to achieve satisfactory voltage regulation within the tolerance band margins.

However, there can be other control objectives imposed by the DSO, e.g. to reduce the grid power losses which are caused by reactive power provision. This can be achieved by optimizing the control settings in a so-called distributed on-line coordination scheme [14]. Since the power output of ReGen plants varies continuously and thereby the voltages in the distribution grid, an Aggregator of grid support services may take over the task to update the controller settings of the ReGen plants continuously in real-time according to the actual operating point.

The involved actors of such coordination scheme are illustrated by means of Fig. 2. The DSO needs to provide the system parameters of the distribution grid. The Aggregator receives measurement signals of voltage, active and reactive power $(V_{meas}, P_{meas}, Q_{meas})$ as well as the available reactive power (Q_{ava}) from all ReGen plants $(1...N)$ and dispatches the droop settings (V_{stp}, droop) for the voltage controllers.

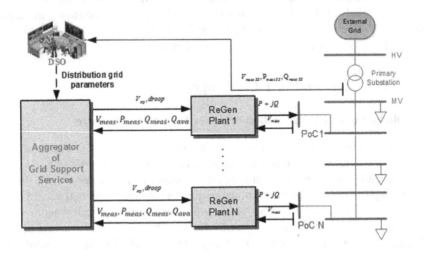

Fig. 2. Scheme for distributed on-line coordination of voltage control functionalities

In this study, an MV distribution grid in the Northern Denmark is used as benchmark test model. It represents a typical radial feeder topology with primary substation (60/20 kV) and four ReGen plants (WPP, PVP 1, PVP 2 and PVP 3), accounting for realistic penetration of renewables in Danish distribution grids in the future (see [4] for more details of the benchmark grid model).

2.2 Communication Network Infrastructure

In order for a ReGen plant to have online coordination with an Aggregator control unit, it should be connected to the Internet via some Internet Service Provider (ISP). This lets the ReGen plant to exchange information with all of the other accessible controllers/ ReGen plants on the Internet. Since here as a base case we are considering the public mobile networks as ISPs, there are, therefore, a number of ISPs available. The ISP used by the ReGen plants can, thus, be different with that used by the Aggregator. The ISPs are usually distinguished by the amount of bandwidth they provide, the service cost and most importantly, the connectivity.

An ISP network consists of long distance transmission lines that interconnect routers at Point-of-Presence (POP) in different cities that the ISPs serve. This equipment is called the backbone of the ISP. If an information packet is destined for a device directly served by the ISP, it is routed over the backbone and delivered to that device. Otherwise, it must be handed over to another ISP [15]. The ISPs are connected to rest of the Internet through Internet eXchange Points (IXP) and exchange information [16]. Thus, for devices on different networks to communicate, the communication traffic needs to go through an IXP, even though the devices are physically right next to each other. These ISPs are said to peer with each other, having a bilateral agreement [16] for the provision of a certain service level. Therefore, in the existing implementation, this change of ISP networks will not have significant effect and the delay may increase up to a few tens of milli-seconds (ranging between 10–50 ms above the normal delay) [17].

Furthermore, in the given benchmark grid scenario (see Sect. 2.1), the Aggregator control unit can be placed at the local primary substation or anywhere else in Denmark. The distance between ReGen plants and the Aggregator, however, can be one of the external influences on latency as well as other communication properties described in [18]. The voltage control information being time critical can, therefore, be effected by the time the signal takes to go from a ReGen plant to the aggregator and a set-point/ reference signal from Aggregator to the ReGen plant. Since the ISPs are deploying faster network technologies [17], e.g. 3G, LTE/4G and HSPA+ etc., this enables higher data transfer rates and quality of service for the network users, and makes the users accustomed to have high speed networks and capable devices. Still, for the heterogeneous networks that are usually shared by a large number of users and data exchange is exposed to stochastic non-controllable delays and packet drops, extra delays can be expected in long distance communication.

2.3   Communication Network Model

In order to get a realistic and accurate model of the network behavior within the benchmark grid area, a system called NetMap [17] is used. NetMap is a mobile-network performance measurement system based on crowd sourcing, which utilizes end user smart devices to automatically measure and gather network performance metrics on mobile networks. The measured metrics include throughput, round trip times, connectivity, and signal strength, accompanied by a wide range of context information about the device state [17]. It offers a Network Performance Map (NPM) based on actual measurements on existing networks using actual end user devices in real end user scenarios. The NPM shows what network performance to expect and provides a more realistic image of what the end system can expect as the measurements are performed with similar devices [17]. According to the NMP in [17], the throughput provided by the existing public network infrastructure is sufficient enough to support voltage control coordination in the said scenario. Therefore, in this paper we base our analysis on the latency a signal might incur while going from the ReGen plants to the aggregator controller (and vice versa) and other connectivity related issues to see the impact on the performance of voltage controller.

NetMap gives the measure of latency in the form of Round Trip Times (RTT) measured using a large number of end devices located at different distances from the Aggregator control unit. Figure 3 shows the real time RTT measurements based on around 3500 TCP-RTT measurement sequences at different distances/locations of the end devices from the Aggregator control unit using different ISPs. These measurements have been obtained over a period of one and a half year with varying number of end devices.

It can be observed in Fig. 3 that for the maximum cases, RTT lies within the range of 30 ms approximately, which means that a minimum of 15 ms delay (half of RTT – assuming the same route for request and reply to/from the server) in the transfer of information update can be expected for the maximum times in daily operations. We, therefore, take this as a normal base case for our future evaluation. However, this network being heterogeneous (and shared by a large number of users), the delay may increase depending on the network conditions. In the worst case, this delay may jump up to 500 ms (RTT), as seen in Fig. 3.

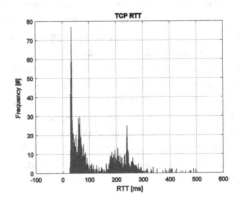

Fig. 3. Distribution of TCP RTT measured around the benchmark region

3   Link Layer Failure

In public wireless communication networks, despite of having several communication masts (base-station) nearby, the ReGen plant usually connects to the nearest communication mast having the strongest signals. While associated with a mast, a plant controller periodically measures the strength of a beacon signal from its nearest mast as well as beacon signals from nearby communication masts that it can hear. These measurements are reported once or twice a second to the controller's current mast [15]. A handoff occurs when an aggregator controller changes its association from one communication mast to another while communicating with any ReGen plant controller.

The handoff occurs due to several reasons, for instance: (a) current communication mast fails to operate, (b) the signal between current communication mast and the plant controller deteriorate to such an extent that the connection between a ReGen plant controller and the aggregator controller is in danger of being dropped or (c) cell becomes overloaded, handling a large number of users [19]. This situation can be dealt by handing off the connected stations to less congested nearby cells. It is worth mentioning that a handoff between masts results not only in the controller transmitting/receiving to/from a new mast, but also in the rerouting of the ongoing communication from a switching point within the network to the new mast. All this would ultimately add to the delays in sending update information from a ReGen plant controller to the aggregator control unit and set-points from Aggregator to ReGen plants.

Therefore, we consider here a test case where, for instance, the radio connection of a plant controller with its base station (cell) suddenly fails. This failure can be due to equipment failure, radio link failure or any other problem within the base station. During such failures, there exist two possibilities: (a) the area is covered by other cells or (b) the area is not covered by other cells.

3.1 The Area Is Covered by Other Cells

The end system detects that there is a problem at the physical layer, when it is out of synchronization for a certain number of consecutive times defined in a parameter set by ISP [20]. A common value of this parameter is 20 times [20]. After detecting a physical layer problem, the user equipment (UE) starts a timer configured by ISP (a typical value is 2 s. [20]). If it recovers synchronization with the serving cell, it resets the timer and everything continues as it was (the recovery was possible). However, if it does not succeed, UE initiates the whole process, look for a suitable cell, connection setup and so on. Putting in nutshell, the whole process may take few seconds to minutes, depending on the severity of the problem.

3.2 The Area Is not Covered by Other Cells

In such a case, the service remains disrupted until the same mast is fixed or communication link is recovered. The delay in service outages may vary from few minutes to hours depending upon the type of problem incurred.

While considering the worst cases, it is worth mentioning a problem seen a couple of years back in Norway at part state-owned telecoms firm Telenor that left around 3 million users without coverage for up to 18 h, caused by a signal storm [21]. Although rare, but such outages must also be considered when targeting to design resilient communication systems.

From the above discussion and the test-cases defined, it can be remarked that the network architecture/setup can introduce signal delays in the range of milli-second to seconds, while failures in communication may impose latencies in the range of minutes up to hours, depending on how severe the failure is. Table 1 summarizes the latencies in communication, resulting from all considered test cases.

Table 1. Resulting performance metrics for test cases

Test cases	Category	Latency (RTT)
Base case	Normal	30–50 ms
	Worst	500 ms
Link layer failure	Normal	Seconds to few minutes
	Worst	Minutes to several hours

4   Assessment of Voltage Control Coordination

As mentioned in Sect. 2, distributed voltage control can increase the power losses in the grid due to reactive power loadings of the lines. The total power losses occurring in the cables/lines are evaluated based on the total active power generation by the ReGen plants in a certain distribution grid, as given in 1:

$$P_{loss,tot,\%} = P_{loss,tot} \cdot 100\% = \frac{\sum P_{loss}}{\sum P_{gen}} \cdot 100\% \tag{1}$$

According to [14], continuously updating the voltage set-points (see Fig. 2) for the ReGen plants is the only effective option to improve the proposed distributed control concept with regard to the power losses within the grid. The idea behind this control concept is that nominal voltage with $V_{stp} = 1\ pu$ does not necessarily have to be targeted, as long as the voltage remains within the tolerance band margins of $\pm 10\%$. Thus, as long as the measured voltage does not exceed a certain critical point, the voltage set-point can be enhanced to avoid unnecessary reactive power support, hence avoiding additional power losses. In this context, the update rate of the voltage set-point will have an impact on the average power losses over a certain time period. A more detailed description of this control concept will be given in a separate publication.

4.1   Impact of Latency

The latencies introduced by the communication network lead to delays of measurement signals being sent from the ReGen plants to the Aggregator as well as delays of reference signals being set from the Aggregator to the ReGen plants. The results obtained in [10] show that, for adjusting the voltage set-point, various update rates in the range of seconds to minutes have a minor impact on the resulting power losses within the grid. Hence, with regard to the obtained latencies for the test cases in the communication network (Table 1), it can be remarked that RTTs in the time range of seconds to minutes would not affect the control performance significantly. As, for instance, if the maximum signal delay in worst case reaches to 500 ms (Fig. 3.) is negligible, assuming that the update rate of the voltage set-point is minimum 10 s.

4.2   Impact of Link Failures

Even if a communication failure in the network sustains for several minutes, the local voltage controller of the ReGen plant will apply the last sent set-point, which results in negligible deviations in the power losses in the distribution feeder. However, as revealed in Sect. 3, under certain circumstances connection failures up to several hours can occur which may affect the power losses more significantly. These communication problems can be due to a failing communication mast without having any available back-up cell. For this, taking into account different test cases, we evaluate the extent to which the latencies in communication up to several hours will affect the on-line coordination of voltage control functionalities in distribution grids.

Test Cases. For testing long-lasting communication failures, a benchmark test scenario with a time frame of 24 h is applied [14]. Four test cases are considered in terms of hours of delay caused due to communication failure i.e. 1 h, 6 h, 12 h and 24 h.

Test Results and Analysis. Figure 4 shows the line losses expressed as percentage of the total generated power by all ReGen plants, averaged over the simulation period of 24 h, with and without various communication failures. It can be observed in Fig. 4 that the power losses increase for longer communication failures. The blue-colored bars show the power losses without any voltage control. However, in this case the tolerance band margins of the voltage (±10%) are not fulfilled. Then, voltage regulation with maintained settings for the ReGen plant controllers (off-line, red-colored) leads to a considerable increase of the power losses. By introducing distributed on-line coordination (no fail., green-colored), the losses can be reduced to a significant extent. However, the power losses increase depending on the duration of the communication failure in the system.

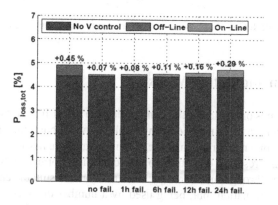

Fig. 4. Average power losses over the simulation period for various durations of communication failure for updating the voltage set-points (Color figure online)

An exemplary voltage profile for a communication failure persisting for 12 h is depicted in Fig. 5. The resulting depression of the voltage profile between 6 a.m. and 6 p.m. is not required as the voltages are sufficiently below the upper limit of 1.1 pu, implicating an undesirable rise in the power losses. After occurrence of the failure at 6:20 a.m., the last sent voltage set-point will be applied during the faulty period. This results in significant reactive power provision, since the voltage set-point is not anymore updated according to the voltage measurements, hence increasing the power losses in the system.

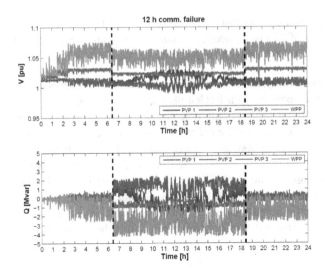

Fig. 5. Voltages of all ReGen plants over one day for a communication failure occurring between 6 a.m. and 6 p.m.

5   Conclusion and Future Work

This paper elaborates on the impact of communication on on-line voltage control coordination in distribution grids using existing public network communication infrastructure. The use of public network communication infrastructure has various aspects associated to it that may result in deviating voltage control performance in the distribution grid. Although, the throughput offered by these networks is suitable enough to support voltage control coordination; but, being used by a number of users at the same time, unexpected/unwanted delays in information exchange may incur. Therefore, several test cases are introduced and evaluated with respect to the related latencies and validity of the signals being exchanged between Aggregator and ReGen plants. According to the results, delays in communication in the range of seconds to minutes have a minor impact on the resulting power losses. However, the delays up to several hours may lead to higher power losses in the grid, increasing the cost of energy which is eventually recovered by the end-consumers of electricity.

In this paper, we only focus on the use of existing public network infrastructure, which leads to the direction of studies in future. For instance, cost estimation to employ these cellular networks for voltage control coordination and then comparing it to the cost of employing other communication networks, such as cable networks. Secondly, securing networks when used in critical infrastructures is crucial. Therefore, the impact of adding security to the information exchange on the controller's performance will also be explored as a next step.

Acknowledgments. This work was carried out by the Department of Electronic Systems in cooperation with the Department of Energy Technology at AAU. Energinet.dk is acknowledged for funding this work in contract number: PSO project 2015 no. 12347, "Ancillary Services from Renewable Power Plants (RePlan)", www.replanproject.dk.

References

1. Cutululis, N., Andrej, G., Keane, A., Hulle, F.V., Holttinen, H.: D2.2 - Ancillary services: technical specifications, system needs and costs (2012)
2. Dohnal, D.: On-Load Tap-Changers for Power Transformers. Maschinenfabrik Reinhausen GmbH (2013)
3. Smartgrid-komponenter til distributionsnettet: Produktkatalog (2014)
4. Petersen, L., Iov, F., Hansen, A.D., Altin, M.: Voltage control support and coordination between renewable generation plants in MV distribution systems. In: Proceedings of the 15th Wind Integration Workshop (2016)
5. Nyt SCADA System - IT sikkerhed og Smartgrid. Net-Sam SCADA A/S, Fredericia, Denmark, November 2013
6. Pineda, I., Wilczek, P., Van Hulle, F.: Economic grid support services by wind and solar PV, September 2014
7. Kuzlu, M., Pipattanasomporn, M., Rahman, S.: Communication network requirements for major smart grid applications in HAN, NAN and WAN. Comput. Netw. **67**, 74–88 (2014)
8. Yang, H.S., et al.: Communication networks for interoperability and reliable service in substation automation system. In: 5th ACIS International Conference on Software Engineering Research, Management Applications (SERA 2007), pp. 160–168 (2007)
9. Study on broadband coverage in Europe (as of 2014), Digital Single Market (2014). https://ec.europa.eu/digital-single-market/en/news/study-broadband-coverage-europe-2014
10. Maskey, N., Horsmanheimo, S., Tuomimäki, L.: Analysis of latency for cellular networks for smart grid in suburban area. In: IEEE PES Innovative Smart Grid Technologies, Europe, pp. 1–4 (2014)
11. Horsmanheimo, S., Maskey, N., Tuomimäki, L.: Feasibility study of utilizing mobile communications for Smart Grid applications in urban area. In: 2014 IEEE International Conference on Smart Grid Communications (SmartGridComm), pp. 440–445 (2014)
12. Kalalas, C., Thrybom, L., Alonso-Zarate, J.: Cellular communications for smart grid neighborhood area networks: a survey. IEEE Access **4**, 1469–1493 (2016)
13. ENTSO-E Network Code for Requirements for Grid Connection Applicable to all Generators. ENTSO-E, March 2013
14. Petersen, L., Iov, F., Shahid, K., Olsen, R.L., Altin, M., Hansen, A.D.: Voltage control support and coordination between ReGen plants in distribution systems. WP2 Deliverable D2, Aalborg, Denmark (2016)
15. Kurose, J.F., Ross, K.W.: Computer Networking: A Top-Down Approach, 6th edn. Pearson, Boston (2013)
16. DIX - Danish Internet eXchange point. http://www.dix.dk/faq/#4. Accessed 21 Nov 2016
17. Mikkelsen, L.M., Thomsen, S.R., Pedersen, M.S., Madsen, T.K.: NetMap - Creating a Map of Application Layer QoS Metrics of Mobile Networks Using Crowd Sourcing (2014)

18. Petersen, L., et al.: D1.1 - Specifications for ReGen plant model and control architecture, Deliverable D1.1, December 2015
19. Tanenbaum, A.S., Wetherall, D.: Computer Networks, 5th edn. Pearson Prentice Hall, Boston (2011)
20. ETSI 3rd Generation Partnership Project (3GPP), Technical Specification - ETSI TS 136 331 V13.2.0, August 2016
21. Signal storm' caused Telenor outages. http://www.newsinenglish.no/2011/06/16/signal-storm-caused-telenor-outages/. Accessed 21 Nov 2016

Energy Management Using a Situational Awareness-Centric Ad-Hoc Network in a Home Environment

Tannaz Monajemi, Ardavan Rahimian, and Kamyar Mehran[✉]

School of Electronic Engineering and Computer Science,
Queen Mary University of London, London, E1 4NS, UK
{a.rahimian,k.mehran}@qmul.ac.uk

Abstract. Energy management theory and techniques for home environments are facing several technical challenges in areas including the real-time scheduling, power distribution, and automation of network of home appliances/renewables for achieving maximum energy efficiency. In this paper, situational awareness (SA) has made this crucial decision making process more efficient, by providing the valuable data about the surrounding environment. In a smart home, apart from the electrical appliances, the intelligent sensors are also consuming energy while transmitting data or when they are in idle mode. In this contribution, our focus is on implementing and analysing a situational awareness-based ad-hoc network in a home environment, in order to reduce the energy consumption, and therefore, increasing the lifetime of these networks. The presented results demonstrate the effectiveness of the proposed SA-centric method, and further confirm the energy consumption in the intended environment is decreased dramatically due to the applied schedule and limitations on the working hours of the devices. Moreover, the sensors are switched to doze mode when there is no data to exchange.

Keywords: Ad-hoc network · Home energy management · Situational awareness

1 Introduction

The energy consumption in wireless networks is recently undergoing an intense study, and several methods and architectures are proposed to manage the energy usage in these ubiquitous networks. Wireless energy analysis, measurement, and management based on the situational awareness (SA) strategies tries to explore the elaboration of schemes for the efficient distributed computing and monitoring of the execution of plans, based on the high-performance techniques [1]. Furthermore, the SA-centric schemes are also employed for the efficient deployment of a number of strategic applications, including the cybersecurity [2, 3], Internet of things (IoT) and big data [4–6], power systems and smart grid [7–14], and computer, communication, and mobile networks [15–18].

There are various questions that SA aims to answer. Some of these questions are about choosing the sensors' allocation method (i.e., dynamically or statically) in mobile ad-hoc networks (MANETs), and the way data can be potentially collected from these

© ICST Institute for Computer Sciences, Social Informatics and Telecommunications Engineering 2017
E.T. Lau et al. (Eds.): SmartGIFT 2017, LNICST 203, pp. 15–24, 2017.
DOI: 10.1007/978-3-319-61813-5_2

sensors through the specified monitoring algorithms, such as the threshold- and value-monitoring. Other questions concerning how to achieve a certain level of SA using the information provided by monitoring methods, and how to mine the collected data using the mining algorithms incorporating the online analytical mining (OLAM) techniques, as well as the stream computing. The aim of this investigation is to demonstrate that a situational awareness-based system could be a very powerful and efficient solution to manage the energy allocation of an ad-hoc infrastructure within a home environment, and to extend the lifetime of batteries used in the employed wireless sensor networks (WSNs). Decision making process is a very challenging task within this platform, since the SA server has to conduct the prediction of the next optimum state of each node, as well as the most efficient path between any source and destination node. Accomplishing these intended objectives is viable using the real-time and accurate data provided by the intelligent sensors utilised as part of the deployment of the SA-centric platform.

2 MANETs and Medium Access Methods

In order for the defined terminals to be able to communicate within a multiple access network over a shared medium, channel access control mechanisms are required which are provided by the medium access protocol (MAC) within the infrastructure. At first, random access protocols did not check the channel availability before any transmission. After some enhancements, another random access method called carrier sense multiple access protocol (CSMA) was proposed, in which nodes sense the transmission medium before exchanging any data. In order to overcome the stumbling blocks of the previous protocols, multiple access with collision avoidance (MACA) protocol was proposed. In this method, two kinds of short-frames are used. The node that plans to transfer its data sends request to send (RTS) message, and the destination node replies by sending the clear to send (CTS) message to clarify that it can receive the data. The neighbour nodes would then recognise these messages, and would not send any data during the intended transmission over the channel. Furthermore, IEEE 802.11 MAC is also designed for a single channel, and network performance and spatial reuse of the wireless channels can take place by using the directional antennas and multiple channels. The newly proposed protocol is called multichannel MAC protocol with directional antennas (MMAC-DA) that benefits from IEEE 802.11 power saving mechanism (PSM). The nodes exchange controlling packets via announcement traffic indication message (ATIM) to choose a data channel and detect a beam direction for exchanging a traffic. This protocol results in a better throughput, packet delivery, and efficient energy consumption, as well as a proper fairness in the network. Each node has two transceivers in a way that one is used for exchanging the controlling packets, and the other is used for data transmission in various channels. This protocol enhances the spatial reuse of a wireless channel, as well as saving the energy of wireless nodes. Moreover, using the bidirectional antennas can also improve the spatial reuse of the medium channels. In order to improve the network capacity, directional network allocation vector (DNAV) is then employed instead of the NAV and by using the circular direction RTS in MAC (CDR-MAC), RTS is transmitted in a directional consecutive fashion, which helps the receiver to identify the location of the sender; then the receiver replies by sending a directional CTS (CTS-MAC) message in the exact direction of the received RTS. All the directional RTS/CTS messages are sent in the multihop directional MAC (MMAC). The sender uses the multihop RTSs in order to set up a connection to the particular destination, then they exchange CTS, data, and ACK in directional mode over a single hop. Considering the RTS/CTS messages, nodes can collect information about the location of their neighbours, the angle of arrival (AoA), as well as the received signal power, so that they could predict the direction and distance of the intended destination, and to form a beam toward it. The time structure of IEEE 802.11 PSM is used to divide time into beacon intervals where each beacon is divided into ATIM window and data window. There are two types of channels in this model, including a controlling channel (CCH) and data channels (DCHs). In previous models, free data channels were wasted since all the nodes had to be on the CCH during the ATIM window. In comparison, the new model allows for the nodes to employ the DCH during the ATIM window. During a high load of the network, some nodes are exchanging controlling packets over the CCH, while others are transmitting data on the chosen DCHs, i.e. the transmission can be extended to the next ATIM window [19].

3   Overview of Situational Awareness

Situational awareness (SA) was first proposed during World War I by Oswald Boelke who defined it as "the importance of gaining an awareness of the enemy before the enemy gained a similar awareness, and devised methods for accomplishing this". More specifically, in an engineering and technical context, SA is defined as the perception of

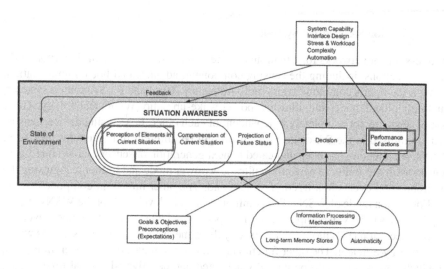

Fig. 1. The generalised model of application-specific situational awareness (This picture is adopted from [12], but customised for our proposed SA-centric framework for energy management in a home environment.), highlighting the primary domain of the focused investigation for the energy management layered framework.

elements in the environment within a volume of time and space and the comprehension of their meaning and a projection of their status in the near future (i.e., Fig. 1) [1, 12].

Wireless sensor networks have been widely employed in diverse environments from battlefields to remote dangerous volcanic areas, to collect appropriate and accurate data and therefore, SA has provided real-time information for better decision making. As such, in order to tackle cyber-attacks, enterprises are benefiting from cyber situational awareness framework based on OODA (i.e., observe, orient, decide, and act) technique [3]. Automatic identification system (AIS) is also employed as the collision avoidance mechanism in the maritime situational awareness by which ships send their presence, identification, and location [21]. Deploying wide-area situational awareness (WASA) for power grids has provided valuable data that is used for monitoring, archiving, and envisioning the state of the dynamic system via connected sensors [7]. In spite of the key role of the monitoring and tracking capabilities in emerging business opportunities, IoT has not been adopted as expected, due to the specific requirements of the systems. In 1999, Tim Bass proposed the cyberspace situational awareness (CSA) concept [5]. In addition, SA is used in WSN that can be formed in a hierarchical framework in which the cluster heads are responsible for a number of tasks including the routing, connection to other clusters and neighbours, and monitoring and administration of the nodes [6]. Dealing with the missing data, by using the information available in an environment where the SA is deployed, interpolation is the best way in order to estimate the missing data for a short period of time, while historic load features are more beneficial when dealing with lost data in a longer time [9]. The other usage of information collected in the SA-centric system is to present the connections of the components of the network using a weighted directed graph, in which the measurements of incidental values are calculated by analysing the mobility of an observer which is moving stochastically from one component to the other, based on the deployed ambient intelligence scenario [18].

3.1 WSNs for SA-Centric Systems

Wireless sensor networks for situational awareness (WSN-SA) systems incorporate six primary sections, including the sensing component, advanced ad-hoc communication, through-the-debris communication, radio frequency (RF) band for SA-centric systems, dual-operational mode, and ultra-low power wake-up radio (WOR) technology. These components are not completely independent of each other. In a sensing device, sensors that are utilised in the SA-centric systems might be different from the ones utilised in WSNs. An attention has been dedicated to next generation of sensors, called intelligent sensors with the ability to perform in ultra-low power mode and further recognising the environmental events in a fraction of a second. The other important component is the dual-operation mode of WSNs. The common protocols developed for the WSNs mainly require nodes to be woken-up several times per second which makes the nodes work in the full-operation (FO) mode, and is exactly the same as the original SA systems which is not energy-efficient. The other functionality mode is called a limited-operation (LO), in which a network would be virtually activated and deactivated several times a day, and nodes would exchange their states to the main SA server in order to examine the intrinsic health of the network. Switching between the FO and LO modes is conducted by commands via a base station (BS). When a disaster is recognised by the local nodes, the efficient environmental deployed sensors are forced to switch to the FO mode.

3.2 Network Design and Performance Analysis

As mentioned earlier, the focus of this investigation has been mainly on the design and performance evaluation of a situational awareness-based ad-hoc network employed for the purpose of reducing the energy consumption in a home environment, which results in the potential increase in the lifetime of these networks. In a smart home environment, the overall energy consumption, denoted as E_t, can be calculated as a combination of the energy used by the home appliances (i.e., E_a), and the energy that sensors consume while they are awake sensing the environment and conducting the data transmission, as well as the consumption rate while in their idle or doze modes (i.e., E_s). Therefore, the total energy consumption in the intended environment can be expressed as follows:

$$\overset{Total}{\rightarrow} E_t = E_a + E_s \tag{1}$$

The SA servers play the most critical roles in the process, since they are considered as the primary decision makers. The most crucial information is provided to these servers by the intelligent sensors so that they can make the most appropriate decisions in a real-time manner. Once the decision is made, the SA server would provide the sensors with the optimum time for the data exchange, best route to the required destination, and list of the neighbours and their location, as well as the angle that each node has to conduct the beamforming during the data exchange process. In addition, to find the pattern of the energy consumption, the SA server would not require the utilised intelligent sensors to be awake continuously, but at certain times of the day that could reduce the energy consumption by the sensors. The SA server would allocate a schedule for each sensor node in order to sense the surrounding environment in the FO mode and after that when no packets are exchanged, nodes would be forced to switch to the LO mode. Hence, by switching to the LO mode, the network would have deactivated and activated several times a day. The sensor nodes consume various amount of energy according to their corresponding status. The intelligent sensor consumes 1.65-W, 1.4-W, and 1.15-W, when functioning in the transmission, reception, and idle modes, respectively [19, 20]. The first simulated scenario shows the energy efficiency enhancement in the SA-centric ad-hoc network versus the conventional ad-hoc network in which nodes that have no packets to exchange would switch to doze mode, in contrast with the idle mode in IEEE 802.11 while facing the same situation. The total number of sensors are 100, data packet size is 512 bytes, packet arrival rate increases over time up to 100 packets per second, and network energy efficiency is calculated using Eq. (2). The upper- and lower-bound network throughputs are considered as 80% and 20%, respectively. In each of these conditions, due to the network topology, various proportion of the nodes might contribute in routing the packets from a source to a destination. The probability of nodes contributing in a routing process varies from 0.3 to 0.6, and each node provides various results for the overall network energy efficiency, as presented in Figs. 2(a) and (b).

$$Network\ Energy\ Efficiency = \frac{Total\ Energy\ Consumption}{Number\ of\ Delivered\ Packets} \qquad (2)$$

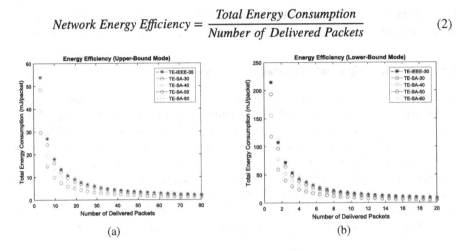

(a)   (b)

Fig. 2. Energy-efficiency plots for the upper- and lower-bounds of the proposed SA-centric ad-hoc system, based on the total energy consumption and number of delivered packets.

According to the presented simulations, implementing the situational awareness-centric ad-hoc network has reduced the network's energy consumption, based on the employed sensors being forced by the SA server to switch into the doze mode, when they do not have any packets to exchange. The intended optimum network performance in both conditions, considering the upper- and lower-bounds, are achieved when the nodes with the cooperation probability of 0.3 are routing the packets. In all the scenarios, energy consumption in the SA-based network is less than the conventional ad-hoc network. As also mentioned earlier, in the newly proposed protocol (MMAC-DA), time is divided into the beacon intervals and at the start of each beacon there is an announcement traffic indication message (ATIM) window; each beacon is divided into an ATIM window and a data window. The controlling messages are transmitted via the CCHs, and the data is transferred by the DCHs. The protocol benefits from the PSM, and has further enhanced it so that more simultaneous packets could be sent over the multiple channel resources. This process is accomplished by using a controlling channel as a data channel during a data window. In the presented simulated scenario, the SA server schedules the beacon interval, ATIM window, and data window. At the start of the interval, the source node (S) checks the status of the destination node (D), and if available, it would send the ATIM message to the destination node in order to perform the channel negotiation, and to provide the information about the transmission power, as well as to detect the beam direction. By analysing this message, node D would understand the beam direction to node S, and would select a data channel. Also, node D sends the ACK message to node S clarifying the chosen data channel and beam direction. Receiving this message, node S confirms the selected channel and beam direction by sending the ATIM reservation (A-RES) message. Once this stage is completed, both nodes S and D would transmit a directional reservation message (DRES) to each other, as the last stage prior to the initiation of the data exchange process. Neighbour nodes would further overhear these handshaking messaged between S and D, and would then update their CUL.

In the data window, S and D would switch to the selected data channel to exchange data and the other nodes would switch to the doze mode in which they consume less energy (i.e., 0.045-W), rather than the defined idle mode. In addition, when the traffic load of the network increases, controlling channels can be used as data channels during the data window, which further results in more successful packets being transferred from the source to the intended destination. This result in the substantial increase in the overall efficient system performance in the SA-based ad-hoc network. Figures 3(a) and (b) presents thoroughly, the simulated scenario, in which the total simulation time is 10 s, and the packet size and number of nodes are 512 bytes and 100, respectively. Also, the total number of channels are 3. The probability of packets being successfully delivered in each channel considering both the lower- and upper-bounds are 0.55 and 0.85. The network throughput is calculated based on the following Eq. (3), which is increased significantly using more channels for the data exchange operation.

$$Network\ Throughput = \frac{Packet\ Size \times Number\ of\ Delivered\ Packets}{Total\ Simulation\ Time} \tag{3}$$

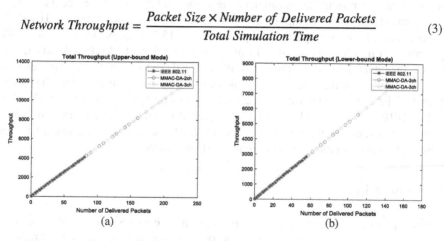

(a)   (b)

Fig. 3. Network throughput plots for the upper- and lower-bounds of the proposed SA-centric ad-hoc system, based on the throughput and number of delivered packets.

The SA server indicates the beacon interval, and then at the start of the ATIM window, the source and destination would initiate the handshaking process using the controlling channel. At the start of the next beacon interval, the SA server would force the utilised sensors to employ this controlling channel in addition to the predefined data channels. This process would result in the increase of the channel's spatial reuse in the intended environment. Consequently, more packets are being transmitted simultaneously, based on the soft-real time (SRT) network framework (i.e., the ability to withstand a certain amount of delay) [22]. Moreover, for the appliances to reduce the energy consumption, they need to use energy only in specific hours of the day. As a case in point, when no one is in the house, the cooling system, television, and lights should be switched off. Detecting this event (i.e., nobody being present in the house), the sensor would activate its cluster head (CH); i.e., the SA node in the hibernation mode; and then would report this waste of energy in that specific surrounding area. Afterwards, the SA node would wake up its CH (i.e., the SA server) via transmitting the beacons specified for this task, for conducting the data transmission. The server would process the data and if required, it would ask for more information from that area of the house, to make decisions.

Hence, by collecting the adequate amount of information, the applied SA server would decide which appliances to switch off. This task is conducted by the supervisory SA agent in the various areas of the house that would give the command to the intelligent sensors to switch off these appliances, which results in an efficient energy consumption. Furthermore, there are a number of factors that should also be taken into account while deploying the physical (PHY) layer elements, for the efficient energy transmission in the network. As a case in point, the path loss elements should be considered (i.e., link budget planning) while the intended scenarios are deployed in a real environment [23]. To demonstrate a functionality assessment of the proposed SA framework, a scenario is considered and analysed, which consists of three utilised intelligent sensors in a home environment controlling the operation of a television, a fan, and a fluorescent light bulb in a room. The power consumption of the utilised devices is 0.06, 0.05, and 0.01 kWh, respectively, and the average electricity unit price is 15.5 pence per kWh. Sensors with power supply of 5-V and current of 14-mA, consume 7.5×10^{-7} kWh in the idle mode. Hence, the total energy consumption of all electrical devices within an hour would be 0.120225 kWh. Assuming the energy could be saved by this mechanism for 3 h per day; as part of the considered SA-centric scenario; at the end of the year, 131.646375 kWh and 21 GBP could be saved. Therefore, by connecting other electrical appliances in a home environment to the proposed SA-centric ad-hoc network, the overall power consumption over a year, would be significantly decreased.

4   Conclusion

We have proposed the thorough design and performance analysis of an ad-hoc network based on the situational awareness framework. The proposed architecture has reduced the energy consumption in a home environment, for the purpose of implementing a regulated and efficient home energy management framework. Moreover, the presented SA platform improves the functionality of wireless networks by providing valuable information about the appropriate way of distributing resources, and also predicts the feasible risks, resulting in a more efficient energy consumption. This investigation can be extended into the case of network modelling and performance analysis based on the SA-based game-theoretical security enhancement, and adaptive dynamic programming (ADP)-based system realisation, within a real-time large-scale architecture.

References

1. Howard, N., Cambria, E.: Intention awareness: improving upon situation awareness in human-centric environments. Hum. Centric Comput. Inf. Sci. **3**, 1–17 (2013)
2. Franke, U., Brynielsson, J.: Cyber situational awareness – a systematic review of the literature. Comput. Secur. **46**, 18–31 (2014)
3. Lenders, V., Tanner, A., Blarer, A.: Gaining an edge in cyberspace with advanced situational awareness. IEEE Secur. Priv. **13**, 65–74 (2015)
4. Wu, J., Ota, K., Dong, M., Li, J., Wang, H.: Big data analysis-based security situational awareness for smart grid. IEEE Trans. Big Data (2016)
5. Gendreau, A.A.: Situation awareness measurement enhanced for efficient monitoring in the internet of things. In: IEEE Region 10 Symposium (TENSYMP), pp. 82–85 (2015)
6. Gendreau, A.A., Barrios, R.M.: Hierarchical-based measurement of situation awareness in the internet of things. In: International Conference on Wireless Networks (ICWN) (2014)
7. Basu, C., Padmanaban, M., Guillon, S., Cauchon, L., De Montigny, M., Kamwa, I.: Situational awareness for the electrical power grid. IBM J. Res. Dev. **60**, 10:1–10:11 (2016)
8. He, X., Qiu, R.C., Ai, Q., Chu, L., Xu, X., Ling, Z.: Designing for situation awareness of future power grids: an indicator system based on linear eigenvalue statistics of large random matrices. IEEE Access. **4**, 3557–3568 (2016)
9. Peppanen, J., Reno, M.J., Thakkar, M., Grijalva, S., Harley, R.G.: Leveraging AMI data for distribution system model calibration and situational awareness. IEEE Trans. Smart Grid **6**, 2050–2059 (2015)
10. Giri, J., Parashar, M., Trehern, J., Madani, V.: The situation room: control center analytics for enhanced situational awareness. IEEE Power Energ. Mag. **10**, 24–39 (2012)
11. Chen, H., Zhang, L., Mo, J., Martin, K.E.: Synchrophasor-based real-time state estimation and situational awareness system for power system operation. J. Mod. Power Syst. Clean Energy **4**, 370–382 (2016)
12. Panteli, M., Kirschen, D.S.: Situation awareness in power systems: theory, challenges and applications. Electr. Power Syst. Res. **122**, 140–151 (2015)
13. Dahal, N., Abuomar, O., King, R., Madani, V.: Event stream processing for improved situational awareness in the smart grid. Expert Syst. Appl. **42**, 6853–6863 (2015)
14. Alcaraz, C., Lopez, J.: WASAM: a dynamic wide-area situational awareness model for critical domains in Smart Grids. Future Gener. Comput. Syst. **30**, 146–154 (2014)
15. Wang, C., Lin, H., Zhang, R., Jiang, H.: SEND: a situation-aware emergency navigation algorithm with sensor networks. IEEE Trans. Mob. Comput. (2016)
16. Eiza, M.H., Owens, T., Ni, Q., Shi, Q.: Situation-aware QoS routing algorithm for vehicular ad hoc networks. IEEE Trans. Veh. Technol. **64**, 5520–5535 (2015)
17. Rolim, C.O., Rossetto, A.G., Leithardt, V.R.Q., Borges, G.A., Geyer, C.F.R., dos Santos, T.F.M., Souza, A.M.: Situation awareness and computational intelligence in opportunistic networks to support the data transmission of urban sensing applications. Comput. Netw. (2016)
18. Roy, S., Dhal, R.: Situational awareness for dynamical network processes using incidental measurements. IEEE J. Sel. Top. Sig. Process. **9**, 304–316 (2015)
19. Dang, D.N.M., Nguyen, V.D., Le Tra, H., Hong, C.S., Choe, J.: An efficient multi-channel MAC protocol for wireless ad hoc networks. Ad Hoc Netw. **44**, 46–57 (2016)
20. Silva, A.R., Liu, M., Moghaddam, M.: WSN-SA: design foundations for situational awareness systems based on sensor networks. In: IEEE Global Humanitarian Technology Conference (GHTC), pp. 179–184 (2013)

21. Papi, F., Tarchi, D., Vespe, M., Oliveri, F., Borghese, F., Aulicino, G., Vollero, A.: Radiolocation and tracking of automatic identification system signals for maritime situational awareness. IET Radar Sonar Navig. **9**, 568–580 (2015)
22. Mehran, F., Rahimian, A.: Physical layer performance enhancement for Femtocell SISO/MISO soft real-time wireless communication systems employing serial concatenation of quadratic interleaved codes. In: 20th Iranian Conference on Electrical Engineering (ICEE), pp. 1188–1193 (2012)
23. Rahimian, A., Mehran, F.: RF link budget analysis in urban propagation microcell environment for mobile radio communication systems link planning. In: International Conference on Wireless Communications and Signal Processing (WCSP), pp. 1–5 (2011)

Interference Assessment for the Spectrum Sharing Between IMT-2020 and Inter-satellite Service

Bo Li[1], Zhaojun Qian[2], Shuaijun Liu[1], Chaowei Wang[1],
Yinghai Zhang[1], and Weidong Wang[1(✉)]

[1] Information and Electronics Technology Lab,
School of Electronic Engineering, Beijing University of Posts
and Telecommunications, Beijing, China
{libol993,wangchaowei,zhangyinghai,
wangweidong}@bupt.edu.cn, lsj_bupt@163.com
[2] The State Radio Monitoring Center, Beijing 100037, China
qianzhaojun@srrc.org.cn

Abstract. This paper analyzes interference coexistence of IMT-2020 (International Mobile Telecommunications-2020) and inter-satellite service where both systems operate in the same spectrum band of 25.25–27.5 GHz. This work can be regarded as a good reference to the research community, industry and regulators which are currently investigating spectrum requirements and technology options for 5G system. Considering the interference scenario between the return inter-orbit link of data relay satellite system and downlink of IMT-2020, we adopt realistic system parameters and radiation pattern, combined with very recent channel from the literature. Simulation results indicate that the interference from IMT-2020 downlink to Data Relay Satellite (DRS) is above the interference level while the LEO spacecraft cause acceptable interference to IMT-2020 downlink.

Keywords: IMT-2020 · Inter-satellite service · Data Relay Satellite (DRS) · Spectrum sharing · Interference coexistence

1 Introduction

The development of IMT for 2020 and beyond is expected to enable new use cases and rapid traffic growth, for which contiguous and broader channel bandwidths would be desirable. This suggests the need to consider spectrum resources in higher frequency ranges [1]. In order to update frequency allocation decisions and other conditions of use of the radio spectrum at the global level, the World Radiocommunication Conference (WRC) is held every two to four years. WRC-15 agenda revolution 238 considers frequency related matters for the future development of IMT-2020 including possible additional allocations to the inter-satellite services on a primary basis of 25.25–27.5 GHz band. However, this band has been allocated on a co-primary basis to inter-satellite service, thus making it necessary and meaningful to study the coexistence of IMT-2020 and inter-satellite services.

© ICST Institute for Computer Sciences, Social Informatics and Telecommunications Engineering 2017
E.T. Lau et al. (Eds.): SmartGIFT 2017, LNICST 203, pp. 25–34, 2017.
DOI: 10.1007/978-3-319-61813-5_3

Inter-satellite communication has become an important research topic to improve communication signal system and ranging method [2]. It can ensure high speed transmission and high bandwidths. Moreover, it can be multi-layered network, which supports flexible large scale network structure. The unique advantages of inter-satellite links make it play a more and more important role in military and civil communication field. The 25.25–27.5 GHz band is used by the inter-satellite service for transmission from low-orbiting satellites to receivers onboard geostationary DRS [3]. The sharing between DRS systems and other space and terrestrial radio systems is required in all of the preferred frequency bands, identified in [4]. As the numbers of space and terrestrial radio systems using the same bands will increase in the future, this will increase the potential of interference situations.

25.25–27.5 GHz band belongs to the mmWave frequency ranges. Recent studies demonstrate the feasibility of mmWave mobile communications using multiple antenna arrays in order to compensate for propagation losses at high frequencies [5]. Study of coexistence between 5G small cells and Fixed Service (FS) at 39 GHz is done in [6], where required frequency rejection is given for tolerable interference on FS resulting from IMT-2020. The spectrum sharing between IMT-2020 and Fixed Satellite Service (FSS) at 28 GHz is simulated in [7]. However, few studies have addressed on spectrum sharing of IMT-2020 and inter-satellite service. It is then important to study the coexistence between inter-satellite service and cellular network to understand whether IMT-2020 operating within these frequencies may affect the inter-satellite service. Similar investigations have been proposed by the International Telecommunication Union (ITU) for spectrum sharing between inter-satellite service and fixed service. The technical and operational requirements that facilitate sharing between point-to-point systems in the fixed service and the inter-satellite service in the 25.25–27.5 GHz are demonstrated in [8].

Different from the literatures above, we both analyze the interference scenario of terrestrial networks to GSO satellite and LEO spacecraft to terrestrial networks. We consider the propagation model, antenna radiation patterns and parameters provided by ITU, 3GPP and other newest publications. Existing work can be guide on our study, but still many challenges are still undergo. In this work, first we verify the interference scenario of IMT-2020 and clarify interference cases in detail. Then we analyze the single point interference and lumped interference. Using the illustrated method, we simulate interference scenario and evaluate interference level.

This paper is organized as follows, Sect. 2 describes the model considered focusing on the interference scenario, interference calculation model and propagation model. Section 3 gives the interference analysis method. Section 4 provides the simulation parameters and gives the performance evaluation. Section 5 concludes the paper.

2   System Model

2.1   Interference Scenario

In this section, we discuss reference system for data relay satellite system and sharing scenario between inter-satellite service and IMT-2020.

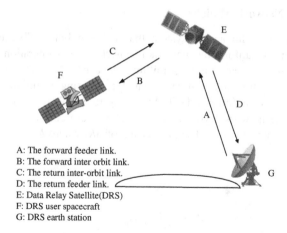

A: The forward feeder link.
B: The forward inter orbit link.
C: The return inter-orbit link.
D: The return feeder link.
E: Data Relay Satellite(DRS)
F: DRS user spacecraft
G: DRS earth station

Fig. 1. Data relay satellite system

Figure 1 shows the reference system for data relay satellite system. According to the ITU-R Recommendation SA.1018 [9], the reference system for data relay system should consist of four cases:

(a) The forward feeder link, from the earth station to the data relay satellite.
(b) The forward inter orbit link, from the data relay satellite to the low-orbiting spacecraft.
(c) The return inter-orbit link, from low-orbiting spacecraft to the data relay satellite.
(d) The return feeder link, from the data relay satellite to the earth station.

We assume that IMT-2020 system is sharing the 25.25–27.5 GHz band with inter-satellite service. This frequency range is the operating frequency of the return inter-orbit link where the DRS user spacecraft is in mainly low-earth orbit and the data relay satellite is GEO. To assess whether the frequency band can be allocated to the inter-satellite service and the IMT-2020 system on a primary basis, we consider the interference between IMT-2020 downlink and the return inter-orbit link as is depicted in Fig. 2. Therefore two interference links will be discussed in this paper, that is

(e) The interference from IMT-base station to data relay satellite.
(f) The interference from DRS spacecraft to the UE.

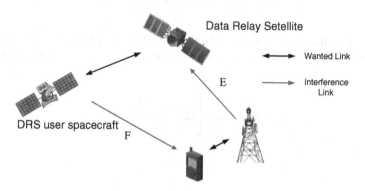

Fig. 2. Sharing scenario between IMT-base station and data relay satellite

2.2   IMT-2020 Network Model

IMT-2020 is a multi-radio access system that will combine LTE and 5G features (i.e., multi-antenna, beamforming, new radio interface, and operation at higher frequencies) [10]. Since the wavelength of millimeter wave frequencies are very small, so it will utilize polarization and different spatial processing techniques like massive MIMO and adaptive beamforming [11]. According to 3GPP, we mainly refer to LTE deployment and the network layout as Fig. 3. The macro cell network is a tri-sector layout placed on a hexagonal grid with distance of $3R$, where R is the cell radius.

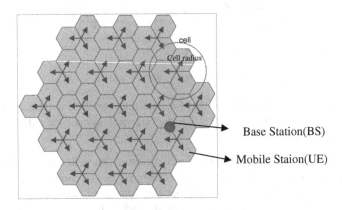

Fig. 3. Network layout

The IMT-2020 system utilizes multiple antennas when operating at high frequencies. Due to the higher path loss at high frequencies, it is important for IMT-2020 to have larger arrays compared with current LTE standards. We use array antennas with 4 columns and 8 rows in this paper. According to 3GPP modeling, the pattern of the radiation element is described as follows

$$A_{E,H}(\phi) = -\min\left[12\left(\frac{\phi}{\phi_{3dB}}\right)^2, A_m\right] \qquad (1)$$

Where ϕ is the azimuth angle defined between $-180°$ and $180°$ is the horizontal 3 dB bandwidth. $A_m = 30dB$ is the front-back radio. $A_{E,H}(\phi)$ is the horizontal pattern of the radiation element.

$$A_{E,V}(\theta) = -\min\left[12\left(\frac{\theta-90}{\theta_{3dB}}\right)^2, SLA_V\right] \qquad (2)$$

Where θ is the elevation angle defined between 0° and 180°. θ_{3dB} is the vertical 3 dB bandwidth. SLA_V is the lower limit. $A_{E,V}(\theta)$ is the vertical radiation pattern of the radiation element.

$$A_E(\phi, \theta) = G_{E,Max} - \min\left\{-\left[A_{E,H}(\phi) + A_{E,V}(\theta)\right], A_m\right\} \tag{3}$$

Where $G_{E,Max}$ is the maximum directional gain of the radiation element.

For DRS antenna pattern, we assumed a tapered circular apertures antenna with uniform distribution, described in (4) with n = 0 [12].

$$G_r(\theta_a) = G_{\max}\left|2^{n+1}(n+1)!\frac{J_{n+1}(\theta_a)}{(\theta_a)^{n+1}}\right|^2 \tag{4}$$

Where a maximum antenna gain of 57.5 dBi is deployed. Considering θ_a to be 10°, and we can get the specific value of the receiving antenna gain of DRS.

2.3 Protection Criteria

ITU-R Recommendation SA.1155 [13] recommends that the maximum aggregate interference power spectral density level from all sources to be exceeded for no more than 0.1% of the time be −178 dB (W/kHz) in the 25.25–27.5 GHz band. This level is based on an I/N = −10 dB and a link margin degradation of 0.4 dB. In the reference bandwidth of 1 MHz, the maximum permissible interference level can be calculated as −118.6 dBm/MHz.

For the co-channel case the interference should not exceed −118 dBm/MHz at the macro base station and −113 dBm/MHz at the UEs according to 3GPP TS 36.101 roughly the same as LTE terminal.

In this paper, we only consider the main beam interference, which is in the case of an IMT-base station radiating towards a DRS and coupling into the main beam of the DRS high gain antenna. The tolerable IMT-base station interference power is calculated under the assumptions of co-channel interference into a GEO DRS orbit. Assuming 3 dB loss due to atmospheric absorption and 3 dB polarization loss, will result in interference level greater than the value specified in [14] when there is direct alignment.

2.4 Propagation Model

The standard model agreed upon this scenario for interference assessment is clearly denoted in the ITU-R Recommendation P. 452 [15], which considers a line-of-sight (LOS) component (modeled as free space propagation). This model including the attenuation due to LOS-propagation as well as the clutter loss in different environment, is used for the frequency sharing study

$$L_p = 92.44 + 20\lg(f) + 20\lg(d) + L_o \tag{5}$$

Where f is the operating frequency (GHz) of the disturbed system and d is the transmission distance (km). L_o means other losses including atmospheric absorption and polarization loss.

3 Interference Analysis

3.1 Single Point Interference

For single point interference, the interference that DRS received can be calculate as

$$I = P_t + G_t(\theta_d) + G_r(\theta_a) - L_p \tag{6}$$

Where P_t is the transmit power of interfering system, $G_t(\theta_d)$ is the transmit antenna gain, $G_r(\theta_a)$ is the receiving antenna gain of disturbed system, L_p is the pathloss component between the interfering system and the disturbed system. θ_d is the angle of departure for transmitting signals, θ_a is the angle of arrival for the receiving signals as illustrated in Fig. 4.

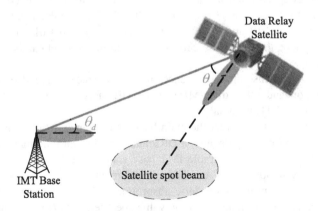

Fig. 4. Antenna radiation pattern for IMT-base station and data relay satellite

3.2 Lumped Interference

In the case of lumped interference, it is required to consider all the ground IMT-BSs covered by the satellite beam to calculate the lumped interference. Therefore, before calculating the lumped interference power, the location and total number of IMT-BSs should be known. Supposing in this case, each IMT BS has the same interference level to the DRS. Under the coverage of satellite, the total interference of M IMT-base stations is

$$I_{lumped} = I + 10\log(M) \qquad (7)$$

The number of IMT-BSs under the satellite coverage area mainly depends on three factors, the satellite coverage area K_{area}, city percentage $K_{percentage}$ and scatter factor per square kilometer IMT-base stations $K_{scatter}$. The total number of IMT-BSs can be obtained from the product of the three factors

$$M = K_{area}K_{percentage}K_{scatter} \qquad (8)$$

An assessment of frequency sharing is based on the concept of permissible interference level at the antenna terminals of a disturbed system and only in-band operation is considered in this paper. To analyze the additional isolation, the specific calculation formula is as follows

$$A_{addiso} = I_{lumped} - I_{limit} \qquad (9)$$

Where I_{limit} is the permissible interference level of the disturbed system.

3.3 The Calculation of Elevation Angle

For interference analysis, the elevation angle of earth station is a main parameter, when calculating the interference level. According to [16], the IMT-base station elevation angle can be calculated as

$$\alpha = \arctan\left(\frac{\cos(|E_E - E_S|)\cos\varphi_E - 0.151}{\sqrt{1 - \cos^2(|E_E - E_S|\cos^2\varphi_E)}}\right) \qquad (10)$$

Where E_E is IMT base station longitude, E_S is DRS longitude, φ_E is earth station latitude.

As the DRS user spacecraft is in low-earth orbit, when the spacecraft and UE are in different geographical position, the distance will change with the latitude and longitude of the two.

$$d = \sqrt{r^2 + R^2 - 2rR\cos(E_E - E_s)\cos\varphi_E} \qquad (11)$$

Where r is the radius of the earth, R is the radius of satellite orbit.

4 Simulation and Discussion

With reference to the ITU-R Recommendation, inter-satellite service system parameters are shown in Table 1 and IMT-2020 system parameters under consideration of sharing between the DRS in the band of 25.25–27.5 GHz is shown in Table 2.

Table 1. Inter-satellite Service System Parameters

Parameter	Value
Center frequency of operation [GHz]	26.375
Receiver bandwidth [MHz]	600
Maximum antenna gain/DRS [dB]	57.5
Maximum antenna gain/Spacecraft	44.5
Maximum power spectral density[dBm/MHz]	−20
Feeder loss [dB]	0
Noise temperature [K]	100
Recommend I/N level [dB]	−10
Boltzmann constant [J/K]	1.38×10^{-23}
Noise level [dB/MHz]	−108.6
Maximum permissible interference [dBm/MHz]	−118.6

Table 2. IMT-2020 System Parameters

Parameter	Value
Center frequency of operation [GHz]	26.375
System bandwidth [MHz]	600
Inter-site distance [m]	200
Transmit power [dBm]	33
Feeder loss [dBm]	−3
polarization isolation [dBm]	−3
City base station activation rate [dBm]	−3
Maximum permissible interference[dBm/MHz]	BS:-118/UE:-113

For area of satellite spot beam and IMT small cell are greatly different in size, and number of IMT-BSs can do make a difference on aggregate interference assessment. We define the Effective Area Percentage (EAP) to describe the deployed IMT area in a spot beam. Assuming the longitude of DRS is 113° E, to analyze the interference power, Fig. 5 shows the interference of IMT-BSs to DRS on different EAP and elevation angle. We observe that the interference power is always above the maximum permissible interference level making it scarcely possible to deploy IMT-2020 downlink with the return inter-orbit link of data relay satellite system.

To evaluate the interference from spacecraft to UE, we consider the worst case scenario. Assuming the spacecraft and UE both in the same longitude, Fig. 6 shows the additional isolation required for the three cities Beijing, Harbin and Wuhan in which the latitude of three cities were 40°, 45° and 30° when spacecraft at different latitude. We observe that the additional isolation is always negative which indicates the forward feeder link may coexist with IMT downlink.

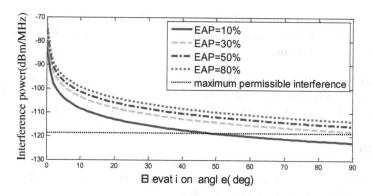

Fig. 5. Interference from IMT BSs to DRS

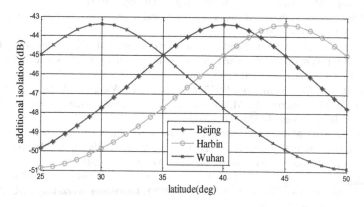

Fig. 6. Additional isolation needed for different cities

5   Conclusion

In this paper, we investigated frequency sharing of IMT-2020 and inter-satellite service in the band between 25.25–27.5 GHz. Focusing on the interference scenario between the return inter-orbit link of data relay satellite system and downlink of IMT-2020. For the interference from IMT-2020 to inter-satellite service, we analyze the interference link from IMT BSs with different elevation angles and density to DRS. For the interference from inter-satellite service to IMT-2020, we mainly evaluate the interference level from DRS user spacecraft to UE. Using the propagation model, antenna radiation patterns and parameters provided by ITU, 3GPP and other newest publications. The results from this study quantify the interference. This work can be a good reference to the research community, industry and regulators which are currently investigating spectrum requirements and technology options for 5G system. However, many challenges are still undergo. Many factors such as power control schemes and antenna deployment can do effect on the spectrum sharing between the two systems.

As future work, we intend to further study the 5G deployment and antenna technology to evaluate the interference level more accurately and provide method for the coexistence of two systems.

Acknowledgement. This work was supported by National Natural Science Foundation of China (61372111), Doctoral Scientific Fund Project of the Ministry of Education of China (20120005110001) and National Nature Science Foundation of China (91438114).

References

1. ITU-R Rep. M.2039, Characteristics of terrestrial IMT-2000 systems for frequency sharing/interference analyses, November 2014
2. Yu, X., Yang, Y., Ding, J.: Satellite network design method applicable to orbit determination and communication for GNSS. In: 2013 4th IEEE International Conference on Software Engineering and Service Science (ICSESS), pp. 886–889 (2013)
3. ITU-R Rec.SA.1019, Preferred frequency bands and transmission directions for data relay satellite systems, June 2001
4. ITU-R Rec.SA.1276, Technical and operational requirements that facilitate sharing between point-to-point systems in the fixed service and the inter-satellite service in the band 25.25-27.5 GHz, December 2013
5. Rappaport, T.S., Sun, S., Mayzus, R., Zhao, H., Azar, Y., Wang, K., Wong, G.N., Schulz, J. K., Samimi, M., Gutierrez, F.: Millimeter wave mobile communications for 5G cellular: it will work! IEEE Access **1**, 335–349 (2013)
6. Kim, J., Xian, l., Maltsev, A., Arefi, R., Sadri, A.S.: Study of coexistence between 5G small-cell systems and systems of the fixed service at 39 GHz band. In: 2015 IEEE MTT-S International Microwave Symposium, Phoenix, AZ, pp. 1–3 (2015)
7. Guidolin, F., Nekovee, M.: Investigating spectrum sharing between 5G millimeter wave networks and fixed satellite systems. In: 2015 IEEE Globecom Workshops (GC Wkshps), San Diego, CA, pp. 1–7 (2015)
8. ITU-R Rec. F.1249, Technical and operational requirements that facilitate sharing between point-to-point systems in the fixed service and the inter-satellite service in the band 25.25-27.5 GHz, September 2015
9. ITU-R Rec SA.1018, Hypothetical reference system for systems comprising data relay satellites in the geostationary orbit and user spacecraft in low Earth-orbits, March 1994
10. Tercero, M., Sharma, S., Coldrey, M, et al.: Coexistence between 5G and Fixed Services. In: 2016 IEEE 83rd Vehicular Technology Conference (VTC Spring), pp. 1–5. IEEE (2016)
11. Rusek, F., Persson, D., Lau, B.K., et al.: Scaling up MIMO: opportunities and challenges with very large arrays. IEEE Signal Process. Mag. **30**(1), 40–60 (2013)
12. ITU-R Rec F.1336, Reference radiation patterns of omnidirectional, sectoral and other antennas for the fixed and mobile services for use in sharing studies in the frequency range from 400 MHz to about 70 GHz, February 2014
13. ITU-R Rec SA.1155, Protection criteria related to the operation of data relay satellite systems, December 2013
14. Stutzman, W.L., Thiele, G.A.: Antenna Theory and Design, 3rd edn, p. 389. Wiley, New York (2012)
15. ITU-R Rec P.452, Prediction procedure for the evaluation of interference between stations on the surface of the Earth at frequencies above about 0.1 GHz, July 2015
16. Li, J., Huang, B., Huang, J.: Electromagnetic Spectrum Engineering. Posts&Telecom Press, June 2008

A Novel Transmission Line Safety Monitoring System for Smart Grid

Chien-Hao Wang, Xiang-Yao Zheng, Yu-Cheng Yang, Ching-Ya Tseng,
Kai-Sheng Tseng, and Joe-Air Jiang[(✉)]

Department of Bio-Industrial Mechatronics Engineering, National Taiwan University,
No. 1, Sec. 4, Roosevelt Road, 10617 Taipei, Taiwan (R.O.C.)
{f01631018,jajiang}@ntu.edu.tw, r99631025@gmail.com,
ji31j6g4cl3bp6@gmail.com,
luisaariel24@gmail.com, tks11111@yahoo.com.tw

Abstract. A smart grid is defined as novel electric power grid infrastructure that improves the efficiency, reliability and safety of the grid, by integrating renewable and alternative energy sources through automated control and novel communication technologies. The increasing demand for more effective electrical power system control has led to the rapid development of smart grids. In this study, a novel transmission line safety monitoring system for smart grid is proposed. The proposed system consists of transmission line sensor modules and wireless communication gateways. To verify the proposed system, a number of experiments are conducted in real extra high-voltage laboratory environment.

Keywords: Smart grids · Transmission line · Safety monitoring system · Sensor modules · Wireless communication gateway

1 Introduction

With the growth of global economy, the demand for electricity increases [1]. To meet the increasing demand, power companies have to supply more electricity. Traditional power systems may face several problems, such as inefficiently manual transmission line inspection and high costs associated with the manual inspection [2]. In Taiwan, most of the power transmission lines pass through the mountain and coast areas. When power towers are destroyed by significant natural disasters, it is difficult to repair malfunctioned towers immediately. Moreover, grid related parameters cannot be monitored and served as a reference for power companies in measuring overhead conductor sags and estimating conductor temperature and line dynamic thermal capacity [3, 4].

To overcome the drawbacks of using traditional power system inspection methods, smart grids, as a next generation of electrical power grids, have been introduced, which integrate modern information, communications, and electronic technologies. The modern communication infrastructure plays an important role in managing, controlling, and optimizing different functional and smart devices and systems in a smart grid. Wireless technologies can be used in different parts of smart grids to achieve flexible and low-cost data communication and networking [5–8]. With the data collected from

© ICST Institute for Computer Sciences, Social Informatics and Telecommunications Engineering 2017
E.T. Lau et al. (Eds.): SmartGIFT 2017, LNICST 203, pp. 35–45, 2017.
DOI: 10.1007/978-3-319-61813-5_4

the real-time monitoring, many useful services which provide power companies advanced information to manage power grids can be developed to make traditional grids become smart grids [9–12].

In this study, a novel transmission line safety monitoring system for smart grid is developed, and the system includes a transmission line sensor modules and wireless communication gateways. At the deployment site, the transmission line sensor modules collect power line information in real-time. Specifically, the optimal cooperative transmission of sensed data in smart grids is considered. The sensed data collected from the sensed modules are transmitted to the gateways located at the towers. The gateways relay the sensed data to the database at the substations and use the big data for data mining in the future. With the transmission line parameters, the central dispatch control center can use complete and accurate information for making decisions on electrical power allocation.

2   Transmission Line Safety Monitoring System

In this study, a transmission line safety monitoring system is proposed, and it can be divided into two subsystems, including transmission line sensor modules and wireless communication gateways. The transmission line sensor modules are attached to the power transmission lines to measure and collect the line-related parameters (e.g. environmental parameters, line temperature, vibration, and current) automatically and periodically. After the sensing data are collected, the transmission line sensor modules transmit the data to the wireless communication gateway on electric towers through the ZigBee protocol, and the wireless communication gateway transmits the data to the database via the 3G/4G protocol. The architecture of the entire transmission line safety monitoring system for smart grid is depicted in Fig. 1. Each subsystem is described in detail in the following subsections.

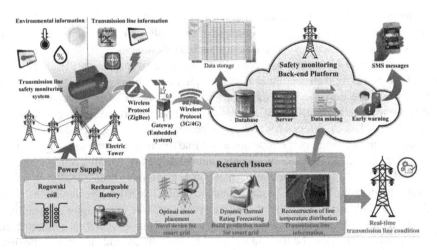

Fig. 1.   The architecture of the IoT-based extra high voltage power grid safety monitoring system

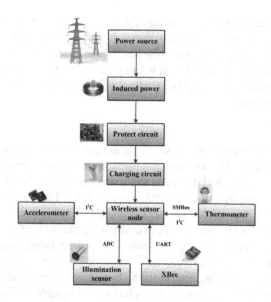

Fig. 2. The architecture of the EHVSM

2.1 Transmission Line Sensor Module

The evolution of sensor technology and communication networks has allowed sensors doing more intelligent jobs. In this study, sensors not only collect data but also perform some local processing tasks and transmit the results through a wireless communication (i.e., radio transmission) module to a gateway. A transmission line sensor module prototype is developed for the system validation, as depicted in Fig. 2. The major circuits/components of the transmission line sensor module and their functions/specifications are briefly described as follows.

(1) *Power module*

Wireless applications, including the proposed transmission line safety monitoring system, still face many challenges. Finding a proper power source is one of the challenges [13, 14]. In this study, the power for sensing device operation cannot be directly supplied by commonly used power sources, because the sensors are placed on the transmission lines and the line voltage is too high. Currently, some studies have utilized an electromagnetic induction sensing device as the power source for the sensing devices deployed on the transmission lines by using a Rogowski coil [15, 16]. The Rogowski coil establishes the electromagnetic coupling between an overhead transmission conductor and the power supply system. The conductor, also the primary side of the coil, delivers the electric energy to the secondary side. The coil is a crucial element in the power module, which determines the amount of power that the power supply can deliver to operate the transmission line sensor module and recharge redundant batteries on the modules.

Moreover, a protection mechanism is designed to prevent lightning surge, overvoltage, and overcurrent caused by channeled to the bypass if an event of lightning or surge occurs, so the electronic components of the proposed system are protected and not compromised. Furthermore, a charging circuit is added to the protection circuit. By improving the power storage capacity of the battery, the endurance of the wireless sensor module is also improved. Such a design not only prevents the EHVSM from electrical damage (such as switching and lightning surge) but also prolongs the operational time of the wireless sensor module.

(2) Sensor module

The sensor module is responsible for sensing and transforming the data to the wireless communication gateway. The transmission line sensor modules are devices capable of performing data acquisition and data processing and transmitting/receiving the data. All subsystems are managed by a microcontroller unit (MCU). There are many commercial microcontrollers. The Atmega328 (Atmel Corporation) [17] is selected as the MCU of the proposed sensor module, because it can easily integrate the sensing devices with the wireless communication module (XBee Series 2, Digi International Inc.) [18].

The transmission line sensor module is equipped with four types of sensors to measure conduct temperature, illumination, 3-axis accelerator, and environmental temperature and humidity. The transmission line sensor module receives and sends the data via a wireless network. After the aforementioned parameters are measured, the sensor board transmits the sensed data to the wireless communication gateway through the ZigBee protocol. The configuration of the sensor module is shown in Fig. 3; where the communication interfaces used in-between the different sensors and the MCU of the transmission line sensor module are also indicated. As illustrated in Fig. 3, the transmission line sensor module will be installed on power grid lines, the problems of electromagnetic compatibility (EMC) and electromagnetic interference (EMI) are inevitable when they are in service.

(3) Communication module

The XBee Series 2 was selected as the communication module in this study to implement the proposed transmission line safety monitoring system. XBee Series 2 modules allow to create networks such as point-to-point and multi-point networks based on the ZigBee

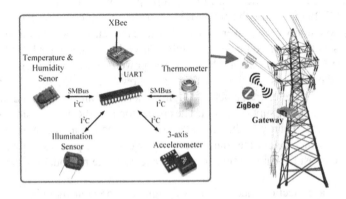

Fig. 3. The configuration of the transmission line sensor module on a power tower.

protocol (IEEE 802.15.4). It could provide a reliable and simple communication between microcontrollers and systems. The XBee Series 2 also had an external I/O board with 6 10-bit ADC input pins and 8 digital IO pins for general purpose input/output, which made the connection of XBee Series 2 mote to other devices or sensors quick and easy. In order to improve the quality of communication, each node was also equipped with a 3 dBi antenna (Maxim Integrated, Inc., Taiwan).

2.2 Wireless Communication Gateway

Wireless communication gateways are responsible for monitoring the changing parameters and rapidly relaying them to the database. The configuration of a wireless communication gateway is illustrated in Fig. 4. Each wireless communication gateway is equipped with a hybrid wireless communication module (ZigBee/3G/4G) to transmit the sensed data to a control center. Moreover, systems designed for monitoring the safety of a grid must be capable of regression analysis results: (a) temperature resisting severe weather variations. For this reason, this study utilizes an embedded-based system, BeagleBoard-Xm [19], with an IP 65 case as the prototype of the wireless communication gateway. The wireless communication gateway is also equipped with algorithms developed earlier to guarantee the quality of service (QoS) for the operation of the transmission line sensor modules deployed in the wild field [20, 21]. In addition, according to the IEEE Std. 738–2006 [22], ambient temperature and wind speed will affect the temperature of the transmission lines, so microclimate variables around the tower need to be monitored. For this purpose, a weather sensing module is integrated into the wireless communication gateway. The gateway was mainly responsible for collecting the sensing data and transmitted them to the database through the mobile communication protocol, i.e., 3G/4G.

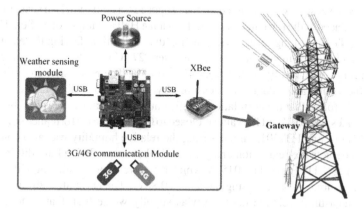

Fig. 4. The configuration of the wireless communication gateway on a power tower.

3   Experiment Results

This study focuses on the reliability of applying a transmission line safety monitoring system to get the real-time transmission line information. The end goal of the study is to provide the transmission line parameters, the central dispatch control center can use complete and accurate information for making decisions on electrical power allocation by using the proposed monitoring system. Thus, the accuracy of the sensors used in the proposed monitoring system must be sufficiently high to obtain accurate analysis results. Before conducting the long-term field trials, the basic performance of the main components/modules used in the transmission line safety monitoring system were first examined, including the calibration of sensors of transmission line sensor module, data delivery rate between transmission line sensor module and wireless communication gateway. The testing and the results are described as follows.

3.1   Sensor Reading Calibration

(1)   *Calibration of temperature/humidity sensors*

A commercial electronic hygrometer (HT-3015, Lutron Electronic Enterprise Co., Ltd.) [23] were employed to conduct the performance comparison with the temperature/humidity sensor (SHT11, SENSIRION.) [24] used in the proposed system. The sensing ranges of SHT11 in temperature (T) and relative humidity (%RH) are from −40 to 123.8 C and from 0 to 100%RH, respectively, and the measurement resolutions in temperature and relative humidity are 0.01 C and 0.05%RH @ 25 C, respectively. The measurement accuracy in temperature and relative humidity of SHT11 and HT-3015, i.e., (T, %RH), are (0.4 C, 3.0%RH) and (0.8 C, 3.0–4.0%RH), respectively.

To conduct the basic performance comparison between the sensors SHT11 and HT-3015, both sensors were mounted on the proposed transmission line sensor module, which were placed at the top balcony of the Tomatake Hall at campus of National Taiwan University (NTU) for long-term environmental data collection. During the experiment, the lowest and highest measured temperature were 27 °C and 35 °C, respectively. The measured relative humidity ranged from 45% to 85%. The regression analysis results between the temperature data sets measured by SHT11 and HT-3015 are shown in Fig. 5(a). It is found that the correlation coefficient of temperature measured by the two sensing devices is 0.9013 and R2 value is closed to 0.8123. The performance comparison between SHT11 and HT-3015 in measuring the relative humidity was also conducted. Figure 5(b) depicts the regression analysis results between relative humidity measurements by using SHT11 and HT-3015, in which the correlation coefficient of the relative humidity measured by both sensing devices is 0.8811. The correlation of both sensing devices in measuring relative humidity was slightly worse than that of temperature measurements, but the test results indicate that the SHT11 still provided satisfactory performance in measuring the relative humidity under outdoor testing environment. The results of performance comparison test imply that the temperature readings provided by SHT11 are reliable and stable, and the data can be served as a reference of follow-up ecological analysis between honey bees' in-and-out activities and environmental factor.

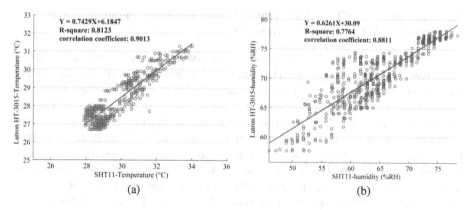

Fig. 5. The regression analysis results: (a) temperature; (b) relative humidity

(2) Calibration of the infrared (IR) thermometer

A commercial electronic thermometer, TM-363 (Tenmars Electronics Co., Ltd.) [25], was employed to conduct the performance comparison with the IR thermometer, MLX90614 (Melexis Semiconductors) [26], used by the proposed system. The sensing range of the TM-363 in temperature is from −200 to 1372 °C, and the measurement resolutions is 0.1%. The sensing range of MLX90614 in temperature (T) is from −70 to 380 °C for object temperature, and the measurement resolution is 0.01 °C.

To conduct the basic sensor calibration experiment between the sensors MLX90614 and TM-363, both sensors were mounted on the proposed sensor module system, and the experiment was conducted at the high-current laboratory of the Taiwan Power Research Institute for conductor temperature data collection. During the experiment, the lowest and highest measured temperature was 25 °C and 54 °C, respectively. The regression analysis results between the temperature measured by MLX90614 and TM-363 are shown in Fig. 6. It is found that the average accuracy of the MLX90614 is 96.71%, and R2 is closed to 0.99555. The results indicate that the two sensed datasets provided by the two sensing devices are very similar. The calibration results imply that the temperature readings provided by MLX90614 is reliable and stable, and the data can be served as a reference for the follow-up smart grid analysis between conductor temperature and DTR.

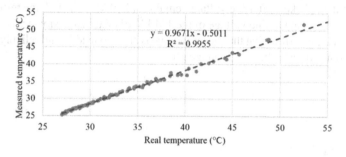

Fig. 6. The correlation and fit curve of the two temperature sensors.

3.2 Communication Test of the Transmission Line Safety Monitoring System in a Real EHV Laboratory Environment

The proposed transmission line safety monitoring system used the ZigBee as a wireless transmission protocol, through which the sensor module was able to communicate with the gateway. However, high-power disturbances cause by HV may affect wireless communication systems and their electronic circuits that operate within the 2.4 GHz industrial-scientific-medical (ISM) band [27]. The power system transients that may interfere with ZigBee networks are crucial for the effective operation of a smart grid [28]. To examine whether the proposed sensor module and gateway was able to stably transmit the sensed data in an extra high voltage environment. This study conducted a wireless communication transmission test in a high voltage environment. The successful data delivery rate served as an index to estimate the reliability of the proposed sensor module. In this study, the successful data delivery rate (DDR) of data delivery for the proposed system in a deployed WSN was defined as

$DataDeliveryRate$

$$= \frac{\sum Packets\ from\ Transmission\ line\ Sensor\ Module\ Recieved\ by\ Gateway}{\sum Packets\ Sent\ by\ Transmission\ line\ Sensor\ Module} 100\%, \quad (1)$$

where the DDR is the successful data delivery rate of the sensor module. Note that the packet size of the sensor data was 43 bytes, which was the same size as the packets that would be transmitted in a real smart grid scenario. The packet included the basic information of the sensor module, such as the header, the cyclic redundancy check (CRC) code, and the sensed data such as transmission line temperature, environmental temperature and humidity, etc.

This experiment was conducted at the high-voltage laboratory of the Taiwan Power Research Institute. During the experiment, the average temperature and relative humidity of the experimental room were 22.8 °C and 40.6%RH, respectively. The maximum test line voltage reached 279 kV. The experimental results were shown in Fig. 8. The test line voltage was from 0 V and then stepwise increased to 120 kV, 173 kV, and finally was up to 279 kV. The time periods that the voltage remained at 120 kV, 173 kV and 279 kV were 9'57", 3'53", and 1'36", respectively, as shown in Fig. 7(a). Moreover, it can be seen from Fig. 7(b), that the data delivery rate reduces to about 90% as the voltage increases, and that when the voltage rises from 173 kV to 279 kV, the MCU would reset. The transmission line sensor module can still stably and continuously transmit the data packets after the voltage remains at 279 kV. The voltage tested in this study was higher than the line voltage of the 161 kV EHV transmission grid in Taiwan. Therefore, this test verifies that the sensor module is able to steadily and reliably transmit monitoring data for an extra high voltage grid.

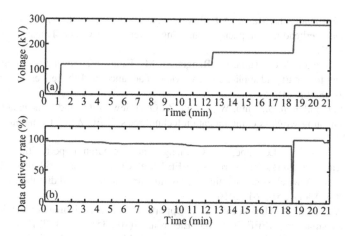

Fig. 7. The transmission line safety monitoring system tested in an extra high voltage environment: (a) the extra high voltage in the experiment; (b) data delivery rates of the EHVSM

4   Conclusion

Based on WSN technology, this study developed a transmission line safety monitoring system for smart grid. The designed system can detect the real-time transmission line parameters such as environmental parameters, conduct temperature. The sensing data collected by the system were transmitted by wireless sensor nodes to the gateway nearby. The gateway then transmitted the data to the database by 3G/4G. This study has successfully implemented an automatic and wireless monitoring prototype system that is suitable to monitor transmission line condition.

Acknowledgments. This work was financially supported in part by the Ministry of Science and Technology, Taiwan, under contract no. MOST 105-2221-E-002-132-MY3, MOST 105-2622-E-002-004-CC2 and MOST 105-3113-E-002-013, MOST 106-3113-E-002-012. The authors would like to give special thanks to Mr. Hung-Wei Lan and Mr. Fang-Cheng Chou at Department of system operation, Dr. Jin-Shyr Yang, Dr. Li-Cheng Wu and Mr. Ching-Jung Liao at Taiwan Power Research Institute, for their great help in providing research data and professional suggestions.

References

1. ExxonMobil 2015: The outlook for energy: A view to 2040 (2015). http://cdn.exxonmobil.com/~/media/global/files/outlook-for-energy/2015-outlook-for-energy_print-resolution.pdf
2. Li, F., Qiao, W., Sun, H., Wan, H., Wang, J., Xia, Y., Xu, Z., Zhang, P.: Smart transmission grid: vision and framework. IEEE Trans. Smart Grid **1**(2), 168–177 (2010)
3. Avendano-Mora, M., Milanovic, J.V.: Monitor placement for reliable estimation of voltage sags in power networks. IEEE Trans. Power Delivery **27**(2), 936–944 (2013)

4. Albizu, I., Fernandez, E., Mazon, A.J., Bengoechea, J.: Influence of the conductor temperature error on the overhead line ampacity monitoring systems. IET Gener. Transm. Distrib. **5**(4), 440–447 (2010)
5. Yigit, M., Gungor, V.C., Tuna, G., Rangoussi, M., Fadel, E.: Power line communication technologies for smart grid applications: a review of advances and challenges. Comput. Netw. **70**(9), 366–383 (2014)
6. Zhu, Z., Lambotharan, S., Chin, W.H., Fan, Z.: Overview of demand management in smart grid and enabling wireless communication technologies. IEEE Wirel. Commun. **19**(3), 48–56 (2012)
7. Ho, Q.D., Gao, Y., Le-Ngoc, T.: Challenges and research opportunities in wireless communication networks for smart grid. IEEE Wirel. Commun. **20**(3), 89–95 (2013)
8. Abdrabou, A.: A wireless communication architecture for smart grid distribution networks. IEEE Syst. J. **10**(1), 251–261 (2016)
9. Gungor, V.C., Lu, B., Hanckeand, G.P.: Opportunities and challenges of wireless sensor networks in smart grid. IEEE Trans. Ind. Electron. **57**(10), 3557–3564 (2010)
10. Matus, M., Saez, D., Favley, M., Suazo-Martinez, C., Moya, J., Jimenez-Estevez, G., Palma-Behnke, R., Olguin, G., Jorquera, P.: Identification of critical spans for monitoring systems in dynamic thermal rating. IEEE Trans. Power Delivery **27**(2), 1002–1009 (2013)
11. Safdarian, A., Degefa, M.Z., Fotuhi-Firuzabad, M., Lehtonen, M.: Benefits of real-time monitoring to distribution systems: dynamic thermal rating. IEEE Trans. Smart Grid **6**(4), 2023–2031 (2015)
12. Shaker, H., Zareipour, H., Fotuhi-Firuzabad, M.: Reliability modeling of dynamic thermal rating. IEEE Trans. Power Delivery **28**(3), 1600–1609 (2013)
13. Liang, C., Yu, F.R.: Wireless network virtualization: a survey, some research issues and challenges. IEEE Commun. Surv. Tutorials **17**(1), 358–380 (2015)
14. Bi, S., Ho, C., Zhang, R.: Wireless powered communication: opportunities and challenges. IEEE Commun. Mag. **53**(4), 117–125 (2015)
15. Zhang, Z.S., Xiao, D.M., Li, Y.: Rogowski air coil sensor technique for on-line partial discharge measurement of power cables. IET Sci. Meas. Technol. **3**(3), 187–196 (2009)
16. Du, L., Wang, C., Li, X., Yang, L., Mi, Y., Sun, C.: A novel power supply of online monitoring systems for power transmission lines. IEEE Trans. Ind. Electron. **57**(8), 2889–2895 (2010)
17. Atmel Corporation: ATmega48A/ PA/ 88A/ PA/ 168A/ PA/328/P Complete. ATmega328 datasheet (2015)
18. Digi International Inc.: XBee/XBee-PRO RF Modules - 802.15.4. XBee datasheet (2009)
19. BeagleBoard.org: BeagleBoard-xM System Reference Manual. BeagleBoard-xM datasheet (2016)
20. Jiang, J.A., Chuang, C.L., Chen, C.P., Lin, T.S., Tseng, C.L., and Yang, E.C.: A topology generator and evolutionary routing algorithm for random deployment of wireless sensor networks. In: Proceedings of The 2008 International Conference on Wireless Networks (ICWN 2008), pp. 698–703, Las Vegas, USA (2008)
21. Jiang, J.A., Lin, T.S., Chuang, C.L., Chen, C.P., Sun, C.H., Juang, J.Y., Lin, J.C., Liang, W.W.: A QoS- guaranteed coverage precedence routing algorithm for wireless sensor networks. Sensors **11**(4), 3418–3438 (2011)
22. IEEE Std. 738–2006 (Revision of IEEE Std 738–1993): IEEE Standard For Calculating The Current-Temperature of Bare Overhead Conductors (2007)
23. Lutron Electronic Enterprise Co., Ltd.: Humidity + Temp. + Dew Point 1000 Data logger. HT-3015 spec. http://www.sunwe.com.tw/lutron/HT-3015.pdf. Accessed 12 Oct 2016

24. SENSIRION: Humidity and Temperature Sensor IC. SHT11 spec (2016). https://www.sensirion.com/fileadmin/user_upload/customers/sensirion/Dokumente/Humidity_Sensors/Sensirion_Humidity_Sensors_SHT1x_Datasheet_V5.pdf. Accessed 12 Oct 2016
25. TENMARS ELECTRONICS CO., LTD: TM-363 N_ K type Thermometer. TM-363N spec (2016). http://www.tenmars.com/webls-en-us/TM-363N.html. Accessed 15 Mar 2016
26. Melexis Semiconductors: MLX90614 family. MLX90614 datasheet (2013)
27. Klünder, C., Haseborg, J.L.: Effects of high-power and transient disturbances on wireless communication systems operating inside the 2.4 GHz ISM band. In: Proceedings of the IEEE International Symposium Electromagnetic Compatibility, pp. 359–363. Fort Lauderdale (2010)
28. Sallabi, F.M., Gaouda, A.M., El-Hag, A., Salama, M.M.A.: Evaluation of ZigBee wireless sensor networks under high power disturbances. IEEE Trans. Power Delivery **29**(1), 13–20 (2014)

Smart Control and Operation

Operation Optimisation Towards Generation Efficiency Improvement in Saudi Arabia, Using Mathematical Programming and Simulation

Mohammad Althaqafi[✉] and Qingping Yang[✉]

College of Engineering, Design and Physical Science, Brunel University London,
London, UB8 3PH, UK
{Mohammad.althaqafi,QingPing.Yang}@brunel.ac.uk

Abstract. The efficiency of fossil power generation has improved during the last decades and technology development has played a significant role in this improvement. However, several factors can affect the efficiency level, such as operation, maintenance and environment, etc. The economic growth in Saudi Arabia in recent years has increased the demand for electricity. On the supply side, despite the reinforcement of generation stock with new units, the generation efficiency of fossil fuel has not improved significantly and is considered as being amongst the lowest in the world. This, as a result, means further consumption of resources and more emissions being produced. For this study, a new merit order has been produced using mathematical models to optimise the operation of power plants and improve the average efficiency. In addition, a simulation model was built to verify the enhancement. The results of the first stage show, on average, 3.5% improvement in generation efficiency and around a 4.95 Mtonnse reduction in total CO_2 produced. In the second stage, the efficiency improved by 6% and the emissions rate dropped by 5.7%.

Keywords: Efficiency · Electricity · Generation · Fossil fuel · Saudi Arabia

1 Introduction

In Saudi Arabia, electricity demand has been growing continuously. A 9.1% rise in peak load was recorded 2013 [1] and around 8% on average during the last decade [2], compared with 2.1% globally. This trend is anticipated to last for the next few years, thus resulting in the need to double the existing generation capacity [3]. Oil and gas are the main sources of electricity in Saudi Arabia. The growing demand for electricity has increased the local consumption of primary energy and Saudi Arabia has become the world's twelfth biggest energy consumer. In addition, local oil consumption has doubled and reached around 38% of total primary energy, making the country the sixth largest oil consumer [4]. 39% and 43% of oil and gas, respectively, are consumed in electricity generation.

The average generation efficiency in the kingdom did not improve significantly during the last two decades, although the generation assets are being reinforced by new units on a yearly basis. Nevertheless, several researchers have reported Saudi Arabia as

© ICST Institute for Computer Sciences, Social Informatics and Telecommunications Engineering 2017
E.T. Lau et al. (Eds.): SmartGIFT 2017, LNICST 203, pp. 49–57, 2017.
DOI: 10.1007/978-3-319-61813-5_5

being among the poorest performing countries in terms of generation efficiency [5, 6]. Regarding which, the average efficiency in the country improved from 26% to 29% (1990–2010), with an annual average of 0.15 of a percentage point. On the other hand, average efficiency in the EU countries reached 46% in the same period [1]. Globally, average efficiency of fossil power generation was 35% in 2003, whilst gas fueled units reached 40% and oil 36% [7].

Efficiency improvement can have significant financial and environmental impact. For instance, the Saudi Electricity Company (SEC), the largest electricity producer in the kingdom, reported 0.12% heat rate reduction in 2011 and 1% in 2014 compared with the previous year. As a result, the fuel saved was worth $28.3 million in 2011 and 12.1 million barrels of oil equivalent in 2014 [8, 9]. This is based on 70% of the country gross electricity produced. Environmentally, achieving 0.1 higher efficiency would reduce the total CO_2 emissions produced by 0.18% to 0.24% [10].

In Saudi Arabia, efficiency has been discussed from a different point of view. The majority of attention has been focused on the consumption side aimed at controlling and reducing the increasing demand [11, 12]. On the supply side, the adoption of renewable energy has been a widely discussed topic [13–15] in relation to mitigating the consumption of fossil fuel in electricity generation. In order to improve the level of generation efficiency, increasing the share of combined cycle (CC) units has been proposed, since they have the ability to generate electricity at a lower heat rate [1, 6] compared to other technologies. However, this option has not shown any significant improvement, for after the doubling of the capacity share of CC units between 2011 and 2013, no marked improvement was observed [16, 17].

The literature has reported several factors that can affect generation efficiency in power plants. Operation is pointed to as the most influencing factor, with up to 7% loss in efficiency, followed by maintenance, subsidies, environment etc. [18–21]. Likewise, among all the influencers, operation has shown the strongest association with the current low efficiency level in Saudi Arabia [22]. It shows high utilisation of less efficient units when compared to the top efficient power plants. In addition, it is acknowledged that the existing generation stock has the potential of reaching a higher level of efficiency. This paper is aimed at improving the efficiency by optimising the operation of power plants in Saudi Arabia and examining the improvement proposed.

The remainder of this paper is structured as follows. Section 2 provides a background, whilst Sects. 3 and 4 describe the methodology employed. Section 5 presents the results obtained and discussion. Finally, Sect. 6 concludes this paper.

2   Operating Criteria of Power Plants

Demand is fed through a mix of different types of power plants with different characteristics and different costs of production. To obtain the optimum operation, power plants are classified according to their cost in generating electricity. Units with the lowest cost of production are located at the top and have priority in operation. This ranking is known as "Merit- Order" [2]. In Saudi Arabia, power plant operation is planned based on the cost of electricity units produced. The main objective is to ensure sufficient production under minimum cost within the security limits. This rule has some exceptions to avoid interruptions, such as shortage in supply, sudden low voltage or unexpected increase on the demand side. The operation of the network is controlled by an LDC (Load Dispatch Centre) located within the SEC, which theoretically means efficiency is a major criterion in operation, since it is related to cost.

3   Simulation

"Simulation is the process of designing a model of a real system and conducting experiments with this model for the purpose of understanding the behavior of the system and/or evaluating various strategies for the operation of the system" [23]. Simulation does not provide solutions; it shows the outcomes of applying different alternatives (scenarios) to the system. This can support the decision makers in evaluating the performance of each choice and acting with high confidence. The main purpose of utilising simulation is to avoid unexpected results in the real world as it predicts system behaviours and outcomes subsequent to any change. Simulation has achieved a 92% satisfaction factor as a tool in supporting decision making [24]. It can be considered as providing risk reduction, efficiency improvement, operation and capital cost saving along with other financial benefits. Furthermore, it is a useful tool for examining hypotheses so as to understand the reasons for a particular phenomenon [23].

A discrete event simulation model has been designed tested and justified following the steps and approach from several studies [25–29]. It was run several times utilising real data obtained from the Electricity and Cogeneration Regulatory Authority (ECRA) in SA [30]. However, only the data for SEC's power plants during the year 2011 were deployed. The data for the simulation comprised 48 power plant names, type, merit order, heat rate and gross actual generation. It is important to mention that this represents around 70% of total production in the kingdom.

The obtained data do not provide exact details of internal consumption (auxiliary) at each power plant. Therefore, 3% was considered as the average for all of them and 10% losses in the transmission and distribution networks, as mentioned in ECRA reports [17, 31]. Fuel consumed and annual load profile was also collected from ECRA annual reports. Finally, the emissions produced and the total cost of fuel were found in [32, 33]. This data will be used to verify the model results.

The simulation report illustrates similar results to the real system by consuming the same amount of fuel and generating a similar amount of electricity at identical efficiency for each unit and on average. Nevertheless, the analysis shows no relation between merit order, efficiency and the actual capacity factor (see Fig. 1). This could be related to the existence of fuel subsidies, which tend to favour less efficient units that are negatively reflected in the average efficiency [1].

In addition, fuel subsidies do not reflect the actual cost of production on the supply side and generate a distorted price pattern [34], which does not support effective decision making for better utilisation of national resources [21, 35, 36], as well as having significant consequences regarding the efficiency. Consequently, a new merit order is

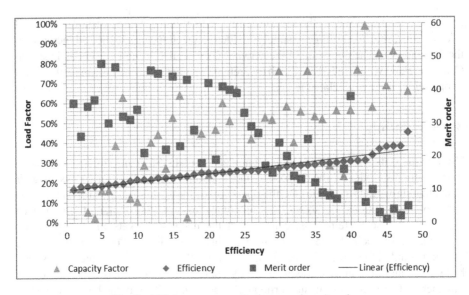

Fig. 1. Efficiency vs capacity factor and merit order

proposed here grounded in a combination of efficiency and a capacity factor using a mathematical model.

4 Mathematical Model in the Electric Power Industry

A mathematical model is a powerful method for helping to understand system performance through equations [37]. It has been utilised to solve issues by recognising the relations within the system or predicting the outcomes of specific variables [38]. Employing such a model requires in depth understanding of the problem to ensure that it is designed appropriately.

4.1 Model 1

In this study, we develop a new merit order by utilising the efficiency (E) and load factor (LF). The mathematical model has been used in order to identify the weight of each factor.

$$E = \sum_{i=1}^{k} (ciei) \tag{1}$$

Where E is the average generation efficiency, k is the number of power plants, e is the efficiency of each power plant and c is the percentage contribution for each power plant, as shown below:

$$c = \frac{PPGP}{TP} \qquad (2)$$

Where TP is total production, PPGP is the power plant gross production.

$$PPGP = LF * NC * 7500h \qquad (3)$$

Where NC is the nominal capacity and 7500 is the maximum operating hours per year for the unit.

$$e = \frac{3412}{HR} \qquad (4)$$

Where HR is the Heat Rate. Hence, we have:

$$E = \sum_{(i=1)}^{k} \frac{LFi*NCi\,3412 * 7500}{(HRi\,TP)} \qquad (5)$$

The actual nominal capacity, total production and average heat rate of the power plants are applied in Eq. (5) to determine the weight both factors in Eq. (6).

$$S = E + (F*LF) \qquad (6)$$

S is the new merit order. By applying Eq. (6) for each power plant individually, using the efficiency and load hours, a new merit order is generated that can be used for operating the power plants.

4.2   Model 2

Alternatively, improvement can be designed based on estimating the required production from each unit that will provide maximum system efficiency.

(1) Total production has been classified into two categories in Eq. (7). Electricity is produced by efficient and non-efficient power plants. The criterion used in classifying the units is the average generation efficiency.

$$TP = \text{Efficient production(EP)} + \text{Non efficient production(NEP)} \qquad (7)$$

(2) Efficient production can be calculated using Eq. (8).

$$EP = \sum_{i=1}^{n} (TPppi) = \sum_{i=1}^{n} (NCppi *7500h) \qquad (8)$$

This means efficient units will be utilised to the maximum

(3) Non-efficient production can be calculated using Eq. (9).

$$NEP = TP - EP \qquad (9)$$

(4) NEP will be distributed to non-efficient units according to their efficiency

Equation (10), which is one of the constraints.

$$EP = \sum_{i=(n+1)}^{m} (NCppi*7500h) \geq Demand \qquad (10)$$

The results will show the required production from each power plant. Nevertheless, this method does not take into consideration the load profile, which can be seen as a drawback and hence, mathematical programming is applied to overcome this issue. Specifically, nonlinear mathematical programming is used to provide the optimum output needed by each power plant to fulfil the total production requirement. The constraints include that the electricity generated by each unit should not exceed its maximum capacity and that there is no less than the minimum needed production to fulfil the load profile. Total production also should not exceed demand by more than 10%. The objective to be minimized is the average heat rate using Eq. (11), which is calculated according to the suggested production by 48 variables.

$$HR = \sum_{i=1}^{k} (cihri) \qquad (11)$$

5   Results and Discussion

The original data have been used on the first mathematical model and generated a new merit order that has been utilised in operating the power plants. This can be used to generate unlimited scenarios regarding implementation by changing the loading hours for each unit. To identify the most optimum scenario, Eq. 7 was applied several times to obtain the required loading hours for each unit. Then, the original simulation model was run and new results were generated. The simulation report shows 3.5% improvement in average generation efficiency. As a result, about 66,189 billion BTU of fuel was saved, worth around one billion US dollars. In addition, the average CO_2 emissions produced per kWh generated were decreased by 3.3%, amounting to 4.95 Mtonnes reduction in the total CO_2 produced by fossil fuel generation.

The second mathematical method combined with the optimisation tool was applied to maximise the utilisation of efficient units and minimise it in the least efficient power plants, without affecting the demand. The obtained utilisation factor was applied to the simulation model and new results were obtained. The second simulation report demonstrates better results than the previous method and the efficiency has improved by 6% compared to the reference scenario. This improvement saves around 1.8 billion US $ by reducing the total fuel consumed by 114 T.BTU (−5.7%). Furthermore, the reduction in the emissions rate is 0.449 kg per kWh, which represents a decrease of 8.5 Mtonnes in CO_2.

Table 1 summarises the results of both methods and compares them to the reference scenario. As can be seen, the difference in the utilisation factor of the efficient units has increased significantly from 78% to 82% in stage 2 and 100% in stage 3. On the other hand, the utilisation of less efficient power plants, has decreased from 40% to 30% in stage 2 and finally, to 25% in stage 3. As a result, the cost of an electricity unit has been reduced to 0.158 $/kWh.

Table 1. Results summary

	Reference scenario S1	1st method improvement	2nd method improvement
Total production (GWh)	189,776.63	189,889.33	189,778.23
Fuel consumed (T.BTU)	2,008	1,942	1,894
Fuel saved (T.BTU)	-----	66	114
Cost of fuel (M.USD)	31,750.15	30,703.70	29,943.79
Saving (M.USD)	-----	1,046.45	1,806.36
Efficiency (%)	32.24	33.36	34.19
Improvement (%)	-----	3.5	6.1
CO_2 emissions (kg/kwh)	0.7888	0.7623	0.7439
Reduction (%)	-----	3.4	5.7
CO_2 emissions (M.Ton)	149.696	144.750	141.176
Reduction (M.Ton)	-----	4.95	8.52
Efficient PP Avg. utilisation factor (%)	78%	82%	100%
NEP PP Avg. utilisation factor (%)	40%	30%	25%
Cost ($)/kWh	0.167	0.162	0.158
Discount (%)	-----	3	5.4

The calculation of average efficiency is affected by the amount of electricity produced by each generating unit (contribution) under specific efficiency. This means that the presence of highly efficient units is not sufficient to improve the average efficiency unless they make a significant contribution, because the increase in the share of production of less efficient units will result in reducing the average efficiency and vice versa. The analysis of the first simulation results show that 52% of gross production was generated by power plants with above average efficiency, but these units were only utilised 78% during the year. On the other hand, several power plants with efficiency below average were being used more than those with high efficiency. This means that SEC's generation assets are not being deployed as efficiently as they could be, which is the main contributor to the low level of average efficiency.

Whilst significant improvement was generated during the implementation of stage 2 and 3, nevertheless, further improvement can be made. According to several studies, the increase in load factor can have significant impact on the unit average efficiency [39, 40]. This study is based on the provided figures of the heat rate for each unit and it was assumed the average figure was fixed in all the scenarios proposed. The results of the new methods indicate higher load hours of the efficient units. This has the potential to increase the average efficiency of each power plant by (1–7% points) or to reduce the fuel consumed by 25%, on average and as a result, this will be positively reflected in the average efficiency. This can open a window for future research.

6   Conclusion

In this paper, the operation of SEC power plants has been analysed using simulation. The results have shown that existing generation stock is not being operated efficiently. Consequently, new merit order has been proposed, using a mathematical model that combines the quality and quantity so as to produce a single measure for operation. Subsequently, simulation models were utilised to implement the new merit order. The average efficiency of power plants improved significantly by optimising the operation. The proposed mathematical model and simulation could be employed in the future with the addition of further parameters.

Acknowledgement. The authors are thankful to the Electricity and Cogeneration Regulatory Authority (ECRA) in Saudi Arabia for providing the data that have been used in this paper.

References

1. Groissböck, M., Pickl, M.J.: An analysis of the power market in Saudi Arabia: retrospective cost and environmental optimization. Appl. Energy **165**, 548–558 (2016)
2. Farnoosh, A., Lantz, F., Percebois, J.: Electricity generation analyses in an oil- exporting country transition to non-fossil fuel based power units in Saudi Arabia. Energy **69**, 299–308 (2014)
3. Sulman, A.: Local consumptiopn of energy represents 38% of the kingdom total production. Aleqtisadiah, RIYADH, 08 February 2016
4. El-katiri, L., Fattouh, B.: A brief political economy of energy subsidies in the middle east and North Africa. Oxford Inst. Energ Study, February 2015
5. Fattouh, B.: Summer Again: The Swing in Oil Demand in Saudi, pp. 1–8, July 2013
6. Alyousef, Y., Abu-ebid, M.: Energy Efficiency Initiatives for Saudi Arabia on Supply and Demand Sides (2012)
7. Graus, W.: Power of Efficiency International comparisons of energy efficiency and CO2 emissions of fossil-based power generation (2010)
8. SEC: Annual Report. RIYADH (2011)
9. SEC: Annual Report. RIYADH (2014)
10. EURELECTRIC: Efficiency in Electricity Generation. Brussels (2003)
11. Khan, S.: Energy efficiency: the first renewable. Oxford (2014)
12. Fattouh, B., El-katiri, L.: Energy and Arab Economic Development (2012)
13. Alnatheer, O.: The potential contribution of renewable energy to electricity supply in Saudi Arabia. Energy Policy **33**(18), 2298–2312 (2005)
14. Aljarboua, Z.: The national energy strategy for Saudi Arabia. World Acad. Sci. Eng. Technol. **3**(9), 472–481 (2009)
15. Al-Saleh, Y.: Renewable energy scenarios for major oil-producing nations: the case of Saudi Arabia. Futures **41**(9), 650–662 (2009)
16. ECRA: Annual Statistical Booklet for Electricity and Sea Water Desalination Industries. RIYADH (2013)
17. ECRA: Annual Statistical Booklet on Electricity and Sea Water Desalination Industries. RIYADH (2011)
18. (Ron) Chan, H.S., Cropper, M.L., Malik, K.: Why are power plants in India less efficient than power plants in the United States? Am. Econ. Rev. **104**(5), 586–590 (2014)

19. Farouk, N., Sheng, L., Hayat, Q.: Effect of ambient temperature on the performance of gas turbines. Int. J. Comput. Sci. Issues **10**(1), 439–442 (2013)
20. De Sa, A., Al Zubaidy, S.: Gas turbine performance at varying ambient temperature. Appl. Therm. Eng. **31**(14–15), 2735–2739 (2011)
21. Krane, J.: Stability versus Sustainability: Energy Policy in the Gulf Monarchies (2013)
22. Althaqafi, M., Yang, Q.: Addressing the factors causing inefficiency of fossil fuel power generation in Saudi Arabia. North Sea Conf. J. **3**(3) (2016)
23. Shannon, R.: Introduction to the art and science of simulation. In: Proceedings of the 1998 Winter Simulation Conference, WSC 1998, vol. 53, pp. 7–14 (1998)
24. Hollocks, B.W.: The impact of simulation in manufacturing decision making. Control Eng. Pract. **3**(1), 105–112 (1995)
25. Banks, J.: Introduction to simulation. In: Proceedings of the 2000 Winter Simulation Conference, no. Riis 1995, pp. 9–16 (2000)
26. Wyland, B., Buxton, K., Fuqua, B.: Simulating the supply chain. IIE Solut. **32**(1), 37–42 (2000)
27. Altiok, T., Melamed, B.: Simulation Modeling and Analysis with ARENA. Academic Press, Burlington (2010)
28. Robinson, S., Brooks, R., Kotiadis, K., Van der Zee, D.-J.: Conceptual Modelling for Discrete-Event Simulation. CRC Press, Boca Raton (2010)
29. Fishwick, P.A.: Simulation Model Design And Execution, 1st edn. Prentice Hall, Upper Saddle River (1995)
30. ECRA: Installed Generation Capacity (2012)
31. ECRA: Activities & Achievements of the Authority (English) (2011)
32. International Energy Agency: CO2 Emissions from Fuel Combustion Highlights (2013)
33. SEC: Annual Report. RIYADH (2012)
34. International Monetary Fund: Energy Subsidies in the Middle East and North Africa: Lessons for Reform. Washington, D.C. (2014)
35. Alyousef, Y., Stevens, P.: The cost of domestic energy prices to Saudi Arabia. Energy Policy **39**(11), 6900–6905 (2011)
36. Fattouh, B., El-katiri, L.: Energy Subsidies in the Arab World. Oxford (2012)
37. El-Haik, B., Al-Aomar, R.: Simulation-based Lean Six-Sigma and Design for Six- Sigma. Wiley, Hoboken (2006)
38. Giordano, F., Weir, M., Fox, W.: A First Course in Mathematical Modelling. Nelson Education (2013)
39. Graus, W., Roglieri, M., Jaworski, P., Alberio, L.: Efficiency and capture- readiness of new fossil power plants in the EU. Utrecht (2008)
40. Graus, W., Worrell, E.: Trend in efficiency and capacity of fossil power generation in the EU. Energy Policy **37**(6), 2147–2160 (2009)
41. ECRA: Revised final report updated generation planning for the Saudi electricity sector (executive summary). Riyadh (2006)

Scheduling Domestic Shiftable Loads in Smart Grids: A Learning Automata-Based Scheme

Rajan Thapa[1], Lei Jiao[1(✉)], B. John Oommen[2], and Anis Yazidi[3]

[1] Department of ICT, University of Agder, Grimstad, Norway
lei.jiao@uia.no
[2] School of Computer Science, Carleton University, Ottawa, Canada
[3] Department of Computer Science,
Oslo and Akershus University College of Applied Sciences, Oslo, Norway

Abstract. In this paper, we consider the problem of scheduling shiftable loads, over multiple users, in smart grids. We approach the problem, which is becoming increasingly pertinent in our present energy-thirsty society, using a novel *distributed* game-theoretic framework. From a modeling perspective, the *distributed* scheduling problem is formulated as a game, and in particular, a so-called "Potential" game. This game has at least one pure strategy Nash Equilibrium (NE), and we demonstrate that the NE point is a global optimal point. The solution that we propose, which is the pioneering solution that incorporates the theory of Learning Automata (LA), permits the total supplied loads to approach the power budget of the subnet once the algorithm has converged to the NE point. The scheduling is achieved by attaching a LA to each customer. The paper discusses the applicability of three different LA schemes, and in particular the recently-introduced Bayesian Learning Automata (BLA). Numerical results (The algorithmic details and the experimental results presented here are limited in the interest of space. More detailed explanations of these are found in [13]), obtained from testing the schemes on numerous simulated datasets, demonstrate the speed and the accuracy of proposed algorithms in terms of their convergence to the game's NE point.

Keywords: Smart Grid · Load scheduling · Potential Game · Nash Equilibrium · Learning Automata

1 Introduction

As society becomes increasingly energy-thirsty, the problems associated with collectively controlling the use of energy resources so that the electrical grids are not overloaded, are becoming more dominant. Power utility companies often

Chancellor's Professor; Fellow: IEEE and *Fellow: IAPR*. This author is also an *Adjunct Professor* with the University of Agder, Norway. The work of this author was partially supported by NSERC, the Natural Sciences and Engineering Research Council of Canada.

© ICST Institute for Computer Sciences, Social Informatics and Telecommunications Engineering 2017
E.T. Lau et al. (Eds.): SmartGIFT 2017, LNICST 203, pp. 58–68, 2017.
DOI: 10.1007/978-3-319-61813-5_6

warn customers to limit their power consumption especially in the warmer summer months. Although this is deemed to be voluntary, these utility companies attempt to enforce it by charging higher rates for the power that is consumed during "peak hours".

Utility companies attempt to monitor and control the use of energy by resorting to so-called "Smart Grids" (SGs). In a SG, loads can be categorized as being either "shiftable" or "non-shiftable". Non-shiftable loads comprise of devices such as bulbs, where there is no room for scheduling, since the power required by the device must be supplied as soon as the device is turned on. Shiftable loads, on the other hand, such as water and floor heaters (which are every-day, commonplace appliances in countries with colder climates), can tolerate a certain amount of delay, permitting the users the possibility to schedule them *when* are turned on. Since these shiftable loads can be adaptively scheduled, the system is capable of smoothing the power consumption curve.

There is a vast body of literature associated with achieving distributed scheduling in SGs, all of which focus on the various facets of the problems encountered in this area [3,4,11]. The main focus of the existing studies that use distributed algorithms is to distribute the computational load to multiple controllers/agents in order to reduce the overall communication and computational complexity, and consequently to "spread them out" to be handled by the individual users. In these cases, the appliances of the end-users (the actual customers) may still be controlled by a local controller/agent.

In our study, various customers are allowed to decide by themselves whether they want to turn a load on or not. To achieve this goal, we propose a distributed Learning Automata (LA)-based approach, where each customer is equipped with a LA to learn from the environment and decide whether to turn on its appliances or not.

The application of LA in SGs has been studied a little, including using them in the underlying communication network in SGs and in the power scheduling approaches. The solution model we propose in this paper is distinct. Firstly, we model the system as a specific type of game and proceed to study its properties. Based on the these properties, we design a distributed LA-based algorithm to solve the game. With regard to solution strategies, we propose the deployment of three LA schemes, explained in the body of the paper. In the case of all these LA-based schemes, the consumers do not need to share information to the provider. Rather, they negotiate the power utilization and make a decision between themselves, implying that the power supplier has to merely perform the task of being a power budget *provider*, rather than also a *scheduler*.

2   System Model

2.1   Problem Formulation

The research undertaken in this research focuses on the domestic smart-grid subnet. The lowest level, i.e., the local domestic network between the transformers and the end customers, is the subnet that we concentrate on. A typical scenario

of this subnet is an apartment building with many families which play the role of
the customers, and where the building is connected to a main power source. This
power source is provided and installed by the power supplier, and it obtains its
power budget from the upper levels of the power network based on the scheduling of the supplier. The objective of the power source is to provide power to the
various families, and at the same time to maintain the overall power consumption
below a given power budget. Following the common practice [6,14], the overall
budget for the shiftable load can be suggested by the source to the customers,
and this quantity is denoted by C_{SL}. Typically, the time index is segmented into
slots, indexed by t, which are of the order of several minutes long. In the beginning
of each time slot, the budget for the shiftable load is offered to all the customers.
But once the customers obtain this budget, they will have to compete with each
other for their own loads. Once a consumer wins the competition, his load will
be served within this time slot. The competition among the various customers is
carried out through mutual communications and information exchange.

Suppose there are N customers with their individual demands
$\{L_1, L_2, \ldots, L_N\}$ for their respective shiftable loads at time slot t. C_{SL}, referred
to above, may not be sufficient to serve all the $\{L_i\}$ loads for all the customers.
It would thus be necessary for the system to figure out which users can be served
such that $\sum_{i=1}^{N} L_i d_i \leq C_{SL}$, where $d_i \in \{1, 0\}$ denotes whether customer i is to
be served or not. In other words, a decision of 1 for a particular customer implies
that the specific customer's demand is to be served by the grid in the current time
slot, while the decision of 0 means that the corresponding load demand will not be
served by the grid in the current time slot. Thus, clearly, all the users who attain the
decision 1 accomplish the sharing of the total shiftable loads' budget, C_{SL}. However, a customer that is not served in the current time slot will eventually be served
in the future time slots. The objective of the distributed scheduling problem is to
determine a proper sub-group of customers whose aggregated demand is as close to
the budget as possible, although it is not allowed to exceed the budget. Formally,
the problem is formulated as follows:

$$\max_{d_i} \sum_{i=1}^{N} (d_i L_i),$$
$$\text{s.t.} \sum_{i=1}^{N} (d_i L_i) \leq C_{SL}, \ d_i \in \{1, 0\}. \tag{1}$$

To simplify the notation, unless explicitly stated, we denote the term
$\sum_{i=1}^{N}(d_i L_i)$ as L_T. Comparing the values of $\sum_{i=1}^{N} L_i$ and C_{SL}, we highlight
the following variations of the problem:

(i) Total shiftable demand is less than shiftable capacity, i.e., $\sum_{i=1}^{N} L_i \leq C_{SL}$.
     Clearly, in this scenario, since the capacity permitted is more than the
     demand, all the loads can be served by the source.
(ii) Total shiftable demand is greater than shiftable capacity, i.e., $\sum_{i=1}^{N} L_i >$
     C_{SL}. This is the condition of greatest concern for both the supplier and the
     set of customers, because, clearly all the demands cannot be served by C_{SL}.

Note that within this case, there is also a special case where the load of certain customers is greater[1] than the available shiftable capacity. Indeed, the scheme that we propose presently can also be applied to it.

The problem described in Case (ii) above (except for the special case where $\forall i, L_i > C_{SL}$), is NP-Hard because it can be deduced to a subset-sum problem. To solve this problem in a distributed manner, the customers need to communicate with each other and to send their respective decisions $\{d_i\}$ (i.e., their decision values of either 1 or 0, meaning "YES" and "NO" respectively), along with their demands $\{L_i\}$. This process is carried out iteratively until a proper common consensus is attained on the usage of the available capacity for all customers, through each customer's individual decision. Once the common consensus is reached, the power source can provide the corresponding power accordingly. Thus, the interactions between the customers is modeled as a game, detailed presently.

3   Modeling and Analysis of the Game

The distributed decision-making problem can be formulated as a game denoted by $\mathfrak{G} = [I, \{d_i\}_{i \in I}, \{U_i\}_{i \in I}]$, where:

- I is the set of customers with shiftable loads $\{1, 2, 3, ...N\}$, with any specific customer being indexed by i.
- $\{d_i\}$ is the set of decision actions taken by the customers, i.e., $D = \{d_1, d_2, ..., d_N\}$, where $d_i \in D$ is the decision/action of customer i. Decision $d_i = 0$ represents the event that customer i does not turn on his load, while $d_i = 1$ represents the condition when customer i does turn it on.
- $\{U_i\}_{i \in I}$ is the utility function of user i, and can be expressed in terms of C_{SL} as in Eq. (2):

$$
U_i(d_i, \mathbf{d}_{-i}) = \begin{cases} \frac{1}{L_i d_i + \sum_{j \in I \setminus i} L_j d_j + C_{SL}}, & C_{SL} < L_i d_i + \sum_{j \in I \setminus i} L_j d_j, \\ \frac{1}{C_{SL} - L_i d_i - \sum_{j \in I \setminus i} L_j d_j}, & C_{SL} \geq L_i d_i + \sum_{j \in I \setminus i} L_j d_j, \end{cases} \tag{2}
$$

where $\mathbf{d}_{-i}$ denotes the set of decisions taken by users other than user i.

The utility function of an individual user is defined from the perspective of the overall system. More specifically, it is beneficial for a user if the sum of the loads based on the current decision of all the users approaches C_{SL} from the left, i.e., whenever the value approaches C_{SL} although it is less than or equal to it. Otherwise, the value of the utility function of each user is reduced.

The formulated game is an exact Potential Game [8] and the reasons are as follows: According to the definition of a Potential Game, the payoff of any player

---

[1] If $\exists i, s.t. L_i > C_{SL}$, our solution is applicable by excluding the users whose demands exceed the capacity. Thus, we will not elaborate on this scenario in any greater detail.

by changing its strategy can be expressed using a single global function, i.e., a so-called potential function. In this particular game, the utility function for each player is defined as a global function, which can be considered to be the potential function itself. Therefore, this game is indeed a Potential Game. Understandably, this game is an exact Potential Game because if a player switches from one action (decision) to another, the change in the potential equals to the change in the utility of that player [8]. From the properties of Potential Games, we see that the game has at least one pure strategy Nash Equilibrium (NE) point. The fact that a global optimal point of the problem is a NE point of the game, and *vice versa*, is proven in [13]. Also, as a global optimal point, it is obvious that any unilateral change of decision of any user at the point will result in a decrease in the utility function.

4   Implementation of LA in Demand Scheduling

In our design, the users improve their decisions based on the rewards/penalties received for the decisions they made in previous iterations, and after sufficient number of iterations, users will, hopefully, converge to the NE point, which is the globally optimal solution of the problem.

4.1   Decisions of Users and Their Effects on Total Load

We invoke a typical working scenario for a LA [9]. It consists of a sequence of interaction cycles between the LA and its environment. In each iteration, the LA selects an action (α_i), which is either rewarded ($R = 1$) or penalized ($R = 0$) by the environment as a response. The most difficult part of designing a LA-based solution for a new application domain is that of determining what the "Environment" is, and then of knowing how the LA itself is "Rewarded" or "Penalized".

In our specific SG-based domain, since a users' decision d_i is either 0 and 1, the load for this user will be either 0 or L_i respectively, and so the total load "L_T" can be calculated by summing up these individual contributions in each iteration. Every iteration yields a new value of L_T. The decision-making process will go through an iterative process so that "L_T" will approach the global optimal C_{SL}. To capture the number of iterations, we denote a new index, $s \in \{1, 2, ..., M\}$ for the number of iterations, where M is the maximum number of iterations permitted. Correspondingly, the decision of user i at the iteration s is denoted by $d_i(s)$, $i \in \{1, 2, ..., N\}$. Similarly, we denote $L_T(s)$ as the current value of the total of the load values at iteration s. Obviously, the value of $L_T(s)$ differs as the values of the decisions $\{d_i(s)\}$ change. As the aim of the game is to achieve a value that is as close as possible to C_{SL} after every iteration, our task is to define the current Reward/Penalty so as to guide the users' decision-making process towards the optimal point.

4.2   Calculation of Reward and Penalty

We shall now consider the intricate problem of determining when the LA should be rewarded or penalized. In order to reach the closest possible value of C_{SL}, it is beneficial if the value of $L_T(s)$ approaches C_{SL} but, at the same time, that it is less than or equal to C_{SL}, as the iterations proceed. In this case, a Reward is applied to all the users. Otherwise, a Penalty is applied (i.e., when $L_T(s)$ is either greater than C_{SL}, or less than the previous value $L_T(s-1)$). The procedure for deciding on a Reward/Penalty is formally outlined in Algorithm 1.

Algorithm 1. Reward/Penalty Assignments

Input:
 – The loads of all the users and their decisions, $\{d_i(s)\}$ at a time instant, s
Output:
 – The assignment of a Reward or a Penalty to all users at the time instant, s
1: **begin**
2:     **for** every user i **do**
3:         Calculate $L_T(s) = \sum_{i=1}^{N} d_i(s)L_i$ based on the information obtained from other users
4:         **if** $L_T(s) \leq C_{SL}$ and $L_T(s) \geq L_T(s-1)$ **then**
5:             Decision $d_i(s)$ leads to a Reward to user i
6:         **else**
7:             Decision $d_i(s)$ leads to a Penalty to user i
8:         **end if**
9:     **end for**
10: **end**

Algorithm 1 is carried out for every decision-making iteration and stopped when the decision-making process ends. This termination phase will be discussed presently. Note that by embarking on this mutual information sharing, each user will be able to *individually* calculate the Reward or Penalty that *he* receives.

4.3   Decision Making on the Actions in the Iteration

Once the Reward/Penalty for each user has been assigned, we need to specify a learning scheme for deciding the action (0 or 1) that he has to make in the next iteration. As mentioned earlier, in this work, we opt to use LA to achieve this, and in this regard, we select three well-established LA to do this learning, namely, the Linear Reward-Inaction (LRI) scheme [9], the Coordination-game Learning Automata (CLA) [7], and the more-recently introduced Bayesian Learning Automata (BLA) [5]. The details of the relevant steps for each of these schemes are included in the formal algorithms described in [13], and omitted here in the interest of space.

Decision Making for the LRI. The way the decisions are made for the LRI scheme is straightforward. The action that each LA makes is based on the action selection probability. Each LA maintains two parameters p_0 and p_1 representing the probability of selecting 0 and 1 respectively, with $p_0 + p_1 = 1$. The quantities are initialized to 0.5. If the chosen action (either 0 or 1) is rewarded, the probability of the alternate action (p_1 or p_0 respectively) is decreased using a user-defined parameter, λ, and thus the probability associated with the chosen action is increased. The LA keeps the action probabilities unchanged in the case of a penalty feedback. The actual decision for scheduling communicated to the SG's power provider will occur after a final decision is attained by the LA-based scheme.

Decision Making for the CLA. The CLA is similar to the LRI since it involves the action probabilities and a learning parameter (denoted by λ), whose value affects the convergence speed and the proximity of the final solution to the optimal point. The CLA-based scheme is different from the LRI (and the BLA) due to the fact that it explicitly uses a *continuous* utility function in the update equation. It is based on the work of Mason on LA with a continuous feedback response [7]. In our particular problem, we need a normalization of the values of the utility to ensure that the feedback is in the interval $[0, 1]$ [7].

Using such a mapping and updating rule, it is possible to prove that the CLA will converge to the pure equilibrium with a probability that approaches unity, as the update parameter is made arbitrarily small. This is a consequence of the work due to Sastry *et al.* [12] since the NE of our Potential Game corresponds to the mode of the payoff matrix. Again, the actual decision communicated to the SG's power provider will occur after a final decision is attained by the CLA-based scheme.

BLA Based Decision Making Process. In the BLA-based scheme, each LA maintains two hyper-parameters $a_{i,j}$ and $b_{i,j}$. These are introduced to count the number of rewards and penalties respectively, where index i is the index of the user and $j \in \{0, 1\}$ denotes the decisions that the LA has made. In each iteration, the LA makes a decision about the choice of the action. Thereafter, the value of $a_{i,j}$ is increased if the decision leads to a reward, and the value of $b_{i,j}$ is increased if the decision leads to a penalty, as shown in Table 1.

Table 1. The effect of the Reward/Penalty responses on the *BLA*'s decision (for user i at iteration s) on its parameters.

	$d_i(s) = 1$	$d_i(s) = 0$
Reward	$a_{i,1} = a_{i,1} + 1$	$a_{i,0} = a_{i,0} + 1$
Penalty	$b_{i,1} = b_{i,1} + 1$	$b_{i,0} = b_{i,0} + 1$

5   Simulation and Experimental Results

To evaluate the performance of the LA-based schemes, we carried out simulations on numerous SGs, where the number of users and the parameters were varied. However, in the interest of brevity and space, we merely cite the results obtained from a subset of these experiments[2]. The experiments were conducted to capture two important metrics, i.e., the accuracy of the convergence and the speed of the convergence.

5.1   The Data Sets

The simulation configuration was derived based on the real-life measurements of the electricity consumption for 28 domestic users [2,10,15], as shown in Table 2.

Table 2. This table lists the demands of 28 user (in KWh) used in our experiments.

L_1	L_2	L_3	L_4	L_5	L_6	L_7	L_8	L_9	L_{10}	L_{11}	L_{12}	L_{13}	L_{14}
242	146	131	111	97	95	92	82	75	74	74	74	71	59
L_{15}	L_{16}	L_{17}	L_{18}	L_{19}	L_{20}	L_{21}	L_{22}	L_{23}	L_{24}	L_{25}	L_{26}	L_{27}	L_{28}
57	55	51	49	42	41	39	37	35	35	31	15	11	11

A word about how the data in Table 2 was obtained is not out of place. Specifically, the annual power consumption in [15] was converted to yield the average consumption for every 15 min timespan [2] considering the scheduling interval in real life. Half of these customers' demands were considered as shiftable loads [10]. In our simulation, we considered the scenario where only a subset of all the users could be selected for the given capacity, i.e., $0 < C_{SL} < \sum L_i$. Although the shiftable capacity of the SG and the shiftable demands were subject to change due to various reasons [1], without loss of generality, we assumed that the capacity of the shiftable load, C_{SL}, was about 70% of the total demand for the shiftable load.

5.2   Average Convergence Characterisitics

To illustrate the average number of iterations before convergence and the average value of the total selected power demands, we present the simulation results of the experiments in Tables 3 and 4. Table 3 illustrates the simulation results with all 28 users while Table 4 summarizes the results when the last 15 users in Table 2 are used. All the results presented in these tables are averaged values of over an ensemble of 400 independent replications. For the cases of the CLA and the LRI,

---

[2] Additional results can be seen from the technical report of the First Author, and can be made available on request.

the results are illustrated for different values of λ. As opposed to this, since the BLA does not depend on any parameter, the results for the BLA are presented, in those tables, in a single line.

Table 3. Simulation results from the BLA and LRI-based algorithms with $i = 28$ and $C_{SL} = 1352$ KWh.

Method	Sum of selected loads		Iterations	
BLA	1351.998		20306	
	LRI	CLA	LRI	CLA
$\lambda = 0.03$	1352.000	1352.000	136737	141411
$\lambda = 0.05$	1352.000	1352.000	60045	61853
$\lambda = 0.08$	1352.000	1352.000	25690	26986
$\lambda = 0.10$	1352.000	1352.000	16906	17863
$\lambda = 0.12$	1352.000	1352.000	11458	12231
$\lambda = 0.14$	1352.000	1352.000	7797	8460
$\lambda = 0.16$	1351.998	1352.000	5391	6409
$\lambda = 0.17$	1351.998	1351.998	4772	5333
$\lambda = 0.2$	1351.946	1351.988	2933	3417
$\lambda = 0.3$	1349.608	1351.408	581	911
$\lambda = 0.4$	1335.400	1348.530	181	300
$\lambda = 0.5$	1289.444	1342.843	92	135

The performances of the LRI and the CLA depend fundamentally on the value of the LA's parameter, λ. With a sufficiently small value for λ, the algorithms can converge to the NE point with high precision at a cost of executing a large number of iterations. Of course, the number of iteration is smaller when λ is relative large, but the convergence accuracy is compromised. If we compare the λ-dependent schemes (i.e., the CLA and the LRI) with the BLA-based algorithms, the number of iterations for the former were smaller than that for the latter, i.e., if the average value of the selected loads was almost identical. For example, when $\lambda = 0.16$ for $i = 15$, the average load was 299.917 after 1,010 iterations for LRI, and 299.947 after 1,142 iterations for the CLA. As opposed to this, the BLA yielded a lower load value of 299.872 after 1,101 iterations. Interestingly, the traditional age-old LRI with $\lambda = 0.16$ was superior to the CLA and the BLA in such a configuration. Similarly, when $i = 28$, both the CLA and the LRI with the parametric setting of $\lambda = 0.17$ yielded a better performance than the BLA. Comparing the λ-dependent schemes, arguably the LRI yielded a slightly better performance than the CLA in most cases, as the CLA needed more iterations to converge.

Although, as demonstrated by the results presented in the tables, comparatively smaller values of λ led to a superior performance for the LRI and the

Table 4. Simulation results from the BLA and LRI-based algorithms with $i = 15$ and $C_{SL} = 300$ KWh.

Method	Sum of selected loads		Iterations	
BLA	299.872		1101	
	LRI	CLA	LRI	CLA
$\lambda = 0.06$	300.000	300.000	5764	6082
$\lambda = 0.08$	300.000	300.000	3763	3767
$\lambda = 0.09$	300.000	300.000	3056	3148
$\lambda = 0.10$	299.997	299.997	2630	2537
$\lambda = 0.12$	299.985	299.995	1772	1930
$\lambda = 0.14$	299.975	299.975	1357	1496
$\lambda = 0.16$	299.917	299.947	1010	1142
$\lambda = 0.2$	299.785	299.722	613	612
$\lambda = 0.3$	298.215	298.347	223	222
$\lambda = 0.4$	294.497	294.882	114	113
$\lambda = 0.5$	285.892	289.745	76	78

CLA, than for the BLA, the λ values could be quite different depending on the system's configurations. Consequently, the issue of determining the ideal value of λ was mandatory for a certain system configuration, whenever the LRI or the CLA was applied. However, the BLA-based approach did not require the setting of any *a priori* configurations, which renders it to be a more practical option in this application domain.

6 Conclusions

In this work, we have studied the problem of the scheduling of loads for domestic users in Smart Grids (SGs) in a distributed manner. This load scheduling problem is NP-Hard, and the distributed scheduling process is formulated as an exact Potential Game that has at least one pure strategy NE point. We proposed a LA-based algorithm which utilized three distinct LA alternatives, i.e., the LRI, the CLA and the BLA. Each of the multiple users utilized a LA to achieve the decision making process, and to thus solve the problem in a distributed manner. The simulations results show that the proposed approaches converge to a solution close to the NE point of the game, which is also the global optimal point. The convergence of all the schemes is comparable.

References

1. Batterberry, T., Miller, M., Jaskolka, K., Toll, R.: Smart grid price response service for dynamically balancing energy supply and demand, June 12 2009. US Patent Ap. 12/483,975

2. Chao, H.-L., Tsai, C.-C., Hsiung, P.-A., Chou, I., et al.: Smart grid as a service: a discussion on design issues. Sci. World J. **2014**, 11 (2014)
3. Chavali, P., Yang, P., Nehorai, A.: A distributed algorithm of appliance scheduling for home energy management system. IEEE Trans. Smart Grid **5**(1), 282–290 (2014)
4. Fan, Z.: A distributed demand response algorithm and its application to phev charging in smart grids. IEEE Trans. Smart Grid **3**(3), 1280–1290 (2012)
5. Granmo, O.-C., Glimsdal, S.: Accelerated Bayesian learning for decentralized two-armed bandit based decision making with applications to the goore game. Appl. Intell. **38**(4), 479–488 (2013)
6. Liu, Y., Hassan, N.U., Huang, S., Yuen, C.: Electricity cost minimization for a residential smart grid with distributed generation and bidirectional power transactions. In: 2013 IEEE PES Innovative Smart Grid Technologies (ISGT), pp. 1–6. IEEE (2013)
7. Mason, L.: An optimal learning algorithm for s-model environments. IEEE Trans. Autom. Control **18**(5), 493–496 (1973)
8. Monderer, D., Shapley, L.S.: Potential games. Games Econ. Behav. **14**(1), 124–143 (1996)
9. Narendra, K.S., Thathachar, M.A.: Learning automata: an introduction. Courier Corporation (2012)
10. Rajakaruna, S., Shahnia, F., Ghosh, A.: Plug in Electric Vehicles in Smart Grids. Springer, Germany (2015)
11. Saad, W., Han, Z., Poor, H.V., Basar, T.: Game-theoretic methods for the smart grid: an overview of microgrid systems, demand-side management, and smart grid communications. IEEE Sig. Process. Mag. **29**(5), 86–105 (2012)
12. Sastry, P., Phansalkar, V., Thathachar, M.: Decentralized learning of Nash equilibria in multi-person stochastic games with incomplete information. IEEE Trans. Syst. Man Cybern. **24**(5), 769–777 (1994)
13. Thapa, R., Jiao, L., Oommen, B.J., Yazidi, A.: A learning automaton-based scheme for scheduling domestic shiftable loads in smart grids. Unabridged Version of this Paper (2016)
14. Zhu, Z., Tang, J., Lambotharan, S., Chin, W.H., Fan, Z.: An integer linear programming based optimization for home demand-side management in smart grid. In: 2012 IEEE PES Innovative Smart Grid Technologies (ISGT), pp. 1–5. IEEE (2012)
15. Zimmermann, J.-P., Evans, M., Griggs, J., King, N., Harding, L., Roberts, P., Evans, C.: Household electricity survey: A study of domestic electrical product usage. Intertek Testing & Certification Ltd. (2012)

An Explicit Battery Discharging Model to Enable Vehicle to Grid Services

Sandford Bessler[✉]

Austrian Institute of Technology (AIT),
Donau-City 1, 1220 Vienna, Austria
sandford.bessler@ait.ac.at

Abstract. With the increased use of electric vehicles, the discharge of electric vehicle (EV) batteries (vehicle to grid, V2G) has been repeatedly proposed as enabler of smart grid services. In this work we describe the weaknesses of current discharging models and propose a model based on explicit discharging tasks. Using simulation in a microgrid control architecture, we realize several V2G use cases that involve aggregated loads and EVs, obtaining promising results.

Keywords: V2G · EV discharging model · Energy flexibility · Charging station · Demand management · Charging optimization · MPC · Microgrid · Mathematical programming

1   Introduction

Following the seminal papers of Kempton and Tomic [1,2] in which the authors present scenarios and business cases for supplying energy to the grid from batteries of plugged-in electric vehicles (PEV), a large number of publications emerged to analyze the benefits and drawbacks of the vehicle to grid (V2G) technology. At the time of writing the trend to efficient and "clean" EVs is unbroken, and the fact that private owned EV remain parked 90% of the time makes the use of the car battery for buffering energy appealing.

One of the most viable scenarios for V2G used in the integration of renewables into the grid to meet peak load by storing the energy from solar peak to the load peak, see [1,12]. Since the renewable power generation rate fluctuates strongly, the power output is often curtailed to reduce the variation. G2V and V2G would help to absorb these variations without curtailing.

In [3] the authors review the revenue opportunities of different use cases for the energy stored in EV batteries: regulation (frequency control), reserve (e.g. spinning capacity kept aside for cases of sudden power loss), renewable energy exploitation. The authors however warn that saturation in the reserve market would probably reduce the attractivity of such services. Although the revenues from V2G can attain several hundred dollars per year and vehicle, the authors of [3,4] arrive to the conclusion that most benefits of V2G can be provided as well through unidirectional, controlled charging.

© ICST Institute for Computer Sciences, Social Informatics and Telecommunications Engineering 2017
E.T. Lau et al. (Eds.): SmartGIFT 2017, LNICST 203, pp. 69–78, 2017.
DOI: 10.1007/978-3-319-61813-5_7

Several works [5,6,11] assume that the battery of an EV can be discharged anytime (if the EV is plugged-in) similarly to a fixed battery. We argue that this mode of operation has serious drawbacks, especially when a fleet of EVs is to be controlled, as we will point out in Sect. 2.

The prevalent model of anytime discharge of a plugged-in EV battery has a main drawback, as the EV owner has no control over the frequency and intensity of charge/discharge operations, as we will explain in the next section.

Therefore, similarly to charging tasks, we propose the introduction of explicit discharging tasks, as elements of future V2G services. These tasks are characterized by start and end times, by the amount of energy to be discharged, or a minimum discharging power required by some services. The user maintains in this way the control over the battery degradation, understands the value of the energy (and of the service) as well as the state of the battery before and after the discharge. Based on this model, a number of V2G use cases are simulated and discussed.

The rest of the paper is as organized as follows: in Sect. 2 we describe the model for explicit discharging tasks, and derive the energy flexibility of EV battery charging and discharging. Section 3 describes the control architecture in which we embed the charging and V2G operations and formulate the optimization problem for a charging station. Section 4 provides simulation results and Sect. 5 summarizes the lessons learned.

2   Flexibility Models for EV Charging and Discharging

2.1   Anytime Discharge

Most of the previous works on bidirectional charging use a model similar to a fixed battery. Mostly controlled in real-time by voltage or energy price, these home batteries may still have a schedule, stating for instance that at a certain time of the day, the state of charge should not fall below a certain value. In general, any trajectory that reaches this value, via charging and discharging is feasible.

EV battery models require more constraints, first of all because of their availability periods. The primary objective is to charge the battery to a certain state of charge, until a given time. Controlled charging allows to achieve this goal via many trajectories and avoids overloading the local grid connection. However if we add the possibility of discharging, the process becomes uncontrollable, especially if the control applies to a whole EV fleet. Therefore, in order to implement energy management functions with V2G, some authors [5,6] use heuristics. It cannot be avoided however, that some of the vehicles have to charge in order to achieve the SoC in time, while other vehicles discharge to provide V2G power. This can be seen as a net transfer of energy from one battery to another and is an undesirable side effect.

Moreover, the number of discharges and their intensity cannot be controlled with this model, therefore the battery deterioration cannot be estimated nor limited and compensation for this degradation cannot be calculated in the business model.

2.2 Explicit Modelling of Charging and Discharging Tasks

The proposed model is applicable to single PEV, a charging fleet or to a general EV service operator.

The mobility pattern has a considerable impact on the effectiveness of V2G operations; for example, in a working and living neighborhood, a part of the vehicles leave in the morning and arrive in the afternoon, while another part arrive in the morning and leave in the afternoon. Without explicit discharge tasks, V2G operations are not possible neither in the morning (because the just arrived cars have to charge first), nor in the afternoon, etc.

Crucial for the charging and discharging operations are energy and power flexibility. In Fig. 1 we illustrate the energy flexibility of a charging task, before the car is available at $t^a = 1$. Charging can be performed with power $p \in [0, p^c_{max}]$, $p^c_{max} = 2\,\text{kW}$, but in order to reach $E^c_{min} = 4\,\text{kWh}$ by the time $t^d = 6$, the car has to start charging at t = 4 at the latest.

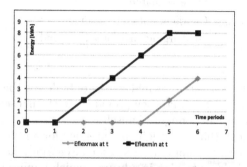

Fig. 1. Energy flexibility of a EV charging task

The first model we introduce is the **Energy based discharge task**. For the qualitative discussion we assume that the EV availability forecast is perfect, and neglect the energy losses of approximatively 12% [12] in charging and discharging.

The proposed discharge model defines a discharge task in a time interval $[t_a, t_d]$, similarly to the charging task. The flexibility of a discharge task as it appears at $t = 0$ is illustrated in Fig. 2 for a vehicle available between $t^a = 1$ and $t^d = 5$. In general the minimum and the maximum amount of energy provided by the battery can be specified. The discharge power is $p \in [0, p^d_{max}]$ with $p^d_{max} = 3\,\text{kW}$. The amount of energy to be injected in the grid during $[t_a, t_d]$ is at least E^d_{min} and is given. How long in advance this information is known to the system and how it is negotiated between EV owner and aggregator, is a matter of the service design and will not be detailed here. In case of peak load leveling or ancillary services (see [3] for an overview of services) the aggregator could for example perform a request for bids.

Table 1. Notation summary

Notation	Description
$j \in N$	Index the time periods
$i \in M$	Index of charging or discharging task
t_i^a, t_i^d	Time interval for task i
p_j^{in}	Injected power from the grid at time j
p_{max}^c	Max. charging power
p_{min}^d	Min. discharging power
p_{max}^d	Max. discharging power
$\underline{P}_{ij}, \overline{P}_{ij}$	Power flexibility
$\underline{E}_{ij}, \overline{E}_{ij}$	Power flexibility
$e_{i,j}$	Energy charged until j
p_{ij}	Power charged/discharged during interval j
SoC^i	State of charge
E_{min}^c, E_{max}^c	Charging minimum demand
E_{min}^d	Discharging guaranteed demand

On a household level, a service would consist of buffering the generated renewable energy in the EV battery and then provide it to the household via discharging tasks that the user can configure himself.

Like any technology that was originally intended for another purpose (charging energy for driving), the approach used for discharging has also drawbacks: it requires the stakeholders to plan in advance, which implies that services with fast response such as grid frequency control or spinning reserve are probably difficult to realize. This applies in general to any stand-by service, as well as to outage or islanding scenarios.

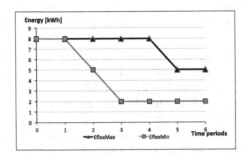

Fig. 2. Energy based EV discharge task

In a variant of the discharge task, the **Guaranteed power discharge task**, a minimum discharge rate p_{min}^d is specified in addition to the minimum energy amount, the maximum discharge rate and time interval. In Fig. 3 the discharge power can be selected between p^d_{min} and p^d_{max}. Any trajectory between the two curves, from the initial state of charge to the final SoC represent the same amount of energy discharged, in our example 28 kWh. The tangent at any point of the trajectory (the charging rate) must however be larger than p^d_{min}. Such a model might be required if a certain minimum power intensity has to be provided as part of the V2G service definition.

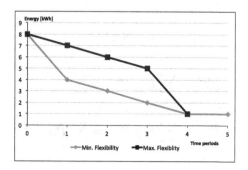

Fig. 3. Guaranteed power EV discharge task

3   Scheduling of Discharge Tasks in a Charging Station

We define a charging station as a parking lot and a fleet of PEVs, each connected to a charging point, so that controlled charging and discharging are possible. The charging station controller has the objective to optimize charging and discharging, such that the total load of the charging station follows the setpoints p^{ref} issued by a central controller (acording to a microgrid control architecture, for details see [7]). A factor that depends on the energy price c_j might be added to the objective. α is the weighting coefficient between the objective components. The local optimization problem at the charging station controller should satisfy the constraints (3), (4), (5), (6). For the schedule calculation, we use a simple model predictive control (MPC) [10] scheme in which the variables p, p^{in}, e, etc. are computed for the future N timeslots in each control loop iteration. It has to be noted that any other model that exploits the flexibility information from the charging and discharging models could be used instead.

$$min : \sum_{j \in N} (\alpha(p^{in}_j - p^{ref}_j)^2 + (1 - \alpha)c_j p^{in}_j) \qquad (1)$$

$$p^{in}_j = \sum_i p_{ij} \qquad (2)$$

$$\underline{P}_{ij} \le p_{ij} \le \overline{P}_{ij}, t_i^a \le j \le t_i^d \tag{3}$$

$$\underline{E}_{ij} \le e_{ij} \le \overline{E}_{ij}, t_i^a \le j \le t_i^d \tag{4}$$

$$e_{i,j} = 1/T p_{i,j-1} + e_{i,j-1} \tag{5}$$

$$e_{i,0} = SoC_i \tag{6}$$

$$\underline{E}_j^{CS} = \sum_i \underline{E}_{ij}; \underline{P}_j^{CS} = \sum_i \underline{P}_{ij} \tag{7}$$

$$\overline{E}_j^{CS} = \sum_i \overline{E}_{ij}; \overline{P}_j^{CS} = \sum_i \overline{P}_{ij} \tag{8}$$

3.1   Aggregation Optimization Model

At the top of the control scheme we use an low voltage grid (or microgrid) aggregation controller that supervises a set R of nodes composed representing residential loads, commercial loads and charging stations.

The limiting constraint in the aggregation function model is the rated power at the transformer (similar to the problem definition in [6]). Using the same model predictive control scheme, the aggregator solves the optimization problem (9, 10, 11) below, in each of the timeslots of the time horizon T, and calculates the setpoints for all the nodes in the microgrid, including the charging station. A setpoint for node i is related to its power consumption prediction by the relation: $p_i^{ref} = p_i^{in} + \beta_i$. p_i^{in} and the flexibility information can be provided by the nodes using a Demand Response communication protocol, such as OpenADR. The model uses the values of $\underline{P}^{CS}$, $\overline{P}^{CS}$, the predicted power consumption P^{in}. In the objective (9), we want to minimize the difference between the setpoint at time t and the setpoint at time t-1, similarly to [9], therefore we denote $p_i^{ref-} = (p_i^{in} + \beta_i)|_{t-1}$

minimize

$$\alpha \sum_{i \in R} \beta_i^2 + (1 - \alpha) \sum_{i \in R} (p_i^{ref} - p_i^{ref-})^2; \alpha \in [0,1] \tag{9}$$

subject to:

$$\sum_{i \in R} (p_i^{in} + \beta_i) \le P^{LV} \tag{10}$$

$$\underline{P}_i \le p_i^{in} + \beta_i \le \overline{P}_i, i \in R \tag{11}$$

4   Simulation Experiments

In the simulation experiments below we use a microgrid control architecture [7]: each charging station and each building has associated an energy management controller (CEMS); these controllers report to an aggregation controller that computes the appropriate setpoints for each facility.

Table 2. Parameters of the EV charging and discharging tasks used in the simulation experiments

Charge task	p^c_{max}	Charge t^a_i	dur[h]	E^c_{min}	Discharge task	Discharge t^a_i	dur[h]	E^d_{min}
C01	11	06:00	6	6	D01	15:00	4	-6
C02	12	07:00	9	8	D02	16:00	5	-8
C03	11	08:00	9	10	D03	17:00	4	-10
C04	12	10:00	2	4	D04	15:00	5	-6
C05	11	09:00	8	6	D05	16:00	4	-8
C06	11	14:00	2	5	D06	15:00	4	-5
C07	11	12:00	2	4	D07	16:00	5	-4
C08	11	07:00	9	8	D08	16:00	4	-8
C09	9	08:00	9	9	D09	16:00	4	-9
C10	12	09:00	8	7	D10	16:00	4	-7
C11	12	06:00	3	6	D11	16:00	4	-6
C12	11	08:00	3	6	D12	16:00	4	-6

In a first set of experiments we show that the load of a charging station can be strongly reduced if needed, thanks to the builtin flexibility. For this purpose, we artificially limit the total load and measure the charging performance of individual charging tasks. The simulation setting consists of 12 EV charging tasks associated to a charging station (see Table 2). The load limit P^{LV} is set to 8, 10 and 15 kW. Figure 4 shows the total charging load. In the 8 kW case the setpoint is not followed exactly, however for all three runs the energy demand E^c_{min} is fully satisfied.

The second experiment illustrates the peak load shaving use case. The same charging station controller manages now 12 discharging tasks which have been planned for the afternoon (3 pm to 8 pm), see Table 2. We assume that the batteries have the necessary amount of energy, for instance because they have been charged previously from PV generated power. For the load we use the models developed in the IRENE project [7,8] in which different buildings with critical and flexible load are available. We have selected two apartment blocks with 24 apartments each, with PV generation and flexible consumption (air condition). The whole microgrid load is limited to 70 kW to simulate the peak shaving requirement. In Fig. 5 we depict the total load after using the V2G discharging tasks and achieve the peak load reduction. It can be seen that the aggregated discharge based on V2G works and reduces the peak that otherwise would reach

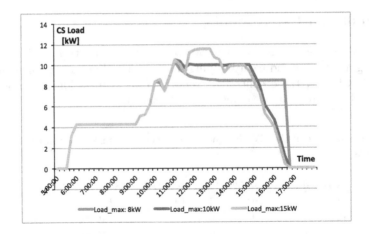

Fig. 4. Limiting the load of 12 charging EVs to 8, 10 and 15 kW

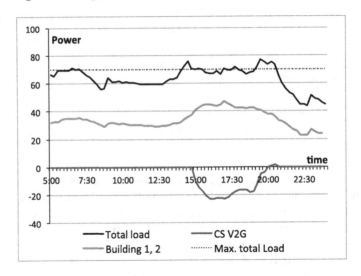

Fig. 5. (a) Charging station discharge only, (b) buildings load, (c) combined load

90 kW. We argue that such a behaviour cannot be achieved with the "anytime discharge" model presented in Sect. 2.1.

Finally, we adapt our simulation system to the use case of a single household that uses V2G for buffering renewable energy between the generation (midday) and consumption time (evening). Figure 6 shows only the discharging schedule: the discharge task is defined as follows: start at 6pm, duration 6 hours, $= E_{min}^d = E_{max}^d = -6$ kWh. If we require that the net power consumption of the house remains positive, then we obtain the behaviour in Fig. 6. The household power consumption is nicely mirrored by the discharge task, except for a few transient spikes.

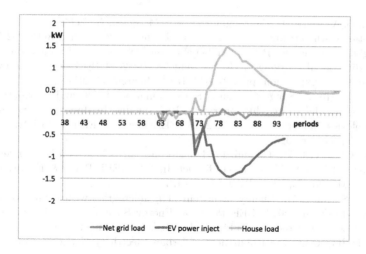

Fig. 6. Renewable integration for single house using a discharge task

5 Discussion and Concluding Remarks

In this work we analyzed two different models for discharging vehicle batteries: the first one ressembles to a home battery model, where no constraints on the number or intensities of discharging operations are imposed, and the second one, described in detail, defines a discharge job with a defined amount of energy.

Using the first model in a peak load shaving scenario we observed that almost no discharging takes place. The are several reasons for that, one is that charging flexibility is normally sufficient to address peak shaving. This holds for the whole charging period, which in case of controlled charging spreads over the whole parking period. In addition, discharging is associated with costs (it degrades the battery life time), therefore it comes as last alternative in achieving the optimization objective [3].

Although many scenarios have been proposed for V2G, three most viable have been simulated using the discharging task model and the results are promising. The discharging tasks can be managed by the user, increasing the acceptance and offer a clear basis for compensation and for estimating the battery degradation.

For the realisation of V2G scenarios that are beneficial to aggregated loads, more research related to the realisation of business models and payment possibilities to compensate the EV owners of the V2G service is needed.

References

1. Kempton, W., Tomic, J.: Vehicle-to-grid power implementation: from stabilizing the grid to supporting large-scale renewable energy. J. Power Sources **144**(1), 280–294 (2005). ISSN 0378–7753, doi:10.1016/j.jpowsour.2004.12.022
2. Kempton, W., Tomic, J.: Vehicle-to-grid power fundamentals: calculating capacity and net revenue. J. Power Sources **144**(1), 268–279 (2005). Elsevier

3. Damiano, A., Gatto, G., Marongiu, I., Porru, M., Serpi, A.: Vehicle-to-grid technology: state-of-the-art and future scenarios. J. Energy Power Eng. **8**(1), 152 (2014)
4. Fasugba, M.A., Krein, P.T.: Cost benefits and vehicle-to-grid regulation services of unidirectional charging of electric vehicles. In: 2011 IEEE Energy Conversion Congress and Exposition, pp. 827–834. IEEE, September 2011
5. Zhang, H., Hu, Z., Song, Y., Moura, S. Coordination of V2G and distributed wind power using the storage-like aggregate PEV model. In: Innovative Smart Grid Technologies Conference (ISGT), 2016 IEEE Power & Energy Society, pp. 1–5. IEEE, September 2016
6. Dang, X.L., Petit, M., Codani, P.: Transformer operating conditions under introduction of PV and EVs in an eco-district. In: 2015 IEEE Power & Energy Society General Meeting, pp. 1–5. IEEE, July 2015
7. Bessler, S., Jung, O.: Energy management in microgrids with flexible and interruptible loads. In: 2016 IEEE Power & Energy Society Innovative Smart Grid Technologies Conference (ISGT), pp. 1–6. IEEE, September 2016
8. IRENE, Improving the Robustness of Urban Electricity Networks. http://www.ireneproject.eu/
9. Sundstrom, O., Binding, C.: Flexible charging optimization for electric vehicles considering distribution grid constraints. IEEE Trans. Smart Grid **3**(1), 26–37 (2012)
10. Parisio, A., Rikos, E., Glielmo, L.: A model predictive control ap- proach to microgrid operation optimization. IEEE Trans. Control Syst. Technol. **22**(5), 1813–1827 (2014)
11. Corchero, C., Cruz-Zambrano, M., Heredia, F.J.: Optimal energy management for a residential microgrid including a vehicle-to-grid system. IEEE Trans. Smart Grid **5**(4), 2163–2172 (2014)
12. Clement-Nyns, K., Haesen, E., Driesen, J.: The impact of vehicle-to-grid on the distribution grid. Electr. Power Syst. Res. **81**(1), 185–192 (2011)

Grid and Components

Intelligent Signal Processing for the Use in Device Identification Using Smart Sockets

Al-Azhar Lalani$^{(\boxtimes)}$, Emilio Mistretta, and Johann Siau

University of Hertfordshire, Hatfield, Hertfordshire AL10 9AB, UK
{a.lalani,e.mistretta,j.siau}@herts.ac.uk

Abstract. In an era, that has seen an increase in smart socket adoption in homes, greater sensor data acquisition and data analytics within the Internet of things (IoT) platforms; new developments in hardware design and converging sensor data with big data introduces new research opportunities in the energy sector. Smart meters currently provide an overall energy usage for a household, by introducing socket level identification of electrical devices an itemised bill or detailed breakdown for device type or category can be achieved. Voltage and current waveforms extracted from sensors within a smart socket is processed using signal processing techniques for the use of pattern recognition. Experimental results for single device identification show that a low equal error rate can be achieved, therefore, increasing the likelihood of a successful device recognition.

Keywords: Smart socket · Signal processing · Pattern recognition · Smart meters · Energy monitoring

1 Introduction

The United Kingdom government has committed to the roll out of 53 million gas and electricity meters to all homes and small businesses by the end of year 2020 [1]. The new smart meters aim to provide a better management for energy use as they can inform the user on how much energy they have been using in near real time via a display in the house linked wirelessly, commonly by 802.11 (Wi-Fi) or 802.15.4 (ZigBee) to the smart meter. With the introduction of device energy monitoring a breakdown can be made of what a typical smart meter provides which is just an overall house usage, this breakdown could be in the form of categories such as lighting, heating, always on devices etc. or a further breakdown of individual appliances such as kettle, toaster or washing machine.

The Smart Systems Research Team at the University of Hertfordshire have developed a smart socket that will be used as the primary testing platform for device identification. Similarly, other smart sockets available on the market provide the ability to remotely control the on/off status of each socket however, with the addition of sensors to monitor the energy that is being drawn by a device. Data can be sent via a wireless transmission to the cloud where algorithms are conducted to provide results of a most likely device match. Obtaining a current waveform allows the system to identify and differentiate between known devices as oppose to the new generation of smart meters, which are only capable of reading overall energy utilised. This research

© ICST Institute for Computer Sciences, Social Informatics and Telecommunications Engineering 2017
E.T. Lau et al. (Eds.): SmartGIFT 2017, LNICST 203, pp. 81–86, 2017.
DOI: 10.1007/978-3-319-61813-5_8

presents the ability for the identification of electrical devices and appliances wired to a traditional UK mains socket. Using a socket as an instrument to monitor, control and measure energy utilisation as a simple means to integrate more sophisticated and smarter devices around a smart home or building [2].

There are key benefits that can help this research contribute to smarter buildings and the future of energy management.

Control and convenience: Having a smart outlet will allow remote control either by individuals or by a local or remote control strategy, for example demand-side management. If the concept of device identification is introduced it could grant a level of security to what can be plugged in to the outlet or control the load as part of an energy saving policy. This could be particularly beneficial to institutions such as hospitals, government buildings or public places by refusing an outlet to supply electricity to either unauthorised or power hungry devices.

Maintenance and business continuity: Digital data is a big part of information gathering and exchange for the majority of businesses and is essential to operations and business continuity. The potential exists for the smart outlet socket to be part of an innovative system that would monitor a device's electrical signature therefore determining its health status; pre-empting a product failure [3].

Electricity monitoring: Finally, a potential significant benefit would be the categorisation of electrical usage by device type. This could offer the energy provider or consumer full disclosure by itemising and categorising electricity consumption by time of day, device, consumption, priority etc. [4].

This paper presents the findings of using a signal processing technique with current waveforms, from varying electrical devices. Section 2 describes the experimental setup as well as the gathering of current waveform data, feature extraction process and the comparison of devices. Section 3 highlights the results of experiments conducted in Sect. 2. Section 4 concludes the results and summarises this paper.

2   Experimental Setup

2.1   Data Acquisition

The smart socket with integrated energy monitoring was utilised to conduct the identification of devices at socket level connected to a single outlet. The internal hardware is capable of measuring voltage waveforms and current measurements from an individual outlet.

Voltage is measured using a fully-differential isolation amplifier to safely insulate high side live electrical connections from the low side logic controllers. A voltage divider circuit is used to step down from 240 VAC to a manageable 3 VAC.

Current measurements were attained using Hall Effect linear based current sensors (Allegro MicroSystems, Inc., Worcester, MA, USA, model ACS758) wired in series between the live electrical feed and socket outlet.

Voltage and current measurements were sampled using a 16-bit analogue-to-digital converter (ADC) (Maxim Integrated, San Jose, CA, USA, model MAX1300) at a sampling rate of 26ksps. Data collected was streamed in near real-time to a microcontroller connected via a personal computer that extracted the measurements and processed the data before being uploaded to a cloud platform that performed a pattern recognition algorithm.

2.2 Device Recognition

For the purpose of this experiment, four common household electrical devices (Table 1) were selected to ascertain different loads. Each device was connected individually to a single outlet ensuring a dedicated and clean signal, which was free from noise induced by other devices. All devices were powered 'on' to their respective operating states. To digitise an analogue signal by using an ADC, a devices waveform is continuously sampled at intervals to capture discrete points along a time domain in order to accurately reconstruct the original sampled signal. By sampling at an insufficient rate, there may not be enough samples to capture the changes in frequency or amplitude; thereby causing a problem where information is getting missed which may

Table 1. Electrical devices used in experiment for training and device identification.

Device	Device type	Figure
1	Desk fan	Fig. 1(a)
2	Incandescent lamp	Fig. 1(b)
3	Personal desktop computer	Fig. 1(c)
4	LCD TV	Fig. 1(d)

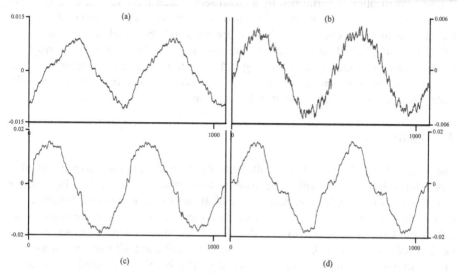

Fig. 1. Current waveforms of tested electrical devices sampled over 40 ms: (a) Desk fan, (b) Incandescent lamp, (c) Personal desktop computer, and (d) LCD TV. X-axis units - # of samples, Y-axis units - mV

also lead to the wrong signal being perceived entirely, this is known as Aliasing [5]. Alternatively, the greater the sampling rate the more accurate the wave reconstruction will be which will result in a higher identification rate amongst known devices.

2.3 Feature Extraction

Measurements were taken simultaneously from all sensors (i.e. one voltage and two current) to maintain that all samples are in sync with one another, thereby accurately detecting if devices connected to the smart socket outlets were resistive, inductive or capacitive loads. Resistive loads are recognised where the voltage and current are in phase; on the contrary, inductive and capacitive loads occur when the voltage and current are out of phase. Inductive loads affect the phase by delaying the current to the device and the opposite happens to the capacitive loads.

Extracted measurements consist of 40 ms analysis windows (European voltage frequency is 50 Hz × 2 cycles), for all sensors and discards data before and after to capture a single waveform. The real power values are also computed from current and voltage measurements using the trimmed analysis windows.

Signal processing techniques were applied to the device waveforms which produced training data that was uploaded to a database. A further experiment was conducted to attain the most suitable parameters by varying the number of coefficients, windowing methods, and percentage of window overlap. A total of 52,800 training data were stored for each device.

2.4 Pattern Classification

Pattern classification is performed by a cloud server after receiving the data from the real-time feature extraction process. This data is compared against trained data stored in the database as a series of clusters. In order for a match to be found, this comparison is calculated using Euclidean distance, the process measures the distance of the resultant features derived by the signal processing technique to provide a distance or error rate closest to a known pattern. A second stage verification is performed on a successful match to determine if the deviation of features are within a known device.

3 Results

The results shown in Figs. 2 and 3 illustrate the normal and cumulative distribution scores for trained devices within the database to determine an acceptable Equal Error Rate (EER) used for an identification threshold. By using the normal distribution scores to establish a successful match vs. an incorrect match, a False Rejection Rate (FRR) and False Acceptance Rate (FAR) plotted onto a cumulative distribution graph can be used to compute an EER where the points of FRR and FAR intersect. In the case of an 'incandescent lamp', the identification algorithm is able to differentiate between a known and an imposter device.

Furthermore, these results illustrate each device grouped by its category type to an individual curve, the curves are plotted against a measure of Euclidean distance

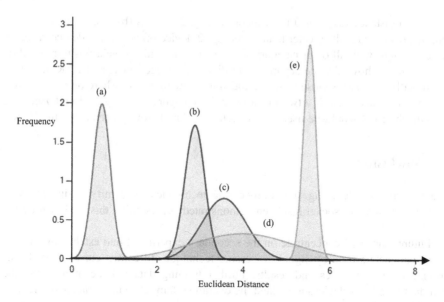

Fig. 2. Normal distribution curves of trained devices compared against an incandescent lamp: (a) Incandescent lamp, (b) LCD TV, (c) Personal desktop computer, (d) All devices, and (e) Desk fan.

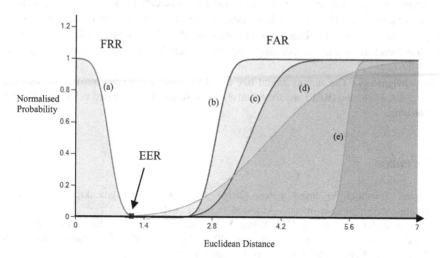

Fig. 3. Cumulative distribution curve of trained devices compared against an incandescent lamp; results show FRR, FAR and EER. (a) Incandescent lamp, (b) LCD TV, (c) Personal desktop computer, (d) All devices, and (e) Desk fan.

returned by the identification algorithm. A distance closest to zero indicates a high probability of a known device, vice versa for devices that are unknown or not identified as the primary device will return a result which is greater than a known device. In the instance of this experiment, Fig. 2 device (a) has been identified as the known device between a distance range of 0 to 1; incorrect Fig. 2 devices (b), (c), (d) and (e) have returned distance results greater than 2. As Fig. 2 device (a) is the sole device category closest to zero with all other categories not intersecting this curve a positive match is made. This is shown by the separation in distance between FRR and FAR in Fig. 3, additionally the EER is close to zero indicating a low threshold where only the known device will be accepted. If a two or more device category curves were to intersect one another, the EER would be used as a threshold value therefore decreasing the FAR.

4   Conclusion

The experiment into using signal-processing techniques to identify a single device plugged into a smart socket has been demonstrated successfully, this is shown by the low EER in Fig. 3.

Future work will concentrate on the secondary experiment into establishing which set of parameters used by signal processing techniques to extract current waveforms provide optimal features and results. Further training data will be attained by the introduction of new devices to expand the overall system recognition rate and fine-tune the EER.

The present results look very encouraging when identifying single devices, however, it becomes challenging when multiple devices are plugged into a single outlet (via an extension cord) as a new current waveform would be created with combined features which the system would not be able to identify. Furthermore, as new devices are added, the probability of new combined waveforms trained to the system would exponentially increase therefore making it increasing difficult to handle multiple devices at this time.

Acknowledgments. The authors would like to acknowledge the funding provide by Building Research Establishment (BRE) and the Smart Systems Research Team based at the University of Hertfordshire.

References

1. Ofgem, Transition to smart meters (2016). https://www.ofgem.gov.uk/gas/retail-market/metering/transition-smart-meters. Accessed 16 April 2016
2. Asare-Bediako, B., Ribeiro, P.F., Kling, W.L.: Integrated energy optimization with smart home energy management systems. In: 2012 3rd IEEE PES Innovative Smart Grid Technologies Europe (ISGT Eur.), pp. 1–8 (2012)
3. Yaqub, R., Hamid, B., Ul Asar, A.: Appliance performance monitoring and warranty alert system. In: ICOSST 2013 - 2013 International Conference on Open Source Systems Technologies Process, pp. 13–17 (2013)
4. Zhou, L., Xu, F.Y., Ma, Y.N.: Impact of smart metering on energy efficiency. In: 2010 International Conference on Machine Learning and Cybernetics, ICMLC 2010, vol. 6, pp. 3213–3218 (2010)
5. Marks, R.J.: Introduction to Shannon Sampling and Interpolation Theory. Springer, New York (1991)

Design of a Seismic Hazard Risk Assessment Model for EHV Transmission Grid

Ching-Ya Tseng, Chien-Hao Wang, Xiang-Yao Zheng,
Huan-Chieh Chiu, and Joe-Air Jiang[(⊠)]

Department of Bio-Industrial Mechatronics Engineering,
National Taiwan University, No. 1, Sec. 4, Roosevelt Road,
Taipei 10617, Taiwan (R.O.C.)
luisaariel24@gmail.com, r99631025@gmail.com,
{f01631018,r05631030,jajiang}@ntu.edu.tw

Abstract. The Chi-Chi earthquake is one of the biggest earthquake occurred in Taiwan and caused a huge damage to the power system, especially the extra-high voltage (EHV) towers. Therefore, seismic hazards for EHV transmission towers should not be underestimated. In particular, earthquakes are especially a significant threat to EHV transmission towers in Taiwan. Thus, this study establishes a quantitative risk assessment model for the seismic hazard analysis on the EHV transmission tower. Fragility curves of EHV towers were established by nonlinear dynamic analysis to describe the probability of structures at different damage levels caused by earthquakes. The damage level of an EHV tower after an earthquake can be accurately estimated by the proposed model, and emergency repair operations can be arranged. In addition, before an earthquake occurs, the proposed model can be used as a tool for estimate the damage potential of EHV towers.

Keywords: Smart grid · Transmission tower · Seismic hazard risk assessment · Nonlinear dynamic analysis · Fragility curve

1 Introduction

Issues regarding power system stability, reliability, and the capability to recover from power failure incidents become more important nowadays. The extra-high voltage (EHV) transmission system, as a core, is the most important lifeline engineering structure for power systems, and its safety is paramount. Taiwan is located in the circum-Pacific seismic belt. Therefore, earthquakes frequently occur. Approximately 23,000 earthquakes strike Taiwan every year. Since 1901, Taiwan has been attacked by 101 disastrous earthquakes [1]. In 1999 a disastrous earthquake, which is the largest earthquake in Taiwan's history, occurred in Chi-Chi, Nantou County, and caused huge damage to Taiwan. The damage of transmission towers and distribution lines caused the Taipower Company losing NT$5.94 billion. And the social cost only in northern Taiwan brought by the constraints on electricity supply was estimated up to NT$63.68 billion [2, 3]. There were 3,741 EHV tower at that time, and a total of 307 EHV transmission towers were damaged by the earthquake [4]. The result showed that the

© ICST Institute for Computer Sciences, Social Informatics and Telecommunications Engineering 2017
E.T. Lau et al. (Eds.): SmartGIFT 2017, LNICST 203, pp. 87–97, 2017.
DOI: 10.1007/978-3-319-61813-5_9

damage of the EHV transmission towers by Chi-Chiearthquake is a unique and far-reaching form of the power system seismic damage in Taiwan [5].

The earthquake loss assessment was proposed to calculate the seismic hazard at all sites of interest and to convolve this hazard with the vulnerability of the exposed building stock such that the damage distribution of the structure stock can be predicted; damage ratios, which relate the cost of repair and replacement to the cost of demolition and replacement of the structures, can then be used to calculate the loss. Constructing an earthquake loss model involves compiling databases of earthquake activity, ground conditions, ground-motion prediction equations, building stock and infrastructure exposure, and vulnerability characteristics of the exposed inventory [6, 7]. For earthquake risk assessments, a fragility curve is used for determining the damage level of a structure and the potential of seismic hazard for a given area. The fragility curve can describe the probability of structures at different damage levels caused by an earthquake. Researchers have been proposed to use four different methods, judgement-based, empirical, analytical, and hybrid, to create the fragility curve according to whether the damage data used in the methods mainly come from observed expert opinions, post-earthquake surveys, analytical simulations [8–11].

Thus, a seismic hazard risk assessment model for EHV transmission towers is established and fragility curves of the EHV transmission tower are created in this paper. And the rationality of the model is verified to provide effective hazard risk assessment for the constructed towers. Therefore the damage level of an EHV power transmission system after an earthquake can be accurately estimated by the proposed model, and emergency repair operations can be fast arranged.

The content of each section is summarized as follows. Section 2 explains the method and procedure to establish the seismic risk assessment model of EHV transmission towers. Section 3 examines the accuracy of the established EHV transmission tower model. Section 4 summarizes the results of this study and describes some research issues for future studies.

2 Seismic Hazard Risk Assessment Model

In order to establish a seismic hazard risk assessment model for 345 kV towers, a research process was developed in this paper. The flowchart of the proposed procedure is shown in Fig. 1. The historical information of seismic stations that measured different intensities of the Chi-Chi earthquake was chosen to be studied. Then, the characteristics and types of EHV towers were classified to establish an EHV tower structural model. And, the seismic damage probability for an EHV tower was analyzed to establish the fragility curve for the tower. Among the methods used to establish fragility curves, the nonlinear dynamic analysis method can more realistically reflect the true response of EHV towers in earthquakes. In the nonlinear dynamic analysis, the tower is viewed to be directly affected by historical earthquakes with varying degrees. In order to establish the tower model and perform the analysis, the finite element analysis software "SAP2000" was used in this study. The SAP2000 is developed by Computers and Structures, Inc., and is widely used in civil engineering, and its credibility is well known in civil engineering [12]. Finally, after considering the maintenance cost of an electrical tower, a

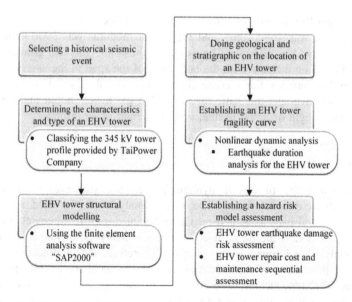

Fig. 1. The flowchart of establishing a seismic hazard risk assessment model for the EHV transmission tower

complete set of the seismic hazard risk assessment model was developed. The established model can increase the speed and efficiency in dealing with seismic incidents for an EHV transmission grid. Each research methods will be sequentially introduced in the following subsections.

2.1   EHV Transmission Tower Structural Modelling

The A4 and the C5 type EHV transmission tower were the most seriously damaged types of towers in the Chi-Chi earthquake, as indicated by Table 1, according to the earthquake statistics [13]. In this study, the A4 EHV transmission tower was studied as an example. According to the detailed information about the A4 provided by Taipower, a three-dimensional tower structural model was established by using the SAP2000. The model components were defined as members and joints, and all elements were established following the exact size and material properties of an A4 tower. The structural members were connected with fastened joints in the simulation. A total 1406 members and 527 joints were used in the A4 tower model. The static load of a tower included the tower self-load and the weight of ground wires, conductors, and insulators. All static load settings were based on the information provided by Taipower.

In order to ensure that the tower model represented the real situation, the weight of the connected plates and bolts was added to the corresponding joints. Moreover, the ground wire used by Taipower was 19NO.8 Aluminum Clad Steel Wire (ACW), the unit weight W_g was 1.062 kg/m, the cross-sectional area A_g was 159 mm2, and the elastic modulus was 10500 kg/mm2. The conductor was 795MCM (26/7) Aluminum

Conductors Steel Reinforced (ACSR), the unit weight Wc was 1.628 kg/m, the cross-sectional area A_g was 468.5 mm^2, and the elastic modulus was 8900 kg/mm^2. The weight of insulator I was 1030 kg. The weight of the conductors and ground wire was evenly distributed on the towers at the both ends of the span in the assessment. And, according to the statistics, the average distance between the 345 kV towers is about 360 m. Thus, on average, the static load of a 345 kV tower should include its own weight and the weight of a 360 m line, and the weight of an insulator.

2.2   Modal Analysis

A modal analysis is the study of the dynamic properties of structures under vibrational excitation without external forces. The modal analysis can be used to determine qualitative structural responses, and provide relevant design requirements of a structural concept. It is also the basis of other dynamic analyses, including the response spectrum analysis and time history analysis. Therefore, the nonlinear time history analysis used the results of the modal analysis as an auxiliary in this study. Many factors affect the dynamic responses of the structure. In addition to the loads and external factors such as environmental conditions (e.g. seismic force) and other internal conditions, the dynamic characteristics of the structure itself (e.g. natural frequency, structural damping) are also related to the dynamic responses of the structure. However, before analyzing the seismic dynamic response of transmission towers, the structural natural vibration duration and frequency and the modal shapes which show the structure vibration form under a certain frequency must be understood, and the parameters can be obtained by using the modal analysis. A modal analysis solves differential equations of motion to obtain the natural frequencies and mode shapes. A transmission tower can be regarded as a degree of freedom (D.O.F.) system. The differential equation of motion can be expressed as

$$\mathbf{M} \cdot \overrightarrow{\ddot{u}}(t) + \mathbf{C} \cdot \overrightarrow{\dot{u}}(t) + \mathbf{K} \cdot \overrightarrow{u}(t) = 0, \tag{1}$$

where $\mathbf{M}$ is the mass matrix, $\mathbf{C}$ is the damping matrix, and $\mathbf{K}$ is the stiffness matrix. $\overrightarrow{\ddot{u}}(t)$, $\overrightarrow{\dot{u}}(t)$ and $\overrightarrow{u}(t)$ are acceleration, velocity, and displacement vector, respectively.

Because the modal analysis does not consider the non-linear factors, the damping is negligible. (1) can be reduced to

$$\mathbf{M} \cdot \overrightarrow{\ddot{u}}(t) + \mathbf{K} \cdot \overrightarrow{u}(t) = 0. \tag{2}$$

The solution of the differential equation of motion is defined as

$$u(t) = u \sin(\omega t). \tag{3}$$

(3) is substituted into (2):

$$(\mathbf{K} - \omega^2 \cdot \mathbf{M}) \cdot \overrightarrow{u} = 0. \tag{4}$$

Table 1. The types and quantity of EHV towers damaged in the Chi-Chi earthquake

Type	Number of damaged towers	Type	Number of damaged towers
A	8	D5	1
A1	1	DH43	5
A4	15	DH48	3
A5	14	E	3
B	2	E5	3
B2	2	E5G	4
C	11	F	7
C2	1	F1	1
C4	1	F5	2
C5	15	FT	1
D	3	G	3
D1	2	G4	5
D3	2	G5	1

(4) represents an eigenvalue problem, and ω^2 is the eigenvalue. The square root of ω^2 is the natural frequency, ω, of the system. The minimum value of ω is the basic natural frequency, and each natural frequency value may correspond to a modal shape. In this study, the modal analysis tools provided by SAP2000 were used to perform the modal analysis. The calculation of the structural weight and mass in the SAP2000 were based on the definitions of the material density, weight, and the setting load.

2.3   Nonlinear Time History Analysis

A time history analysis can simulate the dynamic response of structures in earthquakes. The time-history analysis provides for linear or nonlinear evaluation of dynamic structural responses (displacement, force, stress, spectrum, etc.). This study employed a nonlinear evaluation in the time history analysis. The time functions used in this study were the peak ground acceleration (PGA) data from the Chi-Chi earthquake provided by CWB [14]. The data length of the Chi-Chi earthquake was 90 s, and the sampling rate was 200 Hz. The information of the selected station of the Chi-Chi earthquake is listed in Table 2. After performing a time history analysis, the horizontal displacement of each tower joint as well as the PGA response spectrum of the tower at the Chi-Chi earthquake can be obtained. These data can be used to establish subsequent fragility curves.

2.4   Seismic Fragility Curves

In this study, the seismic fragility curves were developed to provide information necessary for predicting the damage to transmission towers caused by earthquakes. The development of seismic fragility curves requires the synergistic use of nonlinear dynamic structural analysis results. The seismic fragility curves were derived by using

Table 2. The Chi-Chi earthquake data from the selected stations

Station name	Epicenter distance (km)	Intensity	PGA direction		
			X (gal)	Y (gal)	Z (gal)
TCU078	5.53	7	171.00	302.48	439.70
TCU071	15.07	7	415.54	639.00	517.82
CHY006	40.23	6	211.02	351.46	348.00
TCU075	20.06	6	223.88	257.32	325.34
TCU102	44.93	6	173.28	168.98	298.36
CHY025	31.74	5	169.70	152.04	158.56
CHY087	59.94	5	55.14	125.32	132.36
HWA013	80.07	5	61.26	111.26	139.78
TAP010	150.04	5	27.22	85.96	114.90
TCU087	55.07	5	91.10	111.50	119.16
TCU096	105.29	5	36.66	106.00	54.02
CHY070	115.15	4	16.62	47.56	38.04
ILA008	135.06	4	33.32	56.52	77.40
KAU044	159.82	4	10.52	37.74	35.76
TAP024	145.20	4	23.38	75.96	61.60
TAP069	175.01	4	12.08	35.36	25.78
TTN041	85.31	4	38.88	64.24	79.14
TTN044	100.16	4	32.06	54.84	49.22
KAU052	211.22	3	4.84	7.48	10.40
KAU040	184.04	2	6.31	7.64	7.81

the maximum likelihood estimation method in this study. Shinozuka *et al.* assumed that the curves can be expressed in the form of two-parameter lognormal distribution functions, and the estimation of the two parameters (median c and log-standard deviation ζ) was performed with the aid of the maximum likelihood method [15]. For this purpose, the PGA was used to represent the intensity of the seismic ground motion. The likelihood function for the present purpose is expressed as follows:

$$L = \prod_{i=1}^{N} [F(a_i)]^{x_i} [1 - F(a_i)]^{1-x_i}, \tag{5}$$

where $F(\cdot)$ represents the fragility curve for a specific state of damage; a_i represents the PGA value of tower i; $x_i = 1$ or 0 depending on whether or not the tower sustains the state of damage when PGA $= a_i$; and N represents the total number of towers inspected after the earthquake occurred. With the current lognormal assumption, $F(a)$ takes the following analytical form:

$$F(a) = \Phi \left[\frac{\ln\left(\frac{a}{c}\right)}{\zeta} \right] \tag{6}$$

in which a represents PGA; and $\Phi[\cdot]$ is the standardized normal distribution function. The two parameters c and ζ in (6) are computed as c_e and ζ_e satisfying the following equations to maximize $\ln L$ and hence L:

$$\frac{d \ln L}{d c_e} = \frac{d \ln L}{d \zeta_e} = 0. \tag{7}$$

Finally, the value c_e and ζ_e of the curves can be obtained. The story drift ratios of a tower as the damage index produced by time history analysis described the threshold of damage states for the evaluation of fragility curves. If the story drift ratio was greater, the extent of the damage was greater. The story drift ratio was determined by using the time history analysis provided by the SAP2000. The time history analysis outputted the layer horizontal displacement relative to the base, and then the displacement difference between tower layers δ was calculated and divided by the height of tower layers h to obtain the story drift ratio θ as the following formula:

$$\theta = \frac{\delta}{h}. \tag{8}$$

Thus, when a layer of the story drift ratio was particularly high, it may indicated that this weak layer was more likely to suffer from the damage. The HAZUS MR4 represented the extent of the damage defined by a different story drift ratio [16]. As mentioned in the document, the damage state from light to heavy was divided into four categories: Slight, Moderate, Extensive, and Complete for 16 basic structural types. The transmission tower used in the analysis belonged to Steel Braced Frame Type (S2). The story drift ratio thresholds of various damage states for S2 are shown in Table 3. Because no other valid damage state specifications for transmission tower were available, this study used the story drift ratio thresholds of HAZUS MR4 to establish fragility curves.

3 Simulation Result

In this study, A4 tower is assumed being mounted on the ground, so the feet edge of tower is set as fastened joint in sap2000. According to the study procedures of Sect. 2, fragility curves of A4 is eventually established by the results of nonlinear dynamic analysis.

3.1 Story Drift Ratio

Through the time history analysis in SAP2000, A4 tower horizontal displacement under the chosen stations can be calculated. Figure 2(a) shows the horizontal displacement under station CHY006. Substituting the horizontal displacements obtained above into (8) story drift ratio can be calculated, as shown in Fig. 2(b). According to

Table 3. The story drift ratio thresholds of various damage states for S2 ates

Building properties		Story drift ratio thresholds of damage states		
Type	Height (m)	Slight	Moderate	Extensive complete
S2L	7.3152	0.0050	0.0100	0.0300 0. 0800
S2 M	18.288	0.0033	0.0067	0.0200 0. 0533
S2H	47.5488	0.0025	0.0050	0.0150 0. 0400

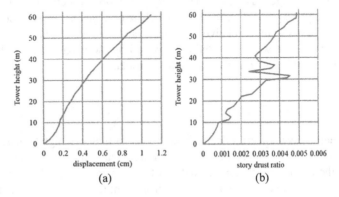

Fig. 2. (a) A4 tower horizontal displacement at CHY006 station, and (b) A4 tower story drift ratio at CHY006 station

the statistics results in the study, the maximum drift ratios are all on the top area of A4 under each station data. It can be presumed that the top area may be the most vulnerable place for transmission towers.

3.2   PGA Response Spectrum

The A4 tower PGA response spectrum under the different station data can also be obtained through the time history analysis. Since the transmission tower belongs to steel structure, the damping ratio choose 2%. Also, the fundamental period of A4 calculated by modal analysis is 0.369985 s. Figure 3 shows the A4 tower PGA response spectrum at different station. The PGA response value of each station which is corresponded to the fundamental period is also listed in Table 4.

3.3   Fragility Curve

In this study, the fragility curves is established inaccordance with the damage state distinguished by story drift ratio provided by HAZUS MR4. Then the calculated story drift ratios combined with the PGA values, and the relationship between story drift ratio

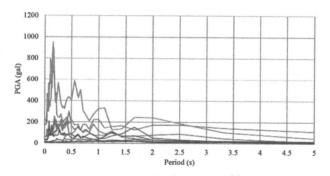

Fig. 3. A4 tower PGA response spectrum at different station

Table 4. PGA response values of the stations at fundamental period point

Station	PGA value	Station	PGA value
TCU078	315.21	TCU096	68.709
TCU071	424.28	CHY070	5.2535
CHY006	340.9	ILA008	81.592
TCU075	365.34	KAU044	27.99
TCU102	198.87	TAP024	65.518
CHY025	192	TAP069	87.343
CHY087	139.24	TTN041	91.018
HWA013	174.96	TTN044	101.61
TAP010	92.258	KAU052	7.0764
TCU087	225.69	KAU040	12.651

Table 5. The medians and standard deviations of each damage state

Damage state	Median c (gal)	Deviation ζ (gal)
Light	275	624
Moderate	551	624
Extensive	1102	615
Complete	2203	615

and PGA has been calculated. According to story drift ratios of A4 the damage state is divided into four categories: slight, moderate, extensive, complete. And the number of each damage state corresponding to the PGA value are counted, and substitute into (6), (7) to calculate the median c and deviation ζ. The medians and standard deviations of each damage state are listed in Table 5, and four fragility curves of A4 are drawn as shown in Fig. 4.

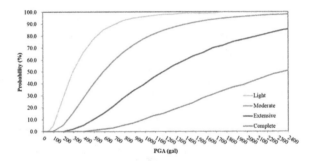

Fig. 4. Fragility curves of A4

4 Conclusions

This study establishes a seismic hazard risk assessment model for A4 tower structure. The damage level of a power transmission system after an earthquake can be accurately estimated by the established fragility curves. However, the seismic hazard risk assessment model is not only for this case. It can be set into any types of transmission towers and easy to build. Therefore, this model is looking forward to be widely used. This model will add the building and maintenance costs of towers in the future. Therefore, the emergency repair operations can be fast arranged. In addition, before an earthquake occurs, the reliable assessment data obtained by the proposed model can be used as a tool for establishing a pre-disaster risk management system for Power Company or the government. Also, In order to be closer to the state of the installed tower, the bases under towers and geological factors will be considered to achieve integrity of simulation.

Acknowledgments. This work was financially supported in part by the Ministry of Science and Technology, Taiwan, under contract no. MOST 105-2221-E-002-132- MY3, MOST 105-2622-E-002 -004-CC2, MOST 105-3113-E-002-013 and MOST 106-3113-E-002-012.

References

1. Central Weather Bureau. Meteorology Encyclopedia FAQ for Earthquake. CWB, Taipei, October 2015. http://www.cwb.gov.tw/V7/knowledge/encyclopedia/eq000.htm
2. Lo, C.H., Huang, C.Y., Wen, K.L., Lin, M.L., Hsiao, C.P., Chang, K.C., Shih, P.C., Hsu, M.H., Lin, C.C., Wang, H.K., Chien, W.Y., Chai, C.F., Teng, C.J., Yeh, C.H., Huang, C.H., Liu, C.Y., Teng, W.H., Chang, S.Y., Yeh, Y.K., Lai, M.J., Wang, S.M., Chung, L.L., Liao, W.Y., Li, C.K., Hsu, C.C.: A Summary Report on the Comprehensive Disaster Relief of the 921 Earthquake, National Center for Research on Earthquake Engineering, Taipei, Technical report NCREE-99-033, December 1999 (Chinese)

3. Hsu, C.Y., Chen, C.S., Tseng, S.W., Ho, H.Y., Sun, S.W., Wei, C.A., Chou, C.H.: Analysis on the Security Policy of China's Electric Power System from "729" and "921" Blackout, Research, Development and Evaluation Commission, Taipei, Technical report RDEC-RES-089-002, February 2000 (Chinese)
4. Hung, H.Y., Wen, C.L., Ko, M.C., Liu, C.Y., Yeh, C.H.: Study on Estimation Model of Underground Pipeline, Transmission Tower and Post-earthquake Fire Disaster. National Center for Research on Earthquake Engineering, Taipei, Technical report NCREE-07-020, Jun. 2007 (Chinese)
5. Liu, C.Y., Wang, Y.J., Liu, C.W.: Study on Estimation Model of Disaster Loss after Earthquake, National Center for Research on Earthquake Engineering, Taipei, Technical report NCREE-08-009, April 2008 (Chinese)
6. Calvi, G.M., Pinho, R., Magenes, G., Bommer, J.J., Restrepo-Vélez, L.F., Crowley, H.: Development of seismic vulnerability assessment methodologies over the past 30 years. ISET J. Earthquake Technol. **43**(3), 75–104 (2006)
7. Kircher, C.A., Nassar, A.A., Kustu, O., Holmes, W.T.: Development of building damage functions for earthquake loss estimation. Earthq. Spectra **13**(4), 663–682 (1997)
8. Shinozuka, M., Feng, M.Q., Lee, J., Naganuma, T.: Statistical analysis of fragility curves. J. Eng. Mech. **126**(12), 1224–1231(2000b)
9. Rossetto, T., Elnashai, A.: Derivation of vulnerability functions for european-type RC structures based on observational data. Eng. Struct. **25**(10), 1241–1263 (2003)
10. Griffin, M.J.: Earthquake performance of nonstructural components and systems difficulties in achieving enhanced earthquake performance. In: Earthquake Engineering Research Institute (EERI), 100th Anniversary Earthquake Conference, San Francisco, California, pp. 18–22, April 2006
11. Rota, M., Penna, A., Strobbia, C.L.: Processing Italian damage data to derive typological fragility curves. Soil Dyn. Earthq. Eng. **28**(10), 933–947 (2008)
12. CSI. SAP2000. Ver. 17.0. Berkeley, California: Computer and Structure, Inc. (2014)
13. Department of Electrical System, Summarization and Review of Damage of Transmission Tower Foundation in the Earthquake of 21 September 1999 (Chinese). Taipei: Taipower Company, pp. 11–42 (2000)
14. Central Weather Bureau. Seismicity. CWB, Taipei, March 2015. http://www.cwb.gov.tw/V7/earthquake/damage_eq.htm
15. Shinozuka, M., Feng, M.Q., Kim, H.K., Kim, S.H.: Nonlinear static procedure for fragility curve development. J. Eng. Mech. **126**(12), 1287–1295 (2000)
16. (NIBS and FEMA) National Institute of Building Sciences and Federal Emergency Management Agency, HAZUS-MH MR4 technical manual, multi-hazard loss estimation methodology earthquake model. Washington, DC: Federal Emergency Management Agency, pp. 184–211 (2003)

A Review of Wireless Power Transfer Electric Vehicles in Vehicle-to-Grid Systems

Chao Liu[✉], Eng Tseng Lau, Kok Keong Chai, and Yue Chen

Queen Mary University of London, Electronic Engineering, London, E1 4NS, UK
{c.liu,e.t.lau,michael.chai,yue.chen}@qmul.ac.uk

Abstract. Wireless power transfer (WPT) for electric vehicles (EVs) provides further ancillary services for Vehicle-to-grid (V2G) system. This paper reviews the current WPT technologies including their principles and applications in EVs for V2G. The current state-of-the-art of WPT techniques, key technical issues and challenges of WPT in V2G system are comprehensively reviewed, and the research challenges and future trends of WPT in V2G systems are identified and discussed.

Keywords: Wireless power transfer · Electric vehicles · Vehicle-to-grid · Inductive coupler

1 Introduction

Smart grid is expected to be the next generation power grid which combines the stand alone microgrids and large-scale electric power plants. By utilising microsources, such as renewable energy sources, smart grid can control and optimise electricity demands in a more economic and reliable way. However, the integration of power generation mixes brings the uncertainty to the grid planning, operation and control [1]. In the meantime, the adoption of Electric Vehicle (EV) is expected to increase tremendously in the coming years. This will inevitably add substantial loads to the smart grid. As a consequence, identifying and designing strategies toward EVs integration are crucial to preserve the stability and resilience of grid system.

The growing EV market has stimulated the demand for more efficient and convenient way to recharge the battery. One of the main limitations of EV development is the wired charging pattern which to make the users stop their routine and wait for EV charging [2]. The inconveniences and insecure traditional charging mechanisms between vehicle and charging device have led to the establishment of wireless power transfer (WPT) techniques. By introducing WPT in EVs, the obstacles of charging time, range and cost are can be mitigated.

By wirelessly transferring energy to the EV, the charging becomes an easier task. For example, for a stationary WPT system, the drivers just need to park and leave the car. For a dynamic WPT system, the EV can be charged while driving [3]. When an EV connects to the grid, it has little effect on the energy grid planning and operation. However as the number of EVs increases, it is predicted that up to 60% of electricity

© ICST Institute for Computer Sciences, Social Informatics and Telecommunications Engineering 2017
E.T. Lau et al. (Eds.): SmartGIFT 2017, LNICST 203, pp. 98–107, 2017.
DOI: 10.1007/978-3-319-61813-5_10

consumption will be consumed by EVs in 2050 [4]. This is a huge and randomized loads to the energy grid. Energy management for the large EVs group is essential for the energy grid in ensuring the balances of supply and demand. Hence, more companies and corporations are increasingly putting their efforts on the EV studies. For instance, the batteries improvement and charging stations [5] with the intention of making EVs towards more prevalent in the near future. Additionally, considering the energy grid distribution that will become essential to the EV system. When EV is connected to the smart grid, it can be operated as active loads that drains energy from the main grid, and as energy storage devices that allows electric energy to be discharged from EV batteries. Thus, the concept of vehicle-to-grid (V2G) is introduced that acts as the provision of energy and ancillary service from an EV to the electric grid [19]. V2G-featured EVs can provide peak shaving, frequency regulation, spinning and non-spinning reserves by optimizing V2G energy scheduling and coordination [6]. These services have been backed up by efforts for standardization of vehicular networking, communication protocols and governmental policies that aim to provide solutions to grid design.

However, the capabilities of WPT EV address not only the attractive potential benefits but also with challenges and possible solutions. For example, the utilisation of adequate WPT technology can enhance the V2G transmission and communication system, and support the EV batteries to be intensively charged/discharged. Among various technical challenges to be overcome such as high mobility of vehicles and multitude of system and application related requirements need to be considered [9]. Such challenges served as the background for studying WPT V2G issues as well as opportunities to increase the grid efficiency. In particular, some of the services, such as energy management model and frequency regulation, are identified to be the most valuable service that EVs can offer in the electricity market [12]. While the aforementioned literatures laid a solid foundation in EV and V2G but limited work has been done in the WPT EV in V2G. In this paper reviews the current WPT technologies, particularly focusing on their principles and applications in relation to EVs for V2G, and identifies the research challenges and future trends of WPT in V2G systems

The remainder of this paper is as follow. In Sect. 2, it presents the fundamentals of WPT techniques for EVs and further addresses different types of charging pattern. In Sect. 3, the V2G system is introduced for the deployment of EV groups and then further investigates the ancillary services and operation challenges. Then, the applications supported by WPT and V2G are discussed in Sect. 4 where technical challenges and trends are addressed. Section 5 concludes and identifies future research problems.

2 Wireless Power Transfer for EV

Figure 1 depicts a typical wireless EV charging system. The basic principle behind the charging system is to utilise the RLC resonators that a high-frequency current in the transmitting coil generates an alternative magnetic field and then transmits to the receiving objects. The efficiency of the energy transaction depends on the number of coils, power electronics convertors and the compensation network [7].

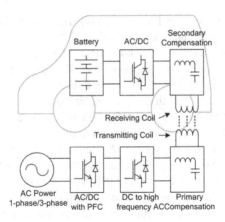

Fig. 1. Typical wireless electric vehicles charging system. Adapted from [2]

There are two main types of WPT technologies, the *near-field* and *far-field* where the energy-carrying medium is the electromagnetic field. The above system utilises the coupled magnetic resonance to transfer power which belongs to the near- field. The far-field technique, on the other hand, uses laser, microwave or radio wave to achieve longer transmission distance. However, the efficiency and controllability are not suitable for EV charging.

By referring to the system as described in Fig. 1 the complex power exchange equation [2] is as follows:

$$\dot{S}_{12} = -\dot{U}_{12}\dot{I}_{12}^* = j\omega\dot{I}_1\dot{I}_2^*$$
$$\dot{S}_{21} = -\dot{U}_{21}\dot{I}_1^* = -j\omega M\dot{I}_2\dot{I}_1^*,$$

(1)

Where $\dot{U}_{12}$ and $\dot{U}_{21}$ denote the voltage for primary and secondary coil (compensation) respectively, $\dot{I}_1^*$ and $\dot{I}_2^*$ are the current in two coils, and $\dot{S}_{12}$ and $\dot{S}_{21}$ + are the apparent power between the transmitting and receiving device coils respectively. The level of transmitted power is proportional to the voltage and current in the conductive coils. With a highly reduced resistance, the resonators can transfer energy more efficiently. To obtain an extended operating range as well as sufficiently high transmission efficiency, coupled magnetic is proposed in [8, 23] to enhance the power transfer.

Moreover, a magnetic gear EV charging technology is also available that uses the mechanical force to carry energy based on the interaction between two synchronized permanent magnets as its main coupling mechanism [24]. In WPT area, such technique was first introduced in powering the medical implant with only 6.6 W transfer power at 1.0 cm air gap [10]. By applying this technique with larger power, it can be scaled up to 1.6 kW at 15 cm which is promising for EV charging application [11].

2.1 Technologies of WPT for EV Charging

A. *Stationary charging*

In a stationary charging, the coupler is usually designed in a pad form. However, in EV charging process, the magnetic coupler is separated to meet the larger power transfer gap. From 1997 to 2011, there has been many achievements in applying coupled magnetic resonance for instance, Conductix-Wampfler in New Zealand, HaloIPT and Qualcomm [14]. Using the inductive power transfer technique, the Plusless Power produced by Evantran could transfer an output power of 3.3 kW across 100 mm which is claimed to be 90% efficient compare to the plug-to-battery efficiency [15]. And at the end of 2012, the Plusless announced a trial called Apollo Launch Program that aims to integrate the WPT stationary charging technique to current on-sale EVs across the United State.

B. *Dynamic charging*

The dynamic charging is a way to charge the EV while driving. The major drawback of this technique is the EV's anxiety range that may be the main reason that limits the market penetration of EVs. In the dynamic charging system, the magnetic components are composed of a primary side magnetic coupler and a secondary side pickup coil [16]. The main difference from the stationary charging is that the primary side coupler is placed aside or under the road. With dynamic charging technique, the EV runs freely on the road. However, the system characteristics should be analysed under the coupling variation to support practice.

KAIST [15] demonstrated a great achievement in the project on-line electric vehicles. An OLEV bus system was demonstrated at Expo 2012 that was able to transfer 100 kW through 20 cm air gap with average efficiency of 75% [14]. The potential of WPT in dynamic charging has been identified that wireless charging and discharging can take place without interfering the movements of EVs.

3 V2G System Requirements and Applications

As the ongoing development of WPT EV, the *V2G concept* is introduced which studies the interaction between mass EV charging and the power grid. The basic concept of V2G power is that the EVs can be both charged and discharged in the grid. In V2G system, each vehicle shall be able to: (1) connect to the grid for electrical energy flow, (2) access and transmit the communication signal from the operator, (3) control the vehicle in response to different scenarios. These requirements vary in according to the operation deployment [28]. The bidirectional WPT can provide advanced performance in V2G applications. Figure 2 illustrates the connection between vehicles and the electrical power grid.

An aggregator can be a utility managing EV groups or a third party operating a virtual power plant. It can be viewed as the market coordinator that passes through system

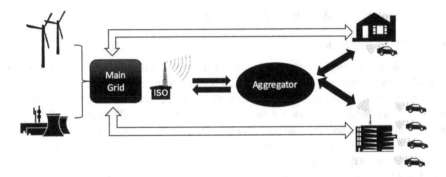

Fig. 2. Smart grid power system with ISO, Aggregator, signal transmission between vehicles, the electric power grid

signals and manages system capacity required to enter the electricity market [27]. Moreover, it is the place that bids with the market participants to provide the most valuable services [6].

The grid operator such as Independent System operator (ISO) broadcasts control signal via cell phone network, direct Internet connection, or power line carrier [28]. The ISO is capable of issuing automatic generation control (AGC) signal to address the ancillary services from EVs. The aggregator manages both the EV fleets and the wholesale market of ISO. In United States, the ISO purchases the regulation capacity service to help aggregators in reducing the financial risk and price volatility [21].

From Fig. 2, the electricity flows from power generators through the grid to electricity users and flows back from EVs to the grid. The ISO sends control signals to the aggregator, and the aggregator develops dispatch algorithms in order to respond the ISO requests. The signal may control the single or multiple EV fleets depending on the request type and dispatch strategy. The batteries in the EVs act as an energy bank which can be connected to the grid more easily, and the bidirectional function of WPT can be realized using the active switch between the rectifiers [30]. Furthermore, studies show that by introducing the WPT technology in V2G design, the drivers are more willing to connect their EVs into the grid [31], which can then maximise the V2G benefits.

3.1   V2G Related Applications and Challenges

V2G system features in transforming EVs from potentially problematic loads into distributed energy sources that generate values for both the utility and EV owners. The electricity sources shall be controlled in real-time by the ISO to ensure the efficiency of power transfer. Some services such as frequency regulation, spinning reserve and load hiding are discussed in this section, along with the challenges associated with the services.

The *frequency regulation* techniques in [6, 21, 26] used to tune the frequency and voltage of the grid by matching generation to load demand. By using the fast-ramping feature of EVs, the regulation can be controlled under the direct real-time control. However, determining the regulation capacity can be difficult in the process as the EV's user behaviour is randomized. Hence, an intelligent dispatch algorithm is required. In [6, 19, 21], the dispatch algorithms were proposed according to the price-based/event-based, incremental/binary or unidirectional/bidirectional charging rate scenarios.

Spinning reserve refers to the additional generating capacity that remains in standby mode to provide power upon request. Spinning reserves are remunerated by the amount of time they are available and ready [28]. In V2G system, the EVs have high response rate and require short time to provide power. The challenge here is to report the number of EVs that can remain online during the contracted/tendered period. Furthermore, the contract length is limited by the state of charge (SoC) in EV battery. The state-of-art stochastic modelling of EV user behaviour were proposed in [4, 17] to calculate the contract/tender length and duration.

V2G system is also suitable in the application of *load hiding* in household electricity consumption profile. The appliance operation activities can be mapped with household routines, which can further be exploited to infer customer preferences and privacy [22], V2G system utilises EV rechargeable battery as controllable load to mitigate the privacy leakage of the customers. The key concept here is to distort the household consumption profile based on different algorithms, such as the best effort in [18], or stepping approach in [18]. However, the current researches are based on a series of idealisation for driving pattern and household base load. The future work should include the uncertainty of household load, EV arrival time and SoC.

4   WPT Supported V2G Applications

Over the past decades, so many efforts have been accomplished to improve conversion and utilisation of energy to reduce the dependency in fossil fuel. However, the fact is that tremendous amount of renewable generations are only able to realise a small portion of utilizable loads. For example, less than 1/3 of wind farms are connected to the grid in China due to the intermittent power dispatch and transmission network limitations [3]. An automatic and bidirectional charging and discharging system is essential for the best interaction between EVs and renewables, where a fleet of EVs need to be simultaneously powered. Especially, the WPT system adds the flexibility to the V2G system which can mitigate the stochastic nature of user behaviour and intermittency of renewable sources.

Involving renewables for compensating the required demand of EVs is an ideal solution for the V2G operation. Several studies have been conducted on the inductive power transfer system with various topologies [32, 33]. The system model with a dynamic multivariate steady-state mathematical model was presented in [34], which is suitable for V2G applications. The representation of the mutual coupling between the circuits shows the effect of the applied control to manage the power transfer. Hence, the study of energy flow between WPT EVs and V2G enhances the grid stability and improves the power quality for further applications.

The V2G power that the system can provide is limited by many factors, such as the infrastructure line capacity limit and vehicle's stored energy. More specifically, the limit is the energy stored on-board divided by the time drawn. It can be expressed as [28]:

$$P_{vehicle} = \frac{\left(E_s - \dfrac{d_d + d_{rb}}{\eta_{veh}} \right) \eta_{inv}}{t_{disp}}, \tag{3}$$

Where $P_{vehicle}$ is the maximum power from V2G in kW, E_s the stored energy available to the inverter, d_d is the distance driven, d_{rb} is the distance of the range buffer, η_{veh} is the vehicle efficiency, t_{disp} is the time where the vehicle's stored energy is dispatched. It is clear that using WPT to minimize the factor t_{disp}, this will increase the power capacity and thus improves the power efficiency.

Furthermore, EV can be used as the supplementary for power delivery system with the help of WPT technology. A mathematically tractable framework is constructed for transporting energy from remote renewable resources to the loads using the dynamic wireless charging [3]. The wireless charging system can be embedded in the pavement and thus transforms roads into public charging facilities. It provides a pervasive and wireless charging platform for integrating the transportation and power networks. The WPT technique allows energy to be transmitted seamlessly with EVs as energy carriers, which provides a new area of WPT EV utilisation in V2G system. The author [35] analyses the transportation and power networks coupled by EVs that electrify the roads as the charging infrastructures. The electrified roads then become nodes in the power flow, and the prices at different nodes will influence the route choices. The optimal calculation towards charging cost, driving routines and power distribution associated with the coupled networks may become complex. With fast- paced technological advancement, this will increase the robustness feature of EV wireless charging capability.

4.1   Challenges and Future Trend of WPT

In V2G system, market penetration of WPT technique is still critical as there are many challenges to be overcome. It can be summarized as three aspects: (1) *achieving high efficiency*: 90% of overall power transmission efficiency is typically to be considered as efficacious for WPT technique. To achieve this, the coil design is the most important part in the whole system. The dimension of coil will define the upper limit of the power capacity and the efficiency will be affected by the quality factor of coil [15]. (2) *alignment tolerance*: A system shall be fairly tolerant of misalignment between transmitter and receiver in both the stationary and dynamic charging. One of the solutions is to adjust configuration of the ferrite cores to achieve better alignment tolerance [30]. (3) *dynamic charging control*: The consistency between the road side and on-board system shall be designed properly at the same time to ensure the consistency and accommodate various vehicle types.

Moreover, when charging an EV battery wirelessly, there is a high frequency magnetic field existing between the transmitting and receiving coils. The large air gap between the two coils causes a high leakage field where can arise safety concerns of such high frequency magnetic field. However, it is clear that the vehicle electrification is unavoidable in the future. The wireless charging techniques would provide the foundation for mass EV market penetration regardless of battery technology.

In EV wireless charging area, there have been many pre-commercial demonstrations and commercial kits that are readily available in the market. And many works have been done to provide an easier way to implement the smart grid functionalities and maximise the V2G benefits. The foreseeing trend of WPT techniques shall focus on the mass adoption of existing available EVs, for example, magnetic structure design, high efficiency RF amplifier and converter control strategy design [16]. International standards and safety regulations must be implemented to ensure the shielding capacity for protecting users. Besides, it is even more important to exchange larger amount of information between the grid and vehicle side wirelessly in the WPT system. The communication design shall be efficient for real- time, large-volume and accurate signal response.

5   Conclusion

This paper presented a review of WPT technology in EVs and the integration of WPT in V2G system. It is clear that introducing inductive WPT into the EV market will accelerate the penetration of transport electrification. Furthermore, the integration of WPT can alter the distribution and operation of V2G system which will inevitably increase the potential of enhancing the power delivery efficiency. Future studies in network communication, WPT technology and V2G topology design are essentially needed in the present, upcoming and future terms.

Acknowledgment.   This work has been supported by the JPI Urban Europe IRENE.

References

1. Liang, H., Zhuang, W.: Stochastic modeling and optimization in a microgrid: a survey. Energies **7**(4), 2027–2050 (2014)
2. Li, S., Mi, C.C.: Wireless power transfer for electric vehicle applications. IEEE J. Emerg. Sel. Top. Power Electron. **3**(1), 4–17 (2015)
3. Lam, A.Y.S., Leung, K.C., Li, V.O.K.: An electric-vehicle-based supplementary power delivery system. In: 2015 IEEE International Conference on Smart Grid Communications (SmartGridComm), Miami, FL, pp. 307–312 (2015)
4. Kriukov, A., Gavrilas, M.: Smart energy management in distribution networks with increasing number of electric vehicles. In: 2014 International Conference and Exposition on Electrical and Power Engineering (EPE), Iasi, pp. 1039–1044 (2014)
5. Lam, A.Y.S., Leung, Y.W., Chu, X.: Electric vehicle charging station placement: formulation, complexity, and solutions. IEEE Trans. Smart Grid **5**(6), 2846–2856 (2014)
6. Yao, E., Wong, V.W.S., Schober, R.: Robust frequency regulation capacity scheduling algorithm for electric vehicles. IEEE Trans. Smart Grid **PP**(99), 1–14
7. Kavitha, M., Bobba, P.B., Prasad, D.: Investigations and experimental study on Magnetic Resonant coupling based Wireless Power Transfer system for neighborhood EV's. In: 2016 IEEE 6th International Conference on Power Systems (ICPS), New Delhi, pp. 1–6 (2016)

8. Kim, J., et al.: Coil design and shielding methods for a magnetic resonant wireless power transfer system. Proc. IEEE **101**(6), 1332–1342 (2013)
9. Karagiannis, G., et al.: Vehicular networking: a survey and tutorial on requirements, architectures, challenges, standards and solutions. IEEE Commun. Surv. Tutorials **13**(4), 584–616 (2011). Fourth Quarter
10. Suzuki, S., Ishihara, M., Kobayashi, Y.: The improvement of the noninvasive power-supply system using magnetic coupling for medical implants. IEEE Trans. Magn. **47**(10), 2811–2814 (2011)
11. Li, W.: High efficiency wireless power transmission at low frequency using permanent magnet coupling (Doctoral dissertation, University of British Columbia) (2009)
12. Huang, S., Wu, L., Infield, D., Zhang, T.: Using electric vehicle fleet as responsive demand for power system frequency support. In: 2013 IEEE Vehicle Power and Propulsion Conference (VPPC), Beijing, pp. 1–5 (2013)
13. Nguyen, H., Khodaei, A., Han, Z.: A Big Data scale algorithm for optimal scheduling of integrated microgrids. IEEE Trans. Smart Grid **PP**(99), 1 (2015)
14. Cirimele, V., Freschi, F., Mitolo, M.: Inductive power transfer for automotive applications: State-of-the-art and future trends. In: 2016 IEEE Industry Applications Society Annual Meeting, Portland, OR, USA, pp. 1–8 (2016)
15. Qiu, C., Chau, K.T., Liu, C., Chan, C.C.: Overview of wireless power transfer for electric vehicle charging. In: Electric Vehicle Symposium and Exhibition (EVS27), 2013 World, Barcelona, pp. 1–9 (2013)
16. Suh, I.S., Kim, J.: Electric vehicle on-road dynamic charging system with wireless power transfer technology. In: 2013 IEEE International Electric Machines & Drives Conference (IEMDC), Chicago, IL, pp. 234–240 (2013)
17. Callaway, D.S., Hiskens, I.A.: Achieving controllability of electric loads. Proc. IEEE **99**(1), 184–199 (2011)
18. Yang, L., Chen, X., Zhang, J., Poor, H.V.: Optimal privacy-preserving energy management for smart meters. In: IEEE INFOCOM 2014 - IEEE Conference on Computer Communications, Toronto, ON, pp. 513–521 (2014)
19. Sortomme, E., Cheung, K.W.: Intelligent dispatch of Electric Vehicles performing vehicle-to-grid regulation. In: 2012 IEEE International Electric Vehicle Conference (IEVC), Greenville, SC, pp. 1–6 (2012)
20. Liu, Q., Golinński, M., Pawełczak, P., Warnier, M.: Green wireless power transfer networks. IEEE J. Sel. Areas Commun. **34**(5), 1740–1756 (2016)
21. Yao, E., Wong, V.W.S., Schober, R.: Risk-averse forward contract for electric vehicle frequency regulation service. In: 2015 IEEE International Conference on Smart Grid Communications (SmartGridComm), Miami, FL, pp. 750–755 (2015)
22. Sun, Y., Lampe, L., Wong, V.W.S.: Combining electric vehicle and rechargeable battery for household load hiding. In: 2015 IEEE International Conference on Smart Grid Communications (SmartGridComm), Miami, FL, pp. 611–616 (2015)
23. Wang, C.-S., Stielau, O.H., Covic, G.A.: Design considerations for a contactless electric vehicle battery charger. IEEE Trans. Industr. Electron. **52**(5), 1308–1314 (2005)
24. Jian, L., Chau, K.T., Jiang, J.Z.: A magnetic-geared outer-rotor permanent-magnet brushless machine for wind power generation. IEEE Trans. Ind. Appl. **45**(3), 954–962 (2009)
25. Etezadi-Amoli, M., Choma, K., Stefani, J.: Rapid-charge electric-vehicle stations. IEEE Trans. Power Delivery **25**(3), 1883–1887 (2010)
26. Ha, D.L., Guillou, H., Martin, N., Cung, V.D., Jacomino, M.: Optimal scheduling for coordination renewable energy and electric vehicles consumption. In: 2015 IEEE International Conference on Smart Grid Communications (SmartGridComm), Miami, FL, pp. 319–324 (2015)

27. Han, S., Han, S., Sezaki, K.: Development of an optimal vehicle-to-grid aggregator for frequency regulation. IEEE Trans. Smart Grid 1(1), 65–72 (2010)
28. Kempton, W., Tomić, J.: Vehicle-to-grid power fundamentals: calculating capacity and net revenue. J. Power Sources **144**(1), 268–279 (2005)
29. Li, H., Dán, G., Nahrstedt, K.: Lynx: authenticated anonymous real-time reporting of electric vehicle information. In: 2015 IEEE International Conference on Smart Grid Communications (SmartGridComm), Miami, FL, pp. 599–604 (2015)
30. Lee, S., Huh, J., Park, C., Choi, N.S., Cho, G.H., Rim, C.T.: On-Line Electric Vehicle using inductive power transfer system. In: 2010 IEEE Energy Conversion Congress and Exposition, Atlanta, GA, pp. 1598–1601 (2010)
31. Huang, X., Qiang, H., Huang, Z., Sun, Y., Li, J.: The interaction research of smart grid and EV based wireless charging. In: 2013 IEEE Vehicle Power and Propulsion Conference (VPPC), Beijing, pp. 1–5 (2013)
32. Kabalo, M., Berthold, F., Blunier, B., Bouquain, D., Williamson, S., Miraoui, A.: Efficiency comparison of wire and wireless battery charging: based on connection probability analysis. In: 2014 IEEE Transportation Electrification Conference and Expo (ITEC), Dearborn, MI, pp. 1–6 (2014)
33. Ayano, H., Yamamoto, K., Hino, N., Yamato, I.: Highly efficient contactless electrical energy transmission system. In: IEEE 2002 28th Annual Conference of the IECON 2002 Industrial Electronics Society, vol. 2, pp. 1364–1369 (2002)
34. Mohamed, A.A.S., Berzoy, A., Mohammed, O.: Power flow modeling of wireless power transfer for EVs charging and discharging in V2G applications. In: 2015 IEEE Vehicle Power and Propulsion Conference (VPPC), Montreal, QC, pp. 1–6 (2015)
35. He, F., Yin, H., Zhou, J.: Integrated pricing of roads and electricity enabled by wireless power transfer. Transp. Res. Part C Emerg. Technol. **34**, pp. 1–15 (2013). ISSN 0968-090X

Data Management and Grid Analytics

Demand Profiling and Demand Forecast Using the Active-Aware-Based Ensemble Kalman Filter

Eng Tseng Lau$^{(\boxtimes)}$, Kok Keong Chai, and Yue Chen

Queen Mary University of London, Mile End Road, London E1 4NS, UK
{e.t.lau,michael.chai,yue.chen}@qmul.ac.uk

Abstract. The concept of demand profiling is established in order to collect, analyse and develop the detailed knowledge of the consumption habits, either in domestic or non-domestic usage. In this paper the state representation of electrical signal is used as the profiling formula to model the diurnal (daily) and annual cycle demand trend of electricity consumption across the grid. The available demand dataset from the public domain is applied as the input for the profiling formula. The developed demand profile is further to be forecast and assimilated using the active-aware-based Ensemble Kalman Filter (EnKF). The resultant EnKF estimations may provide the assessment of nationwide demand within the energy network, thus consider the need for the present and future network reinforcement or upgrades. The ability of EnKF in forecasting the demand is presented, along with the limitations.

Keywords: Demand profiling · Demand forecast · Ensemble Kalman Filter · Data assimilation

1 Introduction

The national energy system is currently experiencing increasing stresses on demand and network load due to: variable heating in colder seasons; the addition of intermittent renewable generators; insufficient storage facilities. Furthermore, the needs to concentrate on balancing the electricity supply, the emission reduction targets, and the affordable operating costs are the current "energy-trilemma" problem [1]. The highest priority in optimising the renewable energy system, for instance, does not guarantee the security of energy supply due to the nature of renewable intermittency [2]. Therefore, various smart initiatives such as the introduction of disruptive technology [3] into the grid utility, decentralised energy distribution, and the high efficient low carbon power plants are deployed in mitigating the trilemma of the energy problem. To this end, the demand profiling concept are established after the inception of the 1950's Electricity Council Load Research and followed by the 1998 Electricity Pool Programme [4]. Such concepts are established to collect, analyse and develop the detailed knowledge of

© ICST Institute for Computer Sciences, Social Informatics and Telecommunications Engineering 2017
E.T. Lau et al. (Eds.): SmartGIFT 2017, LNICST 203, pp. 111–121, 2017.
DOI: 10.1007/978-3-319-61813-5_11

the consumption habits, either in domestic or non-domestic usage [4,5]. The electricity grid operator nowadays use demand profiling as the important strategy to plan the amount of electricity to be provided to the entire network. Additionally, demand profiling also illustrates the capacity trend of the electricity market, whether to power up a more responsive or expensive generation to meet the particular demand [6].

In addition to demand profiling, a good forecasting technique is required in order to provide the demand forecast for few days ahead. In this paper, the Ensemble Kalman Filter (EnKF) is applied in forecasting the demand profile. The EnKF justifies the calculation effort to demand forecasting and also aims to compute demand forecast based on the adequate amount of ensemble sizes for speedy delivery of forecast results. The resultant EnKF estimations may also provide the electrical inventory for assessment of nationwide demand and energy network upgrades.

The organisation of the paper is as follows. Section 2 presents the modelling of demand profile, the introduction and the formulation of EnKF. Section 3 demonstrates the results of demand profiling and EnKF forecast. Section 4 concludes.

2   Methodology

2.1   Modelling of Demand Profile

The electrical consumption representing the demand profile changes periodically with respect to time [7]. Such periodical trend or time series of the electricity data should have diurnal, $D(t)$, and annual, $A(t)$, periodicities [7]. The state representation of the consumed electrical signal can be generally expressed into the formula as follows:

$$X_i(t) = A\left(\frac{t}{T_1}\right) + D_i\left(\frac{t}{T_2}\right) + \varepsilon_i, \tag{1}$$

where $X_i(t)$ is the true state of electrical consumption at time t, $A(t)$ is the annual cycle function, $D_i(t)$ is the diurnal cycle function, T_1 is the annual periodicity that is 365 days, T_2 is the diurnal periodicity that is 24 h, t is the time variable sampled at hourly rate, ε_i is the signal noise, i indexes the types of consumers to be considered.

The $A(t)$ and $D(t)$ are used to describe trends of annual and daily demand profiles. The component of ε is the various influencing factors that affects the overall daily demand profiles. Typical influencing factors are: (1) Seasonal variations; (2) Building characteristics; (3) Weather and temperature effects; (4) Holiday effects; (5) Consumers consumption behaviour. The formula (1) is further used as the profiling formula in developing the complete annual trend of a demand profile representing ith consumer.

Depending the availability of the data, the $A(t)$ and $D(t)$ can be formulated using the real demand data in the public domain (e.g. [8]). In the case of insufficient data required to model the demand profile, the paper by [7] proposed an adaptive seasonal model based on the Hyperbolic tangent function (HTF) to model the electricity consumption for different types of consumers.

2.2   Ensemble Kalman Filter

Based on the historical UK demand reported in [8], the historical demand has shown fluctuations corresponding to different time periods. This is due to the influencing factor that affects the overall energy demand across the grid. Therefore short-term forecast and assimilation of energy demand are necessary. Several existing forecast methodologies are available but with present limitations. According to the author [9], both the Seasonal Autoregressive Integrated Moving Average (SARIMA) and Autoregressive Integrated Moving Average (ARIMA) methods failed to forecast electricity demands with seasonal latent variables. Meanwhile, large numbers of Artificial Neural Networks (ANN) were proposed to handle seasonal variations but with potential drawbacks, where deseasonalising and detrending of pre-processed raw data is required in order to model seasonal trends accurately [10]. Additionally, the forecast using ANN is not always accurate and realistic [11].

Hence, a robust, active-aware-based forecasting mechanism is required to forecast the uncertain trends of the demand, either in long or short term forecast. In order to perform the demand forecast, EnKF is applied in this paper to forecast the demand.

EnKF was first introduced by Evesen [12] and is generally a Monte-Carlo based recursive filter approach for generation of an ensemble of model representations. An ensemble is actually a system representation through a random sampling of the system distribution [12]. EnKF is applied in sequential data assimilation and even a few ensemble members have the ability to exhibit large-scale covariance behaviour of a system considered [13].

2.3   EnKF Formulation

In this paper, formulations of EnKF by [2,14–18] are followed, with only key equations and parameters are outlined. Such EnKF formulation provides the foundation for the demand forecast and assimilation.

EnKF consists of two important steps, the forecast and analysis step. In the forecast step, as the true (actual) state is not always available, new ensemble is created in the state space by forecasting the ensemble mean as the best estimate of the state [14–16]. In other words, a new ensemble is created based on the realisations in each of the model state through the model dynamics (simulator). It is then reflected as the first observation of the actual system that will be incorporated into the model state in (2).

$$y_j^p = y^p + w_j, \tag{2}$$

where j indexes the ensemble member, y^p is the state vector of the model simulator, y_j^p is the new formation of a set of ensemble through the prediction of the model state y^p at ensemble member j, w_j is the model process noise. The superscript p denotes the *priori* state vector.

Instead of adding complex components to y^p, for simplicity the component of y^p can be formulated as:

$$y^p = \begin{bmatrix} m \\ d \end{bmatrix}. \tag{3}$$

In the simulation experiment, m is the model parameters of the energy consumption profile from the dynamical model (1). It is the profiling formula that describes the demand profile for ith consumers. As the component m describes the demand profile, m remain constant throughout the data simulation except the model process noise. This results in similar energy usage pattern from groups of consumers but with varied energy usages. The d is the model prediction of the energy consumption and changes with the simulation at every time step.

The input component of y^p can be further extrapolated as:

$$y^p = \begin{bmatrix} m_{1,1}, m_{2,2}, & ..., & m_{i,t}, & e_{1,1}, & e_{2,2}, & ..., & e_{i,t} \end{bmatrix}^T. \tag{4}$$

The $m_{i,t}$ refers to the component m (3) of the dynamical model (1). The $e_{i,t}$ is the energy demand forecast that also corresponds to the component d. The i indexes the consumer and t is the time step.

As in line with [14], initial ensemble members of y^p are sampled from a normal distribution with the zero mean and standard deviation.

Using (2) and (4) new sets of priori ensemble y_j^p are created. Collections of forecasts y_j^p are stored into a matrix form Y^P to denote the collection of the *priori* ensemble:

$$Y^P = \begin{bmatrix} y_1^p, & y_2^p, & ..., & y_j^p, & ..., & y_{N_e}^p \end{bmatrix}, \tag{5}$$

where N_e is the total number of ensemble member.

During the analysis step, new observations from measurement sets are established through ensemble representations. In order to obtain consistent error propagation the observations have to be considered as random variables [18]. The actual measurement is used as the reference and the random measurement noise is added to the measurement to obtain the perturbed observations [15, 17, 18]. In this paper, the actual measurement set d (also the model prediction) is perturbed using the ensemble representations, this later forms another set of ensemble of perturbed observations denoted by $d_{\text{obs},j}$:

$$d_{\text{obs},j} = d + v_j, \tag{6}$$

where v_j is the measurement noise at jth ensemble member.

Both y_j^p and $d_{\text{obs},j}$ are perturbed with model error: the process noise w with zero mean and covariance Q for Y^P and similarly, the measurement noise v with zero mean and covariance R for d, i.e. values w and v are assumed to be drawn from Gaussian distributions as $w \sim N(0, Q)$ and $v \sim N(0, R)$. The errors are very important to be defined in the EnKF, because without errors the system may be over-specified and no solutions resulting from EnKF propagations obtained [17].

The *priori* ensemble member y_j^p will be assimilated using the EnKF updating formula in order to obtain the updated *posteriori* ensemble y_j^u as follows:

$$y_j^u = y_j^p + C_Y H^T (H C_Y H^T + R)^{-1} (d_{\text{obs},j} - H y_j^p), \qquad (7)$$

where H is the measurement operator that relates to actual state. C_p is the *priori* error covariance. R is measurement covariance error. The $d_{\text{obs},j}$ in this case corresponds to HY^p.

Using the formula (7), the assimilation process is achieved by updating y_j^p, assimilating y_j^p and $d_{\text{obs},j}$ by taking the mean of the perturbed observations $d_{\text{obs},j}$ as the actual observation. Each of the y_j^p ensemble member is updated to obtain y_j^u. The updated y_j^u is stored into a matrix form denoted as Y^u.

In order to examine the performance of EnKF, the root-mean-square error (RMSE) of the ensemble mean y_j^u from the actual state of the model [19] is used in this paper and is calculated as:

$$RMSE = \sqrt{\frac{1}{K} \sum_{k=1}^{K} \left(\overline{Y_k^u} - X_k \right)^2}, \qquad (8)$$

where X denotes the actual state of electrical consumption from the dynamical model (1) and k is the model state variable.

3   Results

3.1   Numerical Simulation of Demand Profile

The half-hourly diurnal profiling data from the UK Elexon portal [20] is adopted in examining the diurnal seasonal demand profiles of spring, summer, autumn and winter correspondingly. The random perturbation of noises are generated to indicate the signal noises as the influencing factors. In this paper, the domestic household profile (out of eight clustered Profile Class) from the UK Elexon portal [20] is selected for further examination of the overall diurnal demand $(D_i(t))$. The clustered Profile Class represents large populations of similar demand profile within consumers [20]. On the other hand, the 2015 annual demand data from the UK National Grid portal [8] is extracted that corresponds to $A(t)$.

The $A(t)$ obtained from the portal [8] is converted to have identical temporal scale with $D_i(t)$. Those $D_i(t)$ will be 'stitched' together with $A(t)$ in order to form a resultant annual trend representing the overall household demand across the grid.

The analytical expressions of $A(t)$ and $D_i(t)$ based on (1) are to be further applied in EnKF for the demand forecast and assimilation process.

Figure 1 shows half-hourly diurnal energy consumption profile for domestic households with seasonal variations. Based on Fig. 1, it can be seen that a

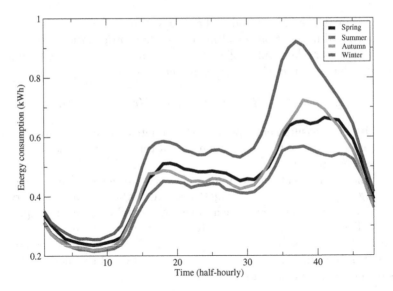

Fig. 1. Diurnal half-hourly energy consumption (demand) cycles for a domestic household.

household electricity consumption drops during the working hours and maximum demand occurs during the peak period (1700–1900). Additionally, the amount of energy consumption during the winter is much higher than other seasons due to the high amount of heating.

The plot from Fig. 1 is aggregated that further forms the half-hourly annual energy consumption as shown in Fig. 2, where $D_i(t)$ is stitched with $A(t)$ to form the complete annual household demand trend. Similarly, Fig. 3 shows the reduced temporal solution plot of Fig. 2, where the average annual-based daily energy consumption for the domestic household is plotted. The total estimated annual energy consumption is 4023kWh and such estimated value is similar to the overall household energy consumption usage as reported by the UK Department of Energy and Climate Change (DECC) [21]. Henceforth, the developed household energy demand trend is a good representation profile for the domestic household consumers.

3.2   EnKF Numerical Simulation

The EnKF simulation in this case involves short-term forecasting and assimilation of the energy consumption using the developed demand profile for the domestic household. The modelled profile of $X_i(t)$ from the dynamical model (1) is the observation that reflects the actual system that will be incorporated into the model state in (3). Since the household demand data is available, variable y^p in (3) contributes to direct model predictions (d) of the energy demand (based on (1) that formulates the household demand profile (m)).

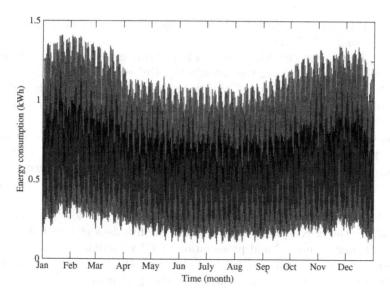

Fig. 2. Annual energy consumption (demand) cycles for a domestic household.

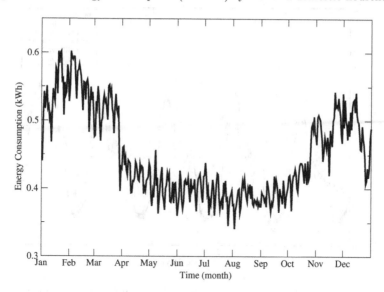

Fig. 3. Average annual-based daily energy consumption (demand) cycles for a domestic household.

The *priori* ensemble y_j^p is created using (2), where $j = 1, 2, ..., N_e$ denotes the ensemble member index and N_e is the total number of ensemble member. Initial ensemble members of y^p are intended to be drawn from a normal distribution with the mean and standard deviation $N(0, 20)$. Additionally, the model error

w is sampled from $w \sim N(0,1)$. The measurement error, on the other hand, is sampled from $v \sim N(0,0.5)$.

In the EnKF, the perturbed observation of demand data $d_{\mathrm{obs},j}$ is based on the model prediction d using the formula (6). Different realisations are created ($N_e = 10, 50, 100, 500, 1000$) and propagated at every time steps. The Y^p in (5) is the collection of the *priori* ensemble y_j^p, which is assimilated along with $d_{\mathrm{obs},j}$ and updated to form the *posteriori* ensemble (y_j^u) through (7).

The ensemble means of the energy demand with different realisations N_e are computed that allow comparison of the convergence in relation to the true (actual) state of the model. The RMSE of the propagated ensemble mean in relative to the actual model state is calculated using (8) in order to examine the robustness of EnKF with different realisations.

For feasibility purpose, total of five days temporal resolutions are adopted to demonstrate the EnKF propagation results. The five days plot with datasets of the actual energy demand and propagation of Y^u with different ensemble sizes is shown in Fig. 4. The figure shows that the larger the ensemble size, the better Y^u estimation converges towards the actual energy demand.

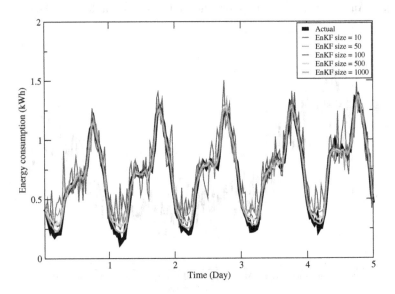

Fig. 4. Five days of household energy demand with different EnKF realisations.

The tabulated RMSE values corresponding to different EnKF realisations are shown in Table 1.

The RMSE values from Table 1 also indicate that the larger the ensemble size, the smaller the RMSE value, and thus the better the EnKF estimations. In this case, an ensemble of size 100 is sufficiently enough to provide accurate demand forecast with acceptable RMSE error.

Table 1. The RMSE value with different EnKF Realisations.

Number of ensemble (N_e)	RMSE value
10	0.180
50	0.087
100	0.050
500	0.035
1000	0.020

4 Conclusions

This paper presents the demand profiling using the available diurnal demand data in the public domain. A domestic household consumer is selected and to be further stitched together with the annual demand trend that is also available in the public domain that forms the annual energy demand for a household consumer. The state representation of electrical signal is used as the profiling formula to model the diurnal and annual demand trend of the domestic household. The profiled annual demand provides the realistic estimation that is comparable with the current UK domestic household energy usage. As there are available demand data in the public domain, this has added the flexibility and simplicity in modelling the overall energy demand with only a few parameters.

The resultant developed household demand profile is further applied in the active-aware-based EnKF field for demand forecasting and assimilation. The EnKF evaluation results demonstrate the capability and robustness of EnKF in forecasting and matching the energy demand, either in real-time or based on prior knowledge and historical records. However, as EnKF is a Monte Carlo type of data assimilation, the low EnKF realisation will result in poor forecast. The realisation of $N_e = 100$ in this example provides the sufficient convergence of EnKF propagations. For this reason, EnKF allows the convergence of data assimilations, on condition that the ensemble size selected is sufficiently large.

As the current EnKF application in this paper is demonstrated in a relatively simple model, the EnKF will however become complex when considering the individual demand profiles (for instance: office, hotel, school, supermarket, restaurant, stadium, and hospital). The nonlinearity in different profiles of consumers will arise and the identification of state variables, initial conditions and prior knowledge of the EnKF model are therefore necessary in order to provide the better demand forecast with minimised EnKF propagation errors.

References

1. E.ON UK. The energy trilemma (2016). https://www.eonenergy.com/for-your-business/large-energy-users/manage-energy/energy-efficiency/decentralised-energy-experts/The-energy-trilemma. Accessed 17 Feb 2016

2. Lau, E.T.: Quantification of carbon emissions and savings in smart grids. Phd thesis, College of Engineering, Design and Physical Sciences, Brunel University London (2016)

3. Plat, R., Williams, J., Pardoe, A., Straw, W.: A new approach to electricity markets - how new, distruptive technologies change everything. Technical report, Institute for Public Policy Research (2014)

4. Elexon. Load profiles and their use in electricity settlement (2013). https://www.elexon.co.uk/wp-content/uploads/2013/11/load_profiles_v2.0_cgi.pdf. Accessed 30 Apr 2016

5. DoE. Module 5: Energy assessment - demand analysis (2011). http://www.energy.gov.za/EEE/Projects/Building%20Energy%20Audit%20Training/Training%20Modules/Building%20Energy%20Auditing%20Module%205_final:pdf. Accessed 30 Apr 16

6. Energy Efficiency Exchange. Understanding your energy requirements (2016). http://eex.gov.au/energy-management/energy-procurement/procuring-and-managing-energy/understanding-your-energy-requirements/. Accessed 30 Apr 2016

7. Lau, E.T., Yang, Q., Forbes, A.B., Wright, P., Livina, V.N.: Modelling carbon emissions in electric systems. Energy Convers. Manage. **80**(59), 573–581 (2014)

8. National Grid. Data explorer (2016). http://www2.nationalgrid.com/UK/Industry-information/Electricity-transmission-operational-data/Data-Explorer/. Accessed 01 May 2016

9. Sumer, K.K., Goktas, O., Hepsag, A.: The application of seasonal latent variable in forecasting electricity demand as an alternative method. Energy Policy **37**(4), 1317–1322 (2009)

10. Zhang, G.P., Qi, M.: Neural network forecasting for seasonal and trend time series. Eur. J. Oper. Res. **160**(2), 501–514 (2005)

11. Hippert, H.S., Pedreira, C.E., Souza, R.C.: Neural network for short-term load forecasting: a review and evaluation. IEEE Trans. Power Syst. **16**, 44–55 (2002)

12. Evensen, G.: Sequential data assimilation with a nonlinear quasi-geostrophic model using Monte-Carlo methods to forecast error statistics. Geophys. Res. **99**(5), 10143–10162 (1994)

13. John, C.J., Mandel, J.: A two-stage Ensemble Kalman Filter for smooth data assimilation. Environ. Ecol. Stat. **15**, 101–110 (2008)

14. Almendral-Vazquez, R., Syversveen, A.R.: The Ensemble Kalman Filter - theory and applications in oil industry. Technical report, Norsk Regnesentral (2006). https://www.nr.no/en/nrpublication?query=/file/4334/Almendral_Vazquez_-_Ensemble_Kalman_Filter_-_theory_and_applications_i.pdf. Accessed 25 Jul 2015

15. Evensen, G.: The Ensemble Kalman Filter: theoretical formulation and practical implementation. Ocean Dyn. **53**(4), 343–367 (2003)

16. Gillijins, S., Barrero Mendoza, O.B., Chandrasekar, J., De Moor, B.L.R., Bernstein, D.S., Ridley, A.: What is the Ensemble Kalman Filter and how well does it work? In: Proceedings of the 2006 American Control Conference, Minneapolis, Minnesota, USA, pp. 4448–4453. IEEE (2006)

17. Jensen, J.P.: Ensemble Kalman Filtering for state and parameter estimation on a reservoir model. Master thesis, Department of Engineering Cybernetics, Norwegian University of Science and Technology, Trondheim (2007)

18. Nævdal, G., Johnsen, L.M., Aanonsen, S.I., Vefring, E.H.: Reservoir monitoring and continuous model updating using Ensemble Kalman Filter. In: SPE Annual Technical Conference and Exhibition, Denver, Colorado, USA, pp. 1–12. SPE (2003)
19. Anderson, J.L.: Localization and sampling error correction in Ensemble Kalman Filter data assimilation. Am. Meteorol. Soc. **140**, 2359–2371 (2012)
20. Elexon. Profiling - Average profiling data per Profile Class (regression data evaluated at 10-year average temperatures (2016). https://www.elexon.co.uk/reference/technical-operations/profiling/. Accessed 30 Apr 2016
21. DECC. Sub-national electricity and gas consumption statistics: analysis tool 2005 to 2014 (2015). https://www.gov.uk/government/publications/sub-national-electricity-and-gas-consumption-statistics-analysis-tool-2005-to-2009. Accessed 22 Mar 2016

A New Approach to the Analysis of Network Observability in Medium and Low Voltage Electrical Grids

Guosong Lin[1,2(⊠)], Sascha Eichstädt[1,2], Dirk Turschner[1,2],
and Hans-Peter Beck[1,2]

[1] Physikalisch-Technische Bundesanstalt, Abbestraße 2, 10587 Berlin, Germany
Guosong_Lin@hotmail.de, Sascha.Eichstaedt@ptb.de,
{Turschner,beck}@iee.tu-clausthal.de
[2] Institut für Elektrische Energietechnik und Energiesysteme, TU-clausthal,
Leibnizstraße 28, 38678 Clausthal-Zellerfeld, Germany

Abstract. Medium and low voltage electrical power grids are typically sparsely instrumented, and thus, not observable in a systems' theory sense. However, this is a requirement to carry out state estimation methods. To this end, many approaches for optimal sensor placement are proposed in the literature. Such methods are typically motivated from a mathematical perspective, not taking the physical properties of the network into account. As a consequence, the dimensionality of the mathematical problem is typically quite large resulting in significant numerical complexity. Therefore, a new approach is proposed here which is based on analyzing the characteristic observable and unobservable nodes by using singular value decomposition (SVD) and the breadth-first search method. The aim of the method is to identify all possibilities for the placement of measuring equipment to achieve observability. The proposed method does render the network observable with a minimal number of sensors. In this way, this reduces the dimensionality for conventional optimal sensor placement algorithms substantially.

Keywords: Electrical grid · State estimation · Singular value decomposition · Breadth-first search · Optimal sensor placement

1 Introduction

Medium and low voltage electrical power grids are typically sparsely instrumented, and thus, such systems are usually not observable in a systems' theory sense [1, 2]. That is, the complete network state cannot be inferred from the available and measured network parameters. There are basically two situations which cause a lack of observability: insufficient measuring equipment and redundant measurements that cannot contribute to the observability of the system. The installation of additional measuring equipment is rather costly, which is why optimal strategies for their placement are of great interest. When additional instrumentation of the network is not feasible, typically pseudo-measurements are used for state estimation instead. Owing to their poor accuracy, it is also important to find the useful placements for such pseudo-measurements in order to achieve good overall estimation quality.

© ICST Institute for Computer Sciences, Social Informatics and Telecommunications Engineering 2017
E.T. Lau et al. (Eds.): SmartGIFT 2017, LNICST 203, pp. 122–131, 2017.
DOI: 10.1007/978-3-319-61813-5_12

Classical sensor placement methods consider the whole network and aim at determining a set of measured nodes which is optimal in the sense of minimal state estimation errors [3–5]. Therefore, typically all possible measurements including redundancy are considered one by one. This process is continued until the network is observable, namely the Jacobian matrix of network has full rank. However, there are many possibilities to install new measuring equipment, resulting in a high-dimensional estimation problem. For practical networks the dimensionality and complexity of this mathematical problem is so large that it results in serious numerical and computational issues. To this end, we propose a new method for determining network nodes at which measurements have to be added in order to achieve network observability. The idea is that based on such kind of pre-processing, the computational complexity of the optimization problem can be reduced significantly (Fig. 1).

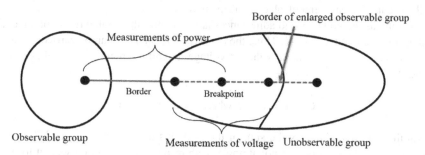

Fig. 1. Possible placements of network based on the proposed observability and voltage flow analysis

The reason for a network being unobservable is that at some nodes the voltage cannot be computed using the forward and backward sweep in the power flow calculation. These nodes are here defined as *breakpoints*. The main idea of the here proposed method is that adding power measurements at the nodes between the border of the observable and the unobservable groups and the breakpoint, adding voltage measurements at the nodes between the border of observable and unobservable groups and border of enlarged observable group or aggregation the nodes on the sides of border will then convert the unobservable group to an observable one. Thus, these nodes are considered as potential points for the placement of extra measuring equipment, pseudo-measurements or aggregation of nodes. In particular for large networks, this pre-determination of appropriate placement positions reduces the dimensionality for conventional optimal sensor placement algorithms substantially.

2 Mathematical Formulation of the Simplified Jacobian

The mathematical model relating measured network parameters z, such as nodal voltage amplitudes, active and reactive power, to the nodal voltage magnitude and phase values x is given by [6]

$$z = h(x). \tag{1}$$

In static state estimation, a linearized variant of this relation is considered, leading to the system of linear equations of a power system

$$z = H \cdot x, \tag{2}$$

where z is the vector of measurements, H is the Jacobian of h with respect to x, and x is vector of $2n - 1$ states. If for the rank r of the Jacobian H it holds that $r < 2n - 1$, then the power system is not observable in a systems' theory sense. To this end, $2n - 1 - r$ measurements have to be introduced in such a way that the resulting Jacobian $H_{new} = \begin{bmatrix} H \\ H' \end{bmatrix}$ has rank $r = 2n - 1$. This can only be achieved efficiently by a well-structured measurement placement method.

As long as the voltages and admittances are non-zero, their value does not affect the rank of the Jacobian matrix H. Thus, the observability analysis can be carried out using the Jacobian matrix with initial value of voltage magnitude being 1 and voltage phase being 0:

$$U = e + \sqrt{-1}f \text{ where } e = 1 \text{ and } f = 0. \tag{3}$$

In the admittance matrix the sum of the elements in each row is zero $\sum_1^n Y_{ij} = 0$. Thus, the partial derivatives of nodal power with respect to nodal voltages that form the Jacobian can be simplified. Hence, the Jacobian matrix for nodal power can be directly written as

$$H = \begin{bmatrix} \frac{\partial P_i}{\partial e} & \frac{\partial P_i}{\partial f} \\ \frac{\partial Q_i}{\partial e} & \frac{\partial Q_i}{\partial f} \end{bmatrix} = \begin{bmatrix} G_i & -B_i \\ -B_i & -G_i \end{bmatrix}. \tag{4}$$

Likewise, the partial derivatives for power from bus i to bus j that form the Jacobian matrix can be simplified. Hence, the part of the Jacobian matrix for power from bus i to bus j is finally given by

$$H = \begin{bmatrix} \frac{\partial P_{ij}}{\partial e} & \frac{\partial P_{ij}}{\partial f} \\ \frac{\partial Q_{ij}}{\partial e} & \frac{\partial Q_{ij}}{\partial f} \end{bmatrix}$$
$$= \begin{bmatrix} & i & & j & & i+n-1 & & j+n-1 & \\ 0 & \cdots & g_{ij} & 0 & \cdots & -g_{ij} & 0 & \cdots & -b_{ij} & 0 & \cdots & b_{ij} & 0 & \cdots \\ 0 & \cdots & -b_{ij} & 0 & \cdots & b_{ij} & 0 & \cdots & -g_{ij} & 0 & \cdots & g_{ij} & 0 & \cdots \end{bmatrix}. \tag{5}$$

where in the row P_{ij} only the element in the columns i is g_{ij}, columns j is $-g_{ij}$, columns $i+n-1$ is $-b_{ij}$ and columns $j+n-1$ is b_{ij}, the other elements in this row are equal to zero. In the row Q_{ij} only the element in the columns i is $-b_{ij}$, columns j is b_{ij}, columns $i+n-1$ is $-g_{ij}$ and columns $j+n-1$ is g_{ij}, the other elements in this row are equal to zero.

3 Determining the Observable and Unobservable Groups

An unobservable power system can always be partitioned into a set of observable groups and a set of unobservable groups. An observable group is defined as a network region where, without additional measurements, the (complex) nodal voltage for all nodes in this region can be calculated. It is assumed that at least the reference (slack) node is observable.

Using the singular value decomposition (SVD) [7], the $m \times 2n - 1$ dimensional Jacobian matrix H can be decomposed into the matrix product

$$H = USV^T. \tag{6}$$

The columns of the $m \times m$ unitary matrix U are the eigenvectors of HH^T; the non-zero elements of the $m \times 2n - 1$ matrix S, which only has non-negative real numbers along the main diagonal, are the square roots of the non-zero eigenvalues of $H^T H$; the columns of the $2n - 1 \times 2n - 1$ unitary matrix V are the eigenvectors of $H^T H$. Assuming the elements $\sigma_{11}, \sigma_{22} \ldots \sigma_{mm}$ of the matrix S are non-zero, the columns $v_1, v_2 \ldots v_m$ of V are the eigenvectors corresponding to the non-zero eigenvalues of $H^T H$, and the columns $v_{m+1}, v_{m+2} \ldots v_{2n-1}$ corresponding to the vanishing eigenvalues. Thus, the columns $v_{m+1}, v_{m+2} \ldots v_{2n-1}$ form an orthonormal basis for the solutions to the homogeneous equation $Hx = 0$. Rows for which all these columns of V have zeros, belong to the observable network nodes. Thus, the remaining nodes are unobservable.

4 Enlarging the Observable Groups

The breadth-first search algorithm [8] can be used to assign connected observable und unobservable nodes to groups. Firstly, for each unobservable group the node which is connected with an observable node is chosen as "top point" in the network topology. From there, all neighbouring nodes up to the first branching point in the network are identified. Say there are n connections $(L_1, L_2 \ldots L_n)$ between the observable und unobservable groups as shown in Fig. 2.

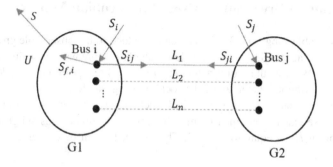

Fig. 2. Observable and unobservable group connected by n lines

In order to identify the points where instrumentation has to be added, the parts of the unobservable groups have to be added to the observable groups by *assumed* or *virtual* measurements.

All values in the observable group G1 are known, but in the group G2 the voltages cannot be calculated due to missing measurements. The bus i from G1 is connected to bus j from G2. For observability, a new virtual measurement, which can be either the complex power S_{ij} from bus i to bus j, the complex power S_{ji} from bus j to bus i, nodal power S_i of bus i or S_j of bus j, has to be added to enable the calculation of the nodal voltage at bus j, so that the observable group can be enlarged.

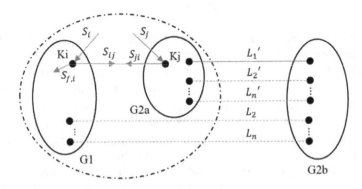

Fig. 3. Enlarged observable group

By adding the virtual measurements to the unobservable group, the observable group will be enlarged and the unobservable group will be decreased. The overall structure of the network can then be illustrated as shown in Fig. 3.

All enlarged observable groups can be determined by repeatedly adding virtual measurements. For radial networks, such as some medium and low voltage network, the lines $L_2, L_3, \cdots L_n$ and $L'_2, L'_3, \cdots L'_n$ in Figs. 2 and 3 should not be considered.

In order to determine the exact placement positions, we analyse the local Jacobian matrices for the unobservable groups as follows.

5 Determining Breakpoints Using the Jacobian Matrix

In the unobservable subgroup G2a, which can be added to the observable group exactly one point exists at which the voltage flow calculation breaks down due to missing measurements. We call this point a *breakpoint*. This breakpoint can be identified by analysing the simplified Jacobian of the local topology as follows.

The Jacobian matrix H_p of G2a, which includes n_p, is extracted from the whole system. Because exactly one measurement is missing to render this subgroup observable, the rank of H_p is equal to $2n_p - 2$. The matrix H_p can be written as

$$H_p = [H_{pRe} \quad H_{pIm}],$$ (7)

where the block-matrix H_{pRe} consists of the partial derivatives of powers $S = (P, Q)^T$ with respect to the real parts of nodal voltage, and H_{pIm} consists of the partial derivatives with respect to the imaginary parts of nodal voltage. The matrices H_{pRe} and H_{pIm}, which have the same rank $n_p - 1$, can be transformed by Gaussian elimination to the form

$$H_{pRe}, H_{pIm} = \begin{bmatrix} 1 & & & & & a_{1,n_p} \\ & 1 & & & & a_{2,n_p} \\ & & \ddots & & & \vdots \\ & & & 1 & & a_{i,n_p} \\ & & & & \ddots & \vdots \\ & & & & 1 & a_{n_p-1,n_p} \end{bmatrix}.$$ (8)

The last column is $a_1, a_2 \ldots a_i \neq -1$ and $a_{i+1}, a_{i+2} \ldots a_{n_p-1} = -1$ for some index i. Assume that the ordering of the Jacobian matrix follows the ordering of nodes in the considered network group. For the successful calculation of the voltage and power flow in the network, the local Jacobian then has to be of the following structure

$$J = \begin{bmatrix} g & -g \\ b & -b \end{bmatrix}.$$ (9)

The elements in the last column after Gaussian elimination, which are equal to -1 indicate that at these nodes this structure is satisfied. Hence, the element a_{i+1} corresponds to the breakpoint for that group. Consequently, a power measurement has to be added between the previously identified border and the breakpoint of the subgroup.

If complex voltage (PMU) can be measured in the subgroup G2a, it means, a new Jacobian matrix H_v with only one row, which has one nonzero element, will be inserted in the Jacobian matrix H_{pRe} and H_{pIm}

$$H'_{pRe} = \begin{bmatrix} H_{pRe} \\ H_v \end{bmatrix}, H'_{pIm} = \begin{bmatrix} H_{pRe} \\ H_v \end{bmatrix}.$$ (10)

No matter which element is nonzero, the new matrices H'_{pRe} and H'_{pIm} have full rank. Hence a complex voltage measurement can be placed at any node of the subgroup to ensure the group becomes observable.

The method of summarising voltages is a special case of complex voltage measurement. The according node s have the same voltage, namely the loss at the line is ignored then. Thus, only the node s at the vicinity of the border should be summarized.

The above steps of identifying and grouping of the remaining unobservable nodes and the subsequent identification of breakpoints have to be repeated until the whole network is observable.

6 Example

For illustrating the application of the proposed method, a 16 buses 15 branches network model is employed. The network is shown in the figure below, where positions of power measurements are marked with blue arrows (Fig. 4).

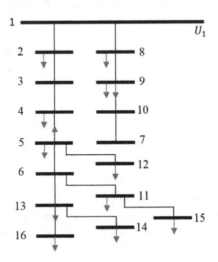

Fig. 4. Topology and measurements of the example network (Color figure online)

The possible placements of power measuring equipment are $\{S_1, S_{1,2}, S_{2,1}...\}$, which are in total 33 possibilities.

The simplified Jacobian matrix is calculated by Eqs. (4) and (5). The observable group and the unobservable group of the network can be determined using the singular value decomposition (SVD) method by Eq. (6). The matrix S is a diagonal 27×31 matrix with number of the non-zero elements $\sigma_1, \sigma_2...\sigma_{27}$, corresponding to the rank of the Jacobian matrix, that 3 measuring equipment are required to let the network observable.

From the 31×31 dimensional matrix V, the non-zero entries in columns $v_{28}, v_{29}, v_{30}, v_{31}$ indicate the elements of the observable group. In the first iteration of the algorithm for this example, the rows $\{1, 8, 9, 10, 23, 24, 25\}$ of these columns of V are zero. Consequently, the resulting observable group include the nodes $\{1, 8, 9, 10\}$ and unobservable group $\{2, 3, 4, 5, 6, 7, 11, 12, 13, 14, 15, 16\}$.

In the considered network topology, the nodes of the observable group are connected to each other. In contrast, the nodes of the unobservable group are partitioned by the breadth-first search algorithm into two groups $\{2, 3, 4, 5, 6, 11, 12, 13, 14, 15, 16\}$ and $\{7\}$, which are separated by the observable group.

The nodes at the border are found to be 1, 2 and 10, 7, for the different groups respectively. Consequently, additional virtual measurements of powers $S_{1,2}$ and $S_{10,7}$ are inserted respectively such that the observable group is enlarged as described in the

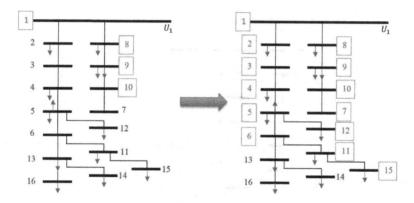

Fig. 5. Observable group before and after first iteration

Sect. 4. The additional nodes in the enlarged groups are then {2, 3, 4, 5, 6, 11, 12, 15}, which before belonged to the unobservable group {2, 3, 4, 5, 6, 11, 12, 13, 14, 15, 16} and node {7}, which before belonged to the unobservable group {7}., see Fig. 5.

Exactly one breakpoint exists in each enlarged group, and it can be found by the Jacobian matrix Eq. (8) as described in the Sect. 5. In our example, the Jacobian matrix of the two enlarged groups {2, 3, 4, 5, 6, 11, 12, 15} and {7} are calculated with the original measurements, which are $\{S_2, S_4, S_5, S_{11}, S_{12}, S_{15}, S_{5,4}\}$ for the first group and no measurement for the second group. For the first group, the Jacobian matrix with respect to the real part with dimension 7×8 of nodal voltage can be simplified by Gaussian elimination to

$$H_{pRe} = \begin{bmatrix} 1 & 0 & \cdots & 0 & -0.5 \\ 0 & 1 & \cdots & 0 & -1 \\ \vdots & \ddots & \ddots & \vdots & \vdots \\ 0 & \cdots & 0 & 1 & -1 \end{bmatrix} \tag{11}$$

From the last column, the breakpoint in this group is identified to be bus 3. In the second group there is no measurement, and hence, the identified breakpoint is bus 7.

This process is to be repeated until the group of observable nodes contains all nodes in the network, see Fig. 6.

Overall, in this example three additional measurements are required in order to achieve observability. The algorithm deduced that power measuring equipment can be installed respectively between bus 1 and 3 for first group, between bus 6 and 13 for the second group and between bus 10 and 7 for the third group. Or measuring equipment of power can be installed in any bus of the three enlarged groups in Fig. 6.

The quantity of possible placements of power measuring equipment is thus reduced by a factor of three from 33 to 11. A optimal placement method can use this information to determine the optimal placement of measuring equipment with respect to the chosen optimality criterion.

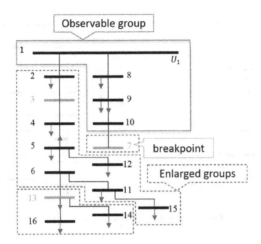

Fig. 6. The result of algorithm

7 Conclusion

In this paper a new algorithm based on the determination of the border between groups of observable and unobservable nodes and so-called *breakpoint* has been proposed to determine placements of measurements by taken into account the physicalities of the network. The observable and unobservable nodes are divided utilizing the Singular Value Decomposition (SVD) and the breadth-first search method. It was shown how adding virtual measurements can enlarge the group of observable nodes. By analysing the Jacobian matrix of the enlarged group, the breakpoint of computable power flow can be identified. The proposed method was illustrated using a 16-bus test system, where the algorithm found the correct minimum number of sensors to be placed and all possible placements of measurements. Using the proposed algorithm, the dimensionality of the optimal placement problem could be reduced by a factor of three.

Classical optimal placement methods are based on solving a complex mathematical discontinuous optimization and problem. The here proposed method utilizes the network topology and technical arguments to determine possible placement settings. The outcome of this algorithm could then be used to overcome the computational complexity of classical placement methods. The clear separation into observable and unobservable nodes and the subsequent algorithmic enlargement of the observable groups can help to make the network observable with fewer measurements, because nodes which do not contribute to the observability can be ignored.

Acknowledgement. This work is part of the European Metrology Research Program (EMRP) Joint Research Project ENG63. The EMRP is jointly funded by the EMRP participating countries within EURAMET and the European Union.

References

1. Heins, W., Ell, N., Beck, H.-P., Bohn, C.: State observation in medium-voltage grids with incomplete measurement infrastructure through online correction of power forecasts. In: Proceeding of European Control Conference (ECC) (2014)
2. Wu, J., He, Y., Jenkins, N.: A robust state estimator for medium voltage distribution networks. IEEE Trans. Power Syst. **28**(2), 1008–1016 (2013)
3. Korres, G., Xygkis, T., Manousakis, N.: Optimal location of measurement devices in distribution grids via Boolean convex optimization, Lyon, 15–18 June 2015
4. Jiang, C., Soh, Y.C., Li, H.: Sensor placement by maximal projection on minimum eigenspace for linear inverse problems. IEEE, June 2015
5. Ketabi, A., Hosseini, S.A.: A new method for optimal harmonic meter placement. ISSN 1546-9239
6. Abur, A., Expósito, A.G.: Power System State Estimation: Theory and Implementation. Marcel Dekker, New York (2004)
7. Wall, M.E., Rechtsteiner, A., Rocha, L.M.: Singular value decomposition and principal component analysis, pp. 99–109. LANL LA-UR-02-4001
8. Leiserson, C.E., Schardl, T.B.: A work-efficient parallel Breadth-First Search Algorithm (or how to cope with the nondeterminism of reducers) (PDF). In: ACM Symposium on Parallelism in Algorithms and Architectures (2010)

Deep Learning Based Consumer Classification for Smart Grid

Kálmán Tornai[1][✉], András Oláh[1], Rajmund Drenyovszki[2], Lóránt Kovács[2], István Pintér[2], and János Levendovszky[3]

[1] Faculty of Information Technology and Bionics,
Pázmány Péter Catholic University, Budapest, Hungary
tornai.kalman@itk.ppke.hu
[2] GAMF Faculty of Engineering and Computer Science,
Pallas Athene University, Kecskemet, Hungary
[3] Department of Networked Systems and Services,
Budapest University of Technology and Economics, Budapest, Hungary

Abstract. Classification of different power consumers is a very important task in smart power transmission grids as the different type of consumers may be treated with different conditions. Furthermore, the power suppliers can use the category information of consumers to forecast better their behavior which is a relevant task for load balancing.

In this paper, we present performance results on the classification of consumers using deep learning based classification scheme in smart grid systems. The results are compared with existing classification methods using real, measured power consumption data.

We demonstrate that consumer classification performed by neural networks can outperform existing, traditional tools as in several cases the correct class assignment rate is greater than 0.97.

Keywords: Classification methods · Consumer classification · Deep learning · Softmax layer network

1 Introduction

Smart power transmission grids efficiently integrate renewable energy sources and can manage the balance between the supply and demand adaptively. The new capabilities inhere in the integrated, intelligent measurement system. In addition, with two-way communication not only the measurements can be collected but the endpoints also can be controlled.

The use of smart meters in the network implies that a vast amount of data is being acquired. These data have to be processed in order to obtain relevant information about the status of the network or the consumer behavior.

The classification of consumers is the basic tool to recognize category changes, consumption behavior changes, or irregularities of the grid. This information can be used (i) for using different pricing for consumers with different behavioral

© ICST Institute for Computer Sciences, Social Informatics and Telecommunications Engineering 2017
E.T. Lau et al. (Eds.): SmartGIFT 2017, LNICST 203, pp. 132–141, 2017.
DOI: 10.1007/978-3-319-61813-5_13

patterns [13]; (ii) for estimating the future consumption better; (iii) in load balancing as the consumers belonging to different classes can be estimated well; (iv) to extract further relevant information about the behavior of different consumer categories.

In this paper, we introduce results on using Deep Learning techniques of recognition of consumer class. The performance of the deep learning based solution is compared with other, existing solutions on real consumption measurements. It will be shown that the proposed method outperforms the existing implementations as it can provide more accurate results compared to other methods. Furthermore, the proposed method is more flexible in the sense that it can handle different scales of the input data as well.

The paper will be organized as follows: in Sect. 2, the existing classification methods will be briefly reviewed. In Sect. 3, the new method will be discussed. In Sect. 4, the performance of the proposed method will be described, finally in Sect. 5, conclusions will be drawn.

2 Related Works

In the followings, based on the review of Zhou et al. [8], the existing classification approaches are summarized. The following reviewed methods are the most commonly used solutions for classifying or clustering power consumption data. The performance of following methods will be compared with the proposed, deep learning based method in Sect. 4.

2.1 K-Nearest Neighbor

Using the k-nearest neighbor (kNN) method [21], the decision is made based on the distance between data elements. For a new object, the distances between the existing objects and new instance have to be calculated. The class assignment problem is solved by seeking the class with smallest (average) distance. The performance of the method is highly influenced by the applied metric [19]. In most cases, the Euclidean distance is used, but special problems require more complicated metrics such as dynamic time warping distance [3,11]. This method is applicable to sequences with non-numerical values, but the data has to be transformed or sequence alignment has to performed. In the case of power consumption classification this method can be applied as it is simple and efficient enough, however it is sensitive to noise and the performance depends on the applied metric highly.

Fuzzy k-NN classification is similar to k-NN classification, but objects have a membership degree for classes. It has the advantage that the algorithm does not assign the object to a class. For example, in a case where a new object lies between two classes this fact is reported by the algorithm and creation of new class or other solutions can be considered [20]. This method has better average performance, however, it can easily happen that a new consumer cannot be assigned to the correct class for sure as the fuzzy membership is not significant enough.

2.2   Artificial Neural Networks

The Artificial Neural Networks (ANN), especially recurrent neural networks (RNN) can model the properties of the time series of classes [15]. These models are constructed for all classes using training sets. With Multilayer Perceptron network (MLP) the data set classification task is solved by using hyperplanes for set separation [6].

Kernel methods such as Support Vector Machines (SVMs) can be used to reduce the number and to extract the features. The kernel-based methods are commonly used to process biological data [10].

Different types of ANNs have been successfully deployed to solve the of power consumer classification [9]. However, there are also certain disadvantages of applying such structures as the performance is affected by weights of network connections the initialization parameters, the order of training samples. Further optimization is possible and new structures can also be deployed, such as introduced in this work.

2.3   Hidden Markov Model Based Classification

The model-based classification methods construct a model for all classes using training sets. The incoming data is classified upon the best fitting model [14]. One of the most popular statistical models is Hidden Markov Model [7]. A trained HMM can reflect the probabilistic relations of the values within the time series thus an HMM represents the structure of the time series. The optimal parameters of an HMM can be found by using the Baum-Welch algorithm.

2.4   Forecast Based Classification

Our previously introduced solution is the forecast based classification method (FBM). This method [18] exploits the different statistical properties of the power consumption time series. For each consumer class, a feed-forward neural network (FFNN) [5] is trained to forecast the time series of the specific class with low error rate. Hence the trained forecaster is able to approximate time series of the same class with low error rate and has a superior error rate in case of time series belonging to different consumer classes.

Newly arriving consumers are classified as follows: each of previously trained forecaster is evaluated on the new time series and the forecast error is calculated as the difference between the forecast and real value of time series. The mean of the forecast error will be used as a decision variable to decide the class where the sequence belongs to.

The advantage of this method is that it utilizes well the temporal property of time series, furthermore short term forecasting is also performed as part of the algorithms. However, this method is highly influenced by the capabilities of the applied forecast method, which affect the performance of the solution. (As the selection and training of the best forecast method is not trivial.)

3 Consumer Classification Using Deep Learning Techniques

Deep learning methods and neural networks are hot topics as the amount of recorded (measured) data increase data day by day. However, the convolutional neural networks (CNN) were invented and first demonstrated by Fukushima Kunihiko in 1980 [4], but they were not applied in practice until 2011 when Yan LeCun applied this method successfully in many different problems [17]. It has been demonstrated that in certain problems they are able to reach a classification accuracy that is comparable to the human performance, or in some cases it can surpass it. In most cases, a series of CNNs are used and a softmax layer is added to determine the resulting class.

Autoencoders (or Diabolo network) [16] with softmax layers are also used for classification. The aim of autoencoders is to learn a representation (model or encoding) for a set of data while the dimensionality of the data is reduced. In this paper, we applied autoencoders with softmax layer to solve the power consumption data classification task.

3.1 Autoencoder Network

The structure of an autoencoder network is a feedforward (without any feedback) neural network (FFNN) with the following properties:

- The input and output layer has the same number of artificial neurons.
- The network has one or more hidden layers between the input layer and output layers.

The network is used for unsupervised learning as the purpose of the output layer is to reconstruct the input data, while the inner layers try to reduce the dimensionality. The structure is demonstrated by Fig. 1.

Autoencoders consists of two parts: (i) encoder and (ii) decoder, which can be described by the following transformations $\Psi : T \rightarrow C$ and $\Phi : C \rightarrow T$. Theses transformation should be defined such that

$$\arg \min_{\Phi, \Psi} \|\mathbf{T} - (\Psi \circ \Phi)\, \mathbf{T}\|^2 . \tag{1}$$

Thus the reconstruction error is minimized. The dimensionality of C should be less than the dimensionality of T in order to extract features from the original data.

Int the neural networks sigmoid activation function

$$\varphi_S(u) = \frac{1}{1 + e^{-\alpha u}}, \tag{2}$$

or rectified linear activation functions are used:

$$\varphi_R(u) = \begin{cases} u, \text{if } u > 0 \\ 0, \text{if } u \leq 0 \end{cases} \tag{3}$$

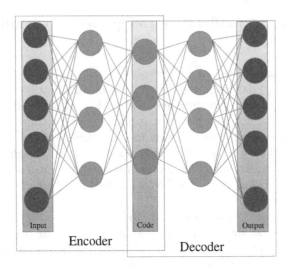

Fig. 1. Structure of autoencoder network

The training of the network can be performed with any of backpropagation algorithms used in feedforward neural networks. In our test, we have used Scaled conjugate gradient backpropagation and Levenberg–Marquardt backpropagation [2] as the first one can be used efficiently on GP-GPU implementation and the execution time of the latter one is often the shortest among of several methods in the case of CPU based simulation.

3.2 Soft Max Layer

This layer consists of artificial neural networks having the soft max function as activation function (or normalized exponential):

$$P\left(\mathcal{C}_r|u\right) = \frac{e^{a_r}}{\sum_{j=1}^{k} e^{a_j}}, \tag{4}$$

where $0 \leq P\left(\mathcal{C}_r|u\right) \leq 1$ and

$$\sum_{j=1}^{k} P\left(\mathcal{C}_j|u\right) = 1.$$

In previous equation $P\left(u|\mathcal{C}_j\right)$ denotes the conditional probability of the sample given class r and $P\left(\mathcal{C}_j\right)$ is the prior probability of the class, and

$$a_r = \ln\left(P\left(u|\mathcal{C}_j\right) P\left(\mathcal{C}_r\right)\right).$$

The softmax function can be considered the multi-class generalization of logistic sigmoid function.

3.3   Proposed Structure

The properties and parameters of the architecture of the neural networks proposed in this paper to solve the power consumer classification problem are overviewed in this section.

Two autoencoders have been applied sequentially in order to reduce the dimensionality of the input time series highly. The number of outputs of the encoder has been determined as the proportion to the original number of inputs. We have investigated the performance of the network using the different ratio of compression.

The encoder of autoencoders has been implemented with rectified linear activation functions and in the output layer, linear activation function was used.

4   Performance Analysis

In this section, the test environment, test data and the performance of the proposed method is introduced and compared to existing solutions.

4.1   Test Environment

The tests of the algorithms have been carried out in Matlab environment [12]. All test has been repeated for several times to have averaged results. Thus the extremely good and bad results are eliminated. The outlier performance values are caused by randomly chosen learning parameters of artificial neural network based algorithms. The available data was randomly split into training data set, test data set and for training purposes validation dataset, with the following ratios of 0.45, 0.45 and 0.1 respectively.

The performance of the proposed method can be evaluated by comparing the results of the method with the known information provided in the database we used for evaluation. (The class assignments made by the database providers are considered as correct solutions.) Hence the performance metrics is the number of correctly classified time series divided by the total number of time series. All performance results are the evaluation of the algorithms on the same test set.

4.2   Real, Measured Consumption Data

Real measurements were obtained from two different sources. First of them is a rather small database. The database was obtained from a large Central-European electricity distribution company, where the power consumption time series was classified into 8 classes by company experts. The consumption was measured at 150 different sites for one year in 2009. Furthermore, as the actual data is trade secret it has been normalized by the company and personal information was removed as well. While the class assignment provided by the power distribution company is unambiguous, the actual classes are overlapping thus automated classification cannot achieve 100% precision.

The second database is "Commercial and Residential Hourly Load Profiles for all TMY3 Locations in the United States" [1]. This dataset contains hourly load profile data for 16 different commercial building types (based on the DOE commercial reference building models) and residential buildings (based off the Building America House Simulation Protocols). The hourly load profiles are available for overall TMY3 locations in the United States. Due to the size of the database, we have reduced the number of classes from 16 to 8 (Hospital, Large office, Medium office, Primary school, Secondary school, Small office, Warehouse, Supermarket) and then the number of sites reduced from 936 to 100 randomly chosen sites.

4.3   Performance Results

We have investigated the influence of actual coding rates of the two autoencoders to the performance of the correct classification capabilities. Several test results with different parameters show that maximal performance can be achieved in the case when the number of nodes of the first encoder's code layer is higher than 90% of the number of the nodes of the input layer. In the case of the second layer the number of nodes has less impact on the performance, however, the best results have been achieved at having the number of code nodes 35% of the input nodes. The results are summarized by Fig. 2. In the following performance test the previous parameters have been used.

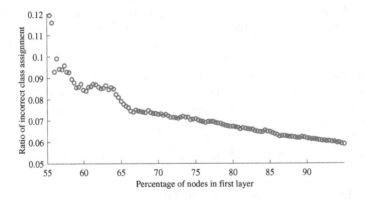

Fig. 2. Performance results in function of the number of nodes in autoencoder network

Results on European Database. As the actual classes are overlapping in some cases we have investigated the performance of the method in four disjoint classes and all classes separately. Figure 3 indicates that the Deep Learning based solution outperforms the other methods in both cases. The correct class assignment ratio is over than 98% in the first case and 95% in the latter case. The classes which are mostly confused by the solutions are investigated using several statistical parameters and the principal components are also compared. It has

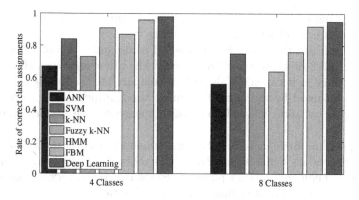

Fig. 3. Performance results of different classification methods executed on the European measurements

been found that the three of the eight classes has several overlapping parameters, as the classification may be acceptable even the class assignment made by algorithms does not match to the manual assignment made by experts. (However in the figure the performance results show the case when we do not take into consideration the overlaps, and if the algorithmic result does not match to the manual assignment the class assignment is considered as a wrong solution.)

Results on US Database. The comparison of the performance of deep learning method to other algorithms is summarized by Fig. 4. The recorded data came from all across the US thus the geographic location may have an influence on the behavior of consumers, as a result, the load profiles may vary between different climate zones. As a result, we have investigated the performance of the

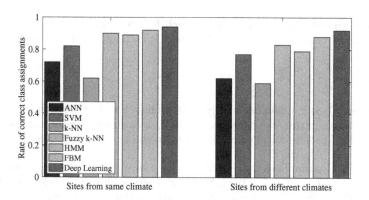

Fig. 4. Performance results of different classification methods executed on the American measurements

algorithms using data sets from the same climate zone (humid subtropical) and using data sets from different climate zones as well.

Results indicate that both in the case of same and different climate zones the deep learning based solution outperforms the other solutions. However, the difference is smaller between the algorithms compared to the European database. It may be explained by the normalization of the European data. Furthermore, the geographic location has only a small influence on the performance of the algorithms.

The algorithm made incorrect class assignments in case of the following pairs of classes: Secondary Schools and Primary Schools; Warehouses and Supermarkets. As the members of these pairs of classes can be considered similar, the number of incorrect class assignments can be acceptable.

5 Conclusion

In this paper, we have introduced performance results on real electricity consumer data of deep learning based power consumption classification scheme. The proposed scheme is capable of classifying the power consumers at very high level in most of the cases.

In addition, the results of the scheme have been compared to existing classification methods, and it has been proven experimentally that the performance of the deep learning method is better than the other available solutions. A further advantage of the solution that is can be efficiently used on data which are previously normalized, and the novel method is more tolerant to deviations of the data set, such as it is capable of recognizing classes which are spanning over different climate zones.

In the future, we are going to investigate whether this scheme can be modified to cluster or rather to automatically categorize the power consumers and it also is going to be tested on additional databases.

Acknowledgment. This publication/research has been supported by PPKE KAP 16-71009-1.2-ITK Grant. This source of support is gratefully acknowledged.

References

1. Commercial and residential hourly load profiles for all TMY3 locations in the united states. http://en.openei.org/datasets/dataset/commercial-and-residential-hourly-load-profiles-for-all-tmy3/locations-in-the-united-states. Accessed 30 Aug 2016
2. Bishop, C.: Pattern Recognition and Machine Learning. Springer, New York (2006)
3. Chan, S., Kao, B., Yip, C., Tang, M.: A brief survey on sequence classification. In: Proceedings Eighth International Conference on Database Systems for Advanced Applications (DASFAA 2003), pp. 119–124. IEEE (2003)
4. Fukushima, K.: Neocognitron: a self-organizing neural network model for a mechanism of pattern recognition unaffected by shift in position. Biol. Cybern. **36**(4), 193–202 (1980)

5. Haykin, S.: Neural Networks, A Comprehensive Foundation, 3rd edn. Pearson, Prentince Hall, Upper Saddle River (2008)
6. Kaefer, F., Heilman, C.M., Ramenofsky, S.D.: A neural network application to consumer classification to improve the timing of direct marketing activities. Comput. Oper. Res. **32**(10), 2595–2615 (2005)
7. Kim, M., Pavlovic, V.: Sequence classification via large margin Hidden Markov Models. Data Min. Knowl. Disc. **23**(2), 322–344 (2011)
8. le Zhou, K., Yang, S.L., Shen, C.: A review of electric load classification in smart grid environment. Renew. Sustain. Energy Rev. **24**, 103–110 (2013)
9. Lo, K.L., Zakaria, Z.: Electricity consumer classification using artificial intelligence. In: 39th International Universities Power Engineering Conference, UPEC 2004, vol. 1, pp. 443–447, September 2004
10. Lodhi, H., Saunders, C., Shawe-Taylor, J., Cristianini, N., Watkins, C.: Text classification using string kernels. J. Mach. Learn. Res. **2**, 419–444 (2002)
11. Maimon, O., Rokach, L. (eds.): Data Mining and Knowledge Discovery Handbook. Springer, New York (2005)
12. MATLAB, version 8.6.0 (r2015b). The MathWorks Inc., Natick, Massachusetts (2015)
13. Noble, P.M., Gruca, T.S.: Industrial pricing: theory and managerial practice. Mark. Sci. **18**(3), 435–454 (1999)
14. Rani, S., Sikka, G.: Recent techniques of clustering of time series data: a survey. Int. J. Comput. Appl. **52**(15), 1–9 (2012)
15. Ruck, D., Rogers, S., Kabrisky, K., Oxley, M., Suter, B.: The multilayer perceptron as an approximation to an optimal Bayes estimator. IEEE Trans. Neural Netw. **1**(4), 296–298 (1990)
16. Rumelhart, D.E., Hinton, G.E., Williams, R.J.: Learning representations by back-propagating errors. Nature **323**, 533–536 (1986)
17. Sermanet, P., LeCun, Y.: Traffic sign recognition with multi-scale convolutional networks. In: Proceedings of International Joint Conference on Neural Networks (IJCNN 2011) (2011)
18. Tornai, K., Kovács, L., Oláh, A., Drenyovszki, R., Pintér, I., Tisza, D., Levendovszky, J.: Classification for consumption data in smart grid based on forecasting time series. Electr. Power Syst. Res. **141**, 191–201 (2016)
19. Xing, Z., Pei, J., Keogh, E.: A brief survey on sequence classification. ACM SIGKDD Explor. Newslett. **12**(1), 40–48 (2010)
20. Zakaria, Z., Lo, K.L., Sohod, M.H.: Application of fuzzy clustering to determine electricity consumers' load profiles. In: IEEE International Power and Energy Conference, pp. 99–103, November 2006
21. Zhang, B., Srihari, S.N.: Fast k-nearest neighbor classification using cluster-based trees. IEEE Trans. Pattern Anal. Mach. Intell. **26**(4), 525–528 (2004)

Grid Resilience Governance of the Future: Analyzing the Role of Associations in Experimental Smart Grid Projects in The Netherlands

Imke Lammers[1] and Alexandr Vasenev[2]([✉])

[1] Department of Governance and Technology for Sustainability (CSTM), 7522 NB Enschede,
The Netherlands
i.lammers@utwente.nl
[2] ServicesCybersecurity and Safety Research Group, University of Twente, 7522 NB Enschede,
The Netherlands
a.vasenev@utwente.nl

Abstract. Local generation decentralizes urban grids. Soon new actors, such as associations, might enter the traditional energy domain. As electrical grids are critical for society, new actors will need to collaborate with other city-level stakeholders to ensure proper grid functioning in times of crisis. Little research has been done about how this collaboration could look like for smart grid projects. This short paper presents for discussion initial analysis on how associations as new actors might approach establishing such collaborations to improve grid resilience. We focus on advances in Dutch governance related to local energy planning projects. First, we outline which stakeholders are currently concerned with grid resilience in the Netherlands. Then, we introduce how innovative smart grid projects can be organized and describe the role of associations within them. Finally, we apply the Institutional Analysis and Development Framework (IAD) to point out what associations might consider to improve grid resilience.

Keywords: Grid resilience · Planning · Governance · Institutional Analysis and Development Framework · Associations · DSO · Security regions

1 Introduction

Ensuring electricity supply to important city-level consumers, such as hospitals, is a task that demands devising plans how a grid should operate in case of blackouts. Collective decision-making might account for how to distribute electricity as a scarce resource during disasters. For this, grid stakeholders can devise 'islanding' strategies [1] to isolate a part of the grid from the main electricity supply and ensure that sufficient local generation is provided [2]. However, it is unclear how smart grid actors can structure their collaboration. This challenge is exacerbated as future grids will see new actors emerge. Specifically, actors like associations that can take over the DSO's role in smart grid projects, as recently introduced for experimental electricity systems in The Netherlands [3]. Based on this, there are questions that have yet to be solved, including defining the

© ICST Institute for Computer Sciences, Social Informatics and Telecommunications Engineering 2017
E.T. Lau et al. (Eds.): SmartGIFT 2017, LNICST 203, pp. 142–148, 2017.
DOI: 10.1007/978-3-319-61813-5_14

specific roles of possible future actors, and how they can structure their interactions with other stakeholders.

The Institutional Analysis and Development (IAD) Framework can help to address these questions [4]. While the Framework is mainly used to study common pool resource (CPR) problems like irrigation systems or fishing grounds [5], it has been applied to understanding energy transitions [6] and kWh can be seen as CPRs [7].

To define electricity grid resilience governance, this paper describes current stake-holders in grid resilience, as well as a new actor (associations) that was introduced by a Dutch Crown Decree to enable experiments for future grids. Afterwards, we present for discussion our analysis on how associations can structure their collaboration with other stakeholders. For this analysis we use constructs from the IAD Framework. Overall, this paper aims to inform researchers about which actors might have a stake in a common grid planning process according to Dutch practices, as well as to show how stakeholders can interact in the future.

2 Background

Ensuring continuity of electricity supply to critical consumers is essential for smart cities of the future. Recently, [2] developed a Collaborative Framework to suggest how urban grid resilience can be improved. This framework deals with threat analysis (e.g., [8, 9]) and the identification of stakeholders. Based on vulnerability and criticality assessments, the stakeholders are to come up with a disaster response plan for establishing a small 'island' of electricity. However, ways in which stakeholders can structure their collab-orations as regards resilience have not been specified in the literature yet. Such a structure can help to structure interactions between stakeholders.

This paper provides initial analysis on how future collaborations can be arranged by taking Dutch practices as an example. To do so, this section overviews actors related to grid resilience, outlines a new actor (associations), and describes the Institutional Anal-ysis and Development Framework that will be used for the analysis.

2.1 Actors Concerned with Grid Resilience in the Netherlands

Distribution system operators (DSOs) are responsible for connecting all consumers to the electricity grid and transporting electricity to them (according to Dutch Electricity Act 1998[1]). They should ensure the safe use of energy and prevent, limit, and fight events that can impact the grid [10]. DSOs work in close connection to the *TSO* (transmission system operator) and *Netbeheer Nederland* (the umbrella organization of all Dutch DSOs) which signs agreements with the *police* and *security regions* to ensure robustness and resilience of the electricity grid.

25 *Security Regions* (in Dutch: veiligheidsregio's) are in charge of reacting to large-scale undesirable events and responsible for protecting critical infrastructure (CIs), with

---

[1] Elektriciteitswet 1998 Wet van 2 Juli 1998, houdende regels met betrekking tot de productie, het transport en de levering van elektriciteit, Stb. 1998, 427, art. 1(g).

special attention to the sectors of electricity, portable water, and surface water [11]. Hereby they are responsible for initiating collaboration between critical sectors in the region, establishing relevant contracts and networks, and reaching agreements with CI operators over communication, information, and measures [11].

Besides the *police, NCTV* is a specialized organization that handles safety on the national level and works together with security regions, if pandemics, terrorist attacks, or, e.g., a blackout in a telecommunication network occur [12]. Additionally, *industry* is an important actor in connection to national safety, as they control about 80% of CI. Thus, collaboration between security regions and the industry is essential [13].

The preferred policy instrument of the Dutch government are covenants between stakeholders [14]. These agreements between actors are important for addressing robustness and resilience issues of the electricity grid. For instance, in the Brabant-Noord region in The Netherlands a covenant was signed by (i.) security region Brabant-Noord; (ii.) the police of Oost-Brabant; (iii.) the DSOs Endinet, Enexis, Liander; (iv.) the TSO TenneT and Gasunie [15]. These four classes of actors indicate stakeholders particularly concerned with grid resilience nowadays.

2.2 Associations as a New Grid Resilience Actor

As decentralized renewable electricity generation continues to change the (previously) centralized electricity grid, it can be expected that the future actor landscape will change in line with it. In the effort to shape future grid-related governance, on April 1, 2015 The Netherlands introduced the Crown Decree 'Besluit experimenten decentrale duurzame elektriciteitsopwekking' (short: Experimentation Decree) [3]. This Decree lifts the ban that no one can take over the tasks of DSOs. Thus, new actors – under specific conditions – are allowed to experiment with the local generation, distribution and sale of renewable energy.

The Decree grants exemptions to *associations,* i.e. owners' associations and energy associations. Associations take over the responsibilities and powers of a *DSO.* They have to comply with DSO-related requirements, including reliability, safety, security of supply, consumer and environmental protection, and technical standards.

Following the two tenders of 2015 and 2016, nine projects were granted an exemption and thus allowed to start smart grid projects (see Table 1).

Seven of the listed projects are defined as 'project grid' (maximum 500 connected consumers), and two others ('Aardehuizen' and 'Kringloopgemeenschap') are 'large grid projects' (up to 10.000 connected entities, 80% of them consumers) in which the DSO remains responsible. For more details see [16].

As these listed projects are rather innovative, the way in which associations might structure their interaction with other stakeholders is not yet clear, especially in regard to disaster response. Analyzing this relation, e.g. with the help of relevant governance frameworks, can be useful to approach the task.

Table 1. List of projects under the Dutch Experimentation Decree

Type of project	Project name (location)	Details
Apartment building complex	Noordstraat 11 Tilburg (Tilburg)	Three apartments with PV panels, solar thermal collectors, ICT
	Villa de Verademing (The Hague)	Apartments with heat pumps, solar thermal collectors, PV panels, small wind turbine, storage, ICT, peer-to-peer supply (p2p)
	Blackjack[a] (Amsterdam)	High-rise apartment complex with PV panels, combined heat and power (CHP), p2p, ICT
	Zwijsen Veghel (Veghel)	115 apartments with PV panels, CHP, ICT, dynamic electricity tariff
Residential area	Endona (Heeten & Raalte)	Solar park with 7.200 PV panels, bio-digester, p2p, ICT
	Green-parq (Reeuwijk)	Recreational homes with PV panels on the roofs of common facilities, heat pumps, p2p
	Schoonschip (Amsterdam)	46 water-homes with PV panels, heat pumps, solar thermal collectors, storage, p2p, ICT
	Aardehuizen (Olst)	Houses with PV panels, collective battery, ICT, p2p, dynamic electricity tariffs
	Kringloopgemeenschap (Bodegraven & Reeuwijk)	2.500 households connected to 2,3 MW wind turbine, 16.000 PV panels, dynamic electricity tariffs

[a] The project was officially discontinued and excluded from participation under the Experimentation Decree in August 2016.

2.3 Rules-in-Use as a Structure to Analyze Stakeholder Interactions

The Institutional Analysis and Development Framework can be employed to analyze interactions between stakeholders for grid resilience. The IAD Framework [4, 5] was developed to find institutional arrangements for the governance of common pool resources. Thus, its aims to overcome the 'tragedy of the commons' [17]. Seven variables (*rules-in-use*) are core elements of the IAD: position, boundary, choice, aggregation, information, payoff, and scope rules (see Table 2). We apply these rules to analyze possible future interrelations between grid resilience stakeholders.

Table 2. An overview of IAD's rules-in-use (based on [4, 18, 19])

Rules-in-use	Definition
Position rules	What positions exist (initiator of meetings, chair, agenda-setter)?
Boundary rules	Which actors need to be involved? Who and how many units withdraw kwh?
Choice rules	Which sets of actions do actors may, must, or must not take?
Aggregation rules	Are decisions made collectively, individually or automated?
Information rules	How much information do actors need? Who shares which information?
Payoff rules	Which costs and benefits do specific actions entail? Is compensation needed?
Scope rules	Which geographic region is affected?

3   Associations as a Grid Resilience Actor: Analysis and Discussions

The rules-in-use can be used to structure stakeholder interactions as follows:

Position rule: In the novel smart grid projects, associations take over the responsibilities of DSOs and energy supply companies in 'project grids', including security. Thus, associations will be responsible for disaster response plans, and will need to organize meetings, establish networks, and initiate contracts.

Boundary rule: Associations might plan how to reduce the impact of electricity supply interruptions, e.g., to perform grid islanding. As developing a disaster response requires knowledge of state-of-the-art solutions and perhaps technical expertise, other parties might need be involved, such as specialized developers or research centers. Thus, similarly to the current Dutch practice, covenants need to be established for public safety in smart grid experiments, e.g. associations might sign agreements with a security region, police, DSO, and TSO (similar to the Brabant-Noord covenant).

Choice rules have to be outlined next. For example, whether an association can decide on behalf of all its members or whether it might need the permission of its members for certain actions. Next, the actors have to specify how they will make agreements (*aggregation rule*), as clear decision-making processes are needed to effectively work together in crisis situations. The agreements have to include: (1) *information rules* (e.g. communications with critical infrastructure operators and citizens); and (2) *payoff rules* related to costs and benefits of certain actions (e.g., withdrawing energy from a private or collective battery can lead to a compensation).

Scope rule: Currently, smart grid projects are rather small and span from one individual building up to the grid of one or two municipalities. In this way, a security region might need to have a number of special agreements within the area concerned. Establishing a significant amount of covenants may lead not only to increased complexity, but might also require additional efforts to coordinate. To counter this, several projects could form a group, which leads to complex stakeholder interactions.

Altogether, the Crown Decree introduces a new actor (associations) into the Dutch electricity production and distribution system. This actor will be an important stakeholder in connection to how electricity should be prioritized in case of black-outs. On the one hand, this might result in easier and faster decision-making, provided that negative outcomes would not strongly interfere with interests of nation-level stakeholders outlined in the document. On the other hand, associations might be inexperienced and lack expertise of DSOs and energy suppliers. To sum up, structuring future stakeholder interactions can be challenging, but devising specific rules-in-use can help to reduce at least part of the governance complexity.

This paper aspires to initiate a discussion. It overviews grid resilience actors in The Netherlands and introduces for the first time (to the authors' best knowledge) how the IAD framework can structure interactions between grid resilience stakeholders. Several future actions can benefit this line of research, including performing additional analysis in from of empirical case studies, overviewing status of resilience governance and trends in other countries, and obtaining feedback from practitioners.

Acknowledgments. This work has been partially supported by the Joint Program Initiative (JPI) Urban Europe via the IRENE project and by the Netherlands Organisation for Scientific Research (NWO) via the URSES-SmaRds project (project number 408-13-005).

References

1. Balaguer, I.J., et al.: Control for grid-connected and intentional islanding operations of distributed power generation. IEEE Trans. Ind. Electron. **58**(1), 147–157 (2011)
2. Jung, O., et al.: Towards a collaborative framework to improve urban grid resilience. In: 2016 IEEE International Energy Conference (ENERGYCON) (2016)
3. MEA, Nota van Toelichting - Besluit van 28 februari 2015, houdende het bij wege van experiment afwijken van de Elektriciteitswet 1998 voor decentrale opwekking van duurzame elektriciteit, M.v.E. Zaken, (ed.). 's-Gravenhage (2015)
4. Ostrom, E.: Background on the institutional analysis and development framework. Policy Stud. J. **39**(1), 7–27 (2011)
5. Ostrom, E.: Governing the Commons: The Evolution of Institutions for Collective Action. Cambridge University Press, Cambridge (1990)
6. Koster, A.M.: An Institutional Approach to Understanding Energy Transitions. Arizona State University, Phoenix (2013)
7. Wolsink, M.: The research agenda on social acceptance of distributed generation in smart grids: renewable as common pool resources. Renew. Sustain. Energy Rev. **16**(1), 822–835 (2012)
8. Vasenev, A., Montoya, L.: Analysing non-malicious threats to urban smart grids by interrelating threats and threat taxonomies. In: 2016 IEEE International Smart Cities Conference (ISC2) (2016)

9. Vasenev, A., Montoya, L., Ceccarelli, A.: A Hazus-Based method for assessing robustness of electricity supply to critical smart grid consumers during flood events. In: 2016 11th International Conference on Availability, Reliability and Security (ARES) (2016)
10. Netbeheer Nederland. Veiligheid (2014). http://www.netbeheernederland.nl/themas/dossier/?dossierid=11010058&title=Veiligheid. Accessed 16 Aug 2016
11. BZK. Bescherming Vitale Infrastructuur: De veiligheidsregio als partner (2008). www.brandweerkennisnet.nl/publish/pages/2206/binder11.pdf. Accessed 16 Aug 2016
12. NCTV. Organisatie. n.a https://www.nctv.nl/organisatie/. Accessed 16 Aug 2016
13. BZK. Informatie Vitale sectoren (2010). https://www.rijksoverheid.nl/documenten/brochures/2010/06/23/informatie-vitale-sectoren. Accessed 16 Aug 2016
14. Minister BZK. Brief minister over het afsluiten van convenanten - Veiligheidsregio's (2008). https://www.parlementairemonitor.nl/9353000/1/j9vvij5epmj1ey0/vi3ubex0seny. Accessed 16 Aug 2016
15. Veiligheidsregio Brabant-Noord. Convenant energiepartijen met Veiligheidsregio Brabant-Noord (2013). https://www.vrbn.nl/. Accessed 16 Aug 2016
16. Lammers, I., Diestelmeier, D.: Experimenting with law and governance for decentralized electricity systems: adjusting regulation to reality? Sustainability 9(2), 212 (2017)
17. Hardin, G.: The tragedy of the commons. Science 162(3859), 1243–1248 (1968)
18. Ostrom, E.: Doing institutional analysis: digging deeper than markets and hierarchies. In: Ménard, C., Shirley, M.M. (eds.) Handbook of New Institutional Economics, pp. 819–848. Springer, Heidelberg (2008)
19. Polski, M.M., Ostrom, E.: An institutional framework for policy analysis and design. In: The Vincent and Elinor Ostrom Workshop in Political Theory and Policy Analysis, (W98–27) (1999)

Invited Papers

Analyzing Cyber Requirements for the Smart Grid Applications

Anurag K. Srivastava[✉]

The School of Electrical Engineering and Computer Science, Washington State University, Pullman, WA 99163, USA
asrivast@eecs.wsu.edu

Abstract. With the development of the smart grid technology, networking technology (NT) plays a significant role in the smart grid. NT enables to realize the smart grid vision mainly focused on (a) wide area monitoring and control for transmission system (b) distribution automation for low voltage distribution system and (c) smart metering for prosumer's participation. Synchrophasor technology enables better situational awareness and decision support and smart meters deployment for end-users constitutes major investment as part of the smart grid development for power distribution system. The two-way communications between 'power utility' and 'smart meters installed near end-user customers' assisted by meter data management systems helps to potentially realize numerous applications for enhanced reliability and efficiency of active distribution system. NT also brings cyber vulnerabilities and it is important to analyze the impact of possible cyber-attacks on the power grid. In this invited talk, networking and data delivery requirements will be discussed for wide area monitoring and smart metering applications as well as a real-time, cyber-physical co-simulation testbed to do cyber-physical analysis.

Keywords: Smart grid · Wide area monitoring and control · Distribution automation · Smart metering · Networking technologies

1 Cyber Requirements for Wide Area Monitoring and Control

The availability of synchronized measurements has made the development of data-driven power system applications possible to enhance the reliability of the power grid [1]. The PMUs provide synchronized time stamped measurements several times a second to enable monitoring of dynamic system response, which was not possible using legacy system, having refresh rate of 4 s [2, 3]. Most of the synchrophasor applications can be classified in several categories following different criteria. Based on the level of adoption by different power system utilities, applications can be classified as (a) existing industry applications and (b) evolving applications. Applications can also be classified based on time criticality, (a) real time online applications and (b) offline applications. Some of the examples of real time applications will be oscillation monitoring, voltage stability monitoring and angle/frequency monitoring, which are already implemented in control centers while examples of offline applications are engineering analysis and includes model validation and post-mortem analysis [2–4]. The data rate and latency

© ICST Institute for Computer Sciences, Social Informatics and Telecommunications Engineering 2017
E.T. Lau et al. (Eds.): SmartGIFT 2017, LNICST 203, pp. 151–154, 2017.
DOI: 10.1007/978-3-319-61813-5_15

required by some applications may be higher than other applications and will require different kind of NT as shown in Table 1.

Table 1. Data and latency requirements for synchrophasors applications

Class	Basic description	Sampling/date rate	Required latency
A	Feedback control	Fast	Fast
B	Open loop control	Medium	Medium
C	Visualization	Medium	Medium
D	Event analysis	Fast	Slow
E	Research/ experimental	N/A	N/A

2 Cyber Requirements for Smart Metering Applications

Cyber requirements for smart meter applications are shown in Table 2.

Table 2. Data and communication requirement for smart meter applications

Application	Quantity	Rate	Data destination	Real time requirements	Criticality	Frequency
Outage detection	High	Few minutes	DMS	Minutes	Low	Frequent
Distribution state estimation	High	Seconds/ minutes	DMS	Second to minutes	Medium to high	Frequent
Billing information	Medium to low	Several days/ month	Billing center/ enterprise	Hours	Very low	Time to time
Voltage control	High to medium	Seconds	Feeder device/ substation/ operating center	Seconds	High	Very frequent
Demand response	High	Seconds	At load/ substation/D MS	Seconds to minutes	High	Frequent
Power quality monitoring	Low to medium	Seconds	Feeder device/ substation/ operating center	Second	Very high	Time to time
Tamper Detection	Medium to low	Days	Billing center	Hours	Very low	Time to time
Load forecasting	Very high	Minutes	Operating center	Hours	Very low	Frequent
Load modeling	High	Minutes	Substation/ operating center	Minutes	Low	Frequent

Requirements are shown in terms of data quantity, rate, data destination, real time requirements, criticality and frequency as shown in Table 2. Applications including outage detection, distribution state estimation, billing information, voltage control, demand response, power quality monitoring, tamper detection, load forecasting, load modeling have been discussed in Table 2. Most of these applications assume tight integration of smart meter data and SCADA data [5]. Communication technologies to meet the requirements include WiFi, Zigbee and several other technologies [6] as highlighted in Table 3.

Table 3. Communication technology for smart meter applications

Comm. Tech.	Application domain	Coverage range	Data rate	Benefits	Limitations
PLC	HAN, NAN, WAN	1–3 km	2–3 Mbps	No extra cabling fee, high security	High noise, low scalability
WiFi	HAN, WAN	100 m, 1 km	Up to 54 Mbps	Free license, mature development	Low security, low scalability
ZigBee	HAN	<50 m	250 kbps	Low cost, easy implementation	Low security, short range, low data rate
Cellular Network (3G, LTE)	HAN, NAN, WAN	1–10 km	Up to 70 Mbps	Mature development, long range	Low security, low costly spectrum fees, low scalability

Acknowledgments. Author would like to thank his colleagues for number of brainstorming sessions related to cyber infrastructure for the smart grid specially Dr. Hauser, Dr. Bakken, Dr. Hahn and Dr. Liu at Washington State University and Prof. Roy at University of Washington.

References

1. Tushar, Banerjee, P., Srivastava, A.K.: Synchrophasor applications for load estimation and stability analysis. In: IET Power and Energy Series, Synchronized Phasor Measurements for Smart Grids (2017)
2. Liu, R., Goodfellow, R., Srivastava, A.K.: A testbed for closed loop cyber-physical-social system simulation and security analysis. In: Cyber-Physical-Social Systems and Constructs in Electric Power Engineering. IET (2016)
3. Liu, R., Vellaithurai, C., Biswas, S., Gamage, T., Srivastava, A.: Analyzing the cyber-physical impact of cyber events on the power grid. IEEE Trans. Smart Grid 6(5), 2444–2453 (2015)
4. Srivastava, A., Morris, T., Ernster, T., Vellaithurai, C., Pan, S., Adhikari, U.: Modeling cyber-physical vulnerability of the smart grid with incomplete information. IEEE Trans. Smart Grid 4(1), 235–244 (2013)

Low-Disruptive and Timely Dynamic Software Updating of Smart Grid Components

Martin Alexander Neumann[✉], Christoph Tobias Bach, Yong Ding,
Till Riedel, and Michael Beigl

Karlsruhe Institute of Technology,
Vincenz-Priessnitz-Str. 1, 76131 Karlsruhe, Germany
{martin.neumann,christoph.bach,
yong.ding,till.riedel,michael.beigl}@kit.edu

Abstract. Components in the power grid require security, high availability and real-time communications for reliable operation. But these components are based on software that contains issues that need to be fixed. Timely installation of software updates allows securing vulnerable software quickly but conventionally disrupts availability and communications. Rolling updates on redundant systems prevent such disruptions but delay update installations as they need to be prepared carefully to update reliably. Dynamic Software Updating shortens the installation duration of updates by implementing them in-memory, allowing timely hot-fixing and installation of new features without service disruption or degradation in soft real-time communications. As the Smart Grid settles on standardization and common technologies for interoperability, the need for timely hot-fixing and updating of software applications and libraries which are in widespread use increases.

In this paper, we discuss requirements of Smart Grid components and their updating opportunities. Afterwards, we present Lusagent, our dynamic updating system for Java 6 to 8 that is based on a novel eager program state transformation approach. We illustrate its programming efforts in a case study on an open-source Java control system framework and on several other server applications. Furthermore, we present performance measurements of dynamically updating these applications. The results demonstrate the potential of our dynamic updating approach in enabling low-disruptive and timely updating of highly available and widespread components at low and only one-time programming efforts.

1 Introduction

The power grid is becoming more connected and intelligent, forming the infrastructure of the Smart Grid. It allows highly frequent measurements at power producers, consumers and in power transmission for real-time monitoring and control. The system can immediately respond to volatile changes in generation and demand, and diagnose faults at high resolution to prevent surges. The goal is to maximize the utilization of the power infrastructure and yet improve

© ICST Institute for Computer Sciences, Social Informatics and Telecommunications Engineering 2017
E.T. Lau et al. (Eds.): SmartGIFT 2017, LNICST 203, pp. 155–171, 2017.
DOI: 10.1007/978-3-319-61813-5_16

its reliability. This requires all grid components to be highly available and inter-connected by real-time communications. Heterogeneous devices, ranging from micro-controllers to cloud servers, and heterogeneous communications, ranging from small-bandwidth unreliable wireless links to high-bandwidth robust cable links are interconnected by standardization and are redundant if applicable.

With the grid becoming more intelligent, the relevance of software in its com-ponents increases. As any other software, the software in the grid infrastructure needs to be updated in the field, either to fix bugs and security features, or to add new features and improve the reliability. These updates must be *low-disruptive* and carefully implemented to not affect the systems' availability and real-time communications. Besides this closed new infrastructure, the grid components are opened up to the Internet forming an open general-purpose platform for services on the Smart Grid. This raises the need to perform updates *timely* to fix bugs and security issues, especially security-critical vulnerabilities.

We discuss Dynamic Software Updating (DSU) as an approach for updating components in the Smart Grid. The goal of DSU is to produce results equivalent to conventional updating but performing updates at runtime in the application's memory to speed up their installation. It uniquely features timely and at the same time low-disruptive updating of highly available applications. Updates can be performed at any time, even at saturated load. System providers and opera-tors are able to immediately push security fixes or new features into the systems without having to wait for low computing load, scheduled maintenance windows or wait for the setup of carefully designed *rolling updates* or *big flips* [2].

Timely updating is vital to open systems and large systems incorporating many components with similar software stacks to make it as a whole practi-cally secure against the exploitation of vulnerabilities. Scheduled maintenance for performing conventional updates (i.e. *fast reboots*) allows straightforward update installation but disrupts the system, which is hardly an option for the components of the Smart Grid. In contrast, big flips or rolling updates allow non-disruptive installation of updates to redundant systems behind load balancers.

But big flips and rolling updates have to be designed carefully to prevent crashing the system during the stretched update period in which old and new program version are running simultaneously—leading to delayed update instal-lations [1]. In addition, with these approaches, the software update must be backwards-compatible to allow both program versions to run concurrently dur-ing the update schedule [2]. DSU provides a simpler update installation proce-dure as it does not require such general backwards-compatibility or comparably complex update scheduling when installing updates to multiple machines.

In the following, we firstly discuss software updating in the Smart Grid and related work about Dynamic Software Updating in Sects. 2 and 3. Afterwards in Sect. 4, we present our DSU system for Java 6 to 8, called Lusagent. Section 5 discusses programming efforts of our approach in a case study on a highly avail-able Java component of an open-source Supervisory Control and Data Acquisi-tion (SCADA) system. Finally in Sect. 6, we evaluate programming efforts for enabling low-disruptive and timely dynamic updates in general, and we assess updating performance on industry-grade Java virtual machines (JVM).

2 Updating Smart Grid Components

Complex SCADA systems for real-time data acquisition, monitoring and control are at the core of Smart Grid infrastructure. As depicted in Fig. 1, nodes at producers, consumers and in the transmission grid connect grid components to each other and to data centers. For example, the nodes implement phasor networks, consisting of PMUs (Phasor Measurement Units) and PDCs (Phasor Data Concentrators) that acquire fine-granular grid state at high frequency. Furthermore, RTUs (Remote Terminal Units) integrate decentralized energy sources into monitoring and control. And, IEDs (Intelligent Electronic Devices) integrate various grid components, such as voltage regulators and circuit breakers. Besides this, the system incorporates highly available generic computing infrastructure, such as databases or message queues and brokers in its nodes and data centers.

Software on these nodes, message queues/brokers, databases and central controllers require updating to fix bugs and to provide new features. Bugs must be fixed quickly to ensure reliability of the grid; security issues need quick care if the components are not entirely sealed in a closed environment; and new features might be interesting to deploy quickly for business or regulatory reasons. Especially, security patches to widespread components, such as cryptographic libraries, are particularly important to deploy quickly, as large parts of a system become vulnerable to the same issue when a vulnerability is disclosed. With the power grid opening up and fostering standardization, the need for timely installation of bug and security patches and other updates increases.

But quick deployment is challenged by high availability requirements, leading to delayed installation and periods of vulnerability. Even if installation is only delayed on a fraction of deployed systems, this may sum up to a large number of vulnerable systems. For example, in case of the heartbleed bug, a duration of 2 weeks has been estimated for its fix to reach 50% of the vulnerable web servers in the public IPv4 space which amounted to 5% of all IPv4 web servers [5].

Updating software on Smart Grid components may either induce downtime at non-redundantly designed systems or maybe enabled hot by rolling updates or application-specific solutions. Rolling updates build on the idea of reliable computing of switching to a hot standby at runtime: such updates low-disruptively switch to a separate instance of the new program version whose state has already been warmed-up. But in contrast to DSU, real-time communications may be challenged by re-establishing (or re-routing) connections to the warmed-up instance. Furthermore, rolling updates require backwards-compatibility of any updates to the application and careful distributed update scheduling. This is also the reason why this scheme is generally found complex to get right [4].

Alternatively, application-specific approaches to live update the parts of an application that make a conventional update take time could be adapted to speed up updating. For example, Facebook's version of memcached is a prominent

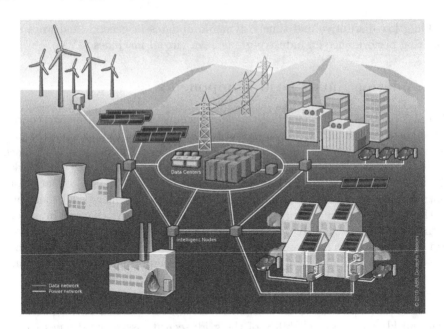

Fig. 1. Power and Computing Components in the Smart Grid (http://www.abb.com/cawp/seitp202/77a7e74be1ea8904c12577050030ab14.aspx)

example that migrates the cache content hot between program versions, effectively hot-swapping the program around cache [12]. Such schemes head towards generic DSU systems by using dynamic updating techniques to perform time-intensive parts of vanilla updates in-memory.

3   Dynamic Software Updating

Systems for Dynamic Software Updates (DSU) may be used by developers when designing new software or to retrofit off-the-shelf applications. They go a step further than application-specific updating approaches by providing generic updating services to an application to update parts of it in-memory [10]. Such DSU systems usually stop the control-flow in program parts affected by an update, transform control-flow and state to the new version and afterwards release the control-flow in the new version. Systems try to provide safety properties such that performed transformations at the point where the control-flow has been stopped—forms of type safety such that no transformations or new program code is able to interact with any unknown/old data structures are usual [16].

DSU systems should require minimal to no programmer intervention to reduce the cost for replacing conventional updates by dynamic ones. For example, no intervention is demonstrated by the DCE VM [18] that aids in Java debugging by applying small changes dynamically. Beyond that, release-level DSU offers tested and efficient generic updating features that aim for high update flexibility in allowing performing any update to any part of a running program. For example, as implemented by JVolve [17], Javelus [8] or Rubah [13] for Java. DSU may complement application-specific updating approaches or be used as a standalone feature for new applications or be retrofitted into off-the-shelf applications. The high flexibility aimed for in the provided generic DSU mechanisms may be less efficient than tuned application-specific solutions (e.g. Facebook's version of memcached), but DSU mechanisms complement such solutions by offering to update even those parts the application-specific ones cannot update.

Besides such flexibility, DSU systems try to be timely in performing updates right away when updates are released. But entire-program DSU systems offering such flexible and timely updates usually require programming: timely updating requires an application to be instrumented to reach a safe point for updating quickly when an update is available [9], and flexible updating requires update code that implements the necessary transformations in-memory. But when considering that such instrumentations and update codes have to be developed for widespread components, as in the context of the Smart Grid, we think, that the benefits outweigh the necessary efforts: all installations could update immediately without additional preparation efforts of the individual installations.

4   Lusagent System

DSU systems perform an atomic swap of an old into a new program in a stop-the-world pause. The transformation of program state is either implemented and finalized *eagerly* (during the stop) or *lazily* (after the stop—while the new program is already running, but before the program is accessing the state).

We present an efficient eager dynamic updating approach for Java. It is based on a novel parallel linear scan of the JVM heap. As previous eager approaches presented in [13,14,17,18], the entire program state is updated in a stop-the-world pause such that no transformation work is left after update which may affect the application performance. In contrast to previous approaches, the heap is sequentially iterated in-between Garbage Collections (GC) instead of traversing its object graph in GC-style. The approach is implemented in our DSU system Lusagent[1]. It is a native plugin to stock Oracle and OpenJDK JVMs for Java 6 to 8 that causes no steady-state overhead by design.

Vanilla applications need an explicit programmer-provided instrumentation with update points [11,13] for enabling dynamic updates but are not modified any further. Update code to transform programs during DSUs can be programmed in our Domain-Specific Language (DSL) for Object Transformers (OT).

---

[1] Code of Lusagent and evaluated applications: https://github.com/lusagent

4.1 Parts of Lusagent

- *Static analyses of old and new program*
    (1) determine mappings and categorizations for classes and fields (Sects. 4.2)
    (2) determine efficient auto-transformations (Sects. 4.3 and 4.5)
    (3) build type universe for type-safe OT programming/execution (Sect. 4.4)
- *Programming environment for object transformers* (Sects. 4.6 and 4.7)
- *Updating runtime* (Sect. 4.8).

4.2 Class Mapping

Classes in the new program, i.e. in namespace $V_1 = \{t_1^1 \dots t_m^1\}$, are firstly mapped
to classes in the old program, i.e. in namespace $V_0 = \{t_1^0 \dots t_n^0\}$. Lusagent by
default does so by their name: equally-named classes are mapped. The programmer may add custom mappings to change the defaults or add renamed classes.
Let these **mapped classes** be defined by a relation $\mathbf{M_t} := (V_0 \times V_1) \cup (V_1 \times V_0)$.
Furthermore, classes in external and standard libraries form namespace C_F
(called foreign classes). Let our type universe be closed and consist of V_0, V_1
and C_F, such that $T = V_0 \cup V_1 \cup C_F$ holds. M_t is not allowed to define mappings
on C_F.

Fields in old classes are mapped to fields in new classes. Lusagent by default
does so by their name and type: equally-named fields are mapped if their types
are mapped by M_t. The programmer may add custom mappings to change the
defaults or add renamed fields to a class mapping. Definition of **mapped fields**
($\mathbf{M_f}$): let F be the set of all fields; let $\pi(f)$ be the name of field f; let $\tau(f)$ be the
type of field f; let $\tau_{def}(f)$ be the defining type of field f; let $\epsilon : T \to F^P$ $\epsilon(t) :=$
$\{f \in F | \tau_{def}(f) = t\}$; let $x \preceq y :\Leftrightarrow x$ instanceof y; let $\xi : T \to F^P$ $\xi(t) :=$
$\bigcup_{s \in T, t \preceq s} \epsilon(s)$; let $x, y \in F$; $(x, y) \in \mathbf{M_f} :\Leftrightarrow \pi(x) = \pi(y) \wedge (\tau(x), \tau(y)) \in M_t \wedge$
$(\tau_{\mathrm{def}}(x), \tau_{\mathrm{def}}(y)) \in M_t$. A mapping between two classes is defined as successful if
all fields are mapped between them. Definition of **successful type mappings**
($\mathbf{M_{st}} \subset M_t$): let $(s, t) \in M_t$; $(s, t) \in \mathbf{M_{st}} :\Leftrightarrow \forall x \in \xi(s) \exists y \in \xi(t) : (x, y) \in M_f$.

4.3 Class Categorization and Auto-transformation

Afterwards, any classes loaded into the JVM, i.e. in our type universe T, are
categorized as follows. Definition of **foreign types** ($\mathbf{C_F} \subset T$): $\mathbf{C_F} := T \backslash (V_0 \cup V_1)$. Definition of **deleted types** ($\mathbf{C_D} \subset V_0$): let $x \in V_0$; $x \in \mathbf{C_D} :\Leftrightarrow \forall y \in T : (x, y) \notin M_t$. Definition of **unmodified types** ($\mathbf{C_U} \subset V_0$): let $x \in V_0$;
$x \in \mathbf{C_U} :\Leftrightarrow \exists y \in T : (x, y) \in M_{st} \wedge (y, x) \in M_{st}$. Definition of **modified types**
($\mathbf{C_M}$): $C_M := V_0 \backslash (C_U \cup C_D)$. Classes in C_F and C_D and their objects are not
transformed as they are not part of the old program or will not be part of the
new program. Classes in C_U and C_M and their objects will be transformed.

Objects of classes in C_U can be directly used in the new program as their
memory layout does not change. Lusagent copies classes in C_U into the new
namespace, but their objects are transformed *in-place* by *patching* their *class-
pointers*. Classes in C_M have changed memory layouts which requires to copy
their field values. Lusagent copies classes in C_M and their objects *out-of-place*.

The layout of objects may be directly or indirectly affected by modified object fields: the modification of object fields is inherited in stock JVMs as the memory layout of an object contains all values of its own fields but also of all object fields of its superclasses. Figure 2 shows an example type hierarchy. It contains the generic superclass `java.lang.Object`, the subclasses `A` (abstract), `C1`, `C2` and `C3`, and the interfaces `I1`, `I2` and `I3`. Given modified class fields of `A`: this affects `A` only, no other classes would be affected. Given modified object fields of `A`, the objects of `C1`, `C2` and `C3` would all be affected by this modification too.

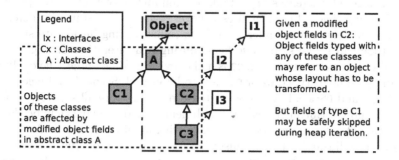

Fig. 2. Example on classes with modified object fields

4.4 Type Universe for Object Transformers

We use a type universe such that programmers can safely (1) access deleted fields in old objects, (2) access old objects of deleted classes, and (3) access new objects which are incompatible to the new fields they are stored in. We leave V_1 as is such that the programmer can safely interact with the new program but we modify V_0 as follows to provide type-safe access in any cases of (1), (2) and (3).

Definition of **foreign-typed fields** ($\mathbf{F_f} \subset F$): let $\tau(f)$ be the type of field f; let $\epsilon : T \to F^P$ $\epsilon(t) := \{f \in F | \tau_{def}(f) = t\}$; let $x \preceq y :\Leftrightarrow x$ `instanceof` y; $\mathbf{F_f} := \{f \in \bigcup_{x \in V_0} \epsilon(x) | \tau(f) \in C_F\}$. Foreign-typed fields in V_0 are not rewritten and always provide type-safe access to old and new objects (assumes that types of new objects are never narrowed by a foreign type which is currently a limitation of our system). Definition of V_0-**typed fields** ($\mathbf{F_0} \subset F$): let $st(t)$ be the set of all subtypes of type t including t; $\mathbf{F_0} := \{f \in \bigcup_{x \in V_0} \epsilon(x) | \tau(f) \in V_0 \land \forall t \in sty(\tau(f)) : t \in C_D\}$. Fields in V_0 are V_0-typed fields and therefore not rewritten if the field can only refer to old objects. Definition of V_1-**typed fields** ($\mathbf{F_1} \subset F$): $\mathbf{F_1} := \{f \in \bigcup_{x \in V_0} \epsilon(x) | \tau(f) \in V_0 \land \forall t \in M_t(\tau(f)) : t \in sty(\tau(M_f(f)))\}$. Field f in V_0 is V_1-typed and therefore rewritten to its mapped new type $\tau(M_f(f))$ if f can only refer to new objects that are compatible to the new type of the field. Definition of **unknown-typed fields** ($\mathbf{F_U} \subset F$) $\mathbf{F_U} := \{f \in \bigcup_{x \in V_0} \epsilon(x) | \tau(f) \in V_0 \land ((\exists t \in M_t(sty(\tau(f))) : t \notin sty(\tau(M_f(f)))) \lor ((\exists t \in sty(\tau(f)) : t \in C_D) \land (\exists t \in M_c(sty(\tau(f))) : t \in sty(\tau(M_f(f))))))\}$. Field f in V_0 is unknown-typed and therefore rewritten to `java.lang.Object` if f can refer to old and new objects, or if f can refer to new objects that are incompatible to its mapped new type $\tau(M_f(f))$. These rewrites allow programmers to access all objects which are incompatible to the typing of the new program safely via fields of old objects.

4.5   Skippable Fields During Heap Iteration

Our heap iteration copies changed objects out-of-place and fixes up any references to these objects. This requires to iterate all fields in all objects and patch values if affected references are found. To minimize costly memory operations when iterating fields, Lusagent uses a novel technique to statically determine which object fields cannot refer to objects copied during an update such that the runtime can safely skip these fields during heap iteration. In Fig. 2, given modified object fields of C2, also C3 is a class with modified object fields. In this case, firstly all fields typed C2 or C3 have to be visited. Secondly, all fields typed I1, I2, I3, A and Object have to be visited too as these are all supertypes of the classes C2 and C3. But in this situation all fields typed C1 may safely be skipped as they cannot refer to an object of a class with modified object fields.

Lusagent's linear heap scan ensures that all objects on the heap are still reached. In contrast, when performing a heap traversal (from the heap roots), no object fields could be skipped, as parts of the heap would become unreachable.

4.6   Programming Model

The programmer can implement OTs, i.e. Java-like code snippets registered on classes in V_1. The OT is called once per object of that class: it provides local variables o0 and o1 to access transformed old and new objects. The OT programmer in general interacts with the new program version only and reads fields of the old version to rescue values. The type universe T is defined as outlined in Sect. 4.4, i.e. types in V_1 are unmodified and types in V_0 have been rewritten for type-safe access. To integrate the classes in V_0 and V_1 into one Java namespace, their names are prefixed by pseudo packages v0 and v1. New fields contain the value that has been transformed into it, except they contain the value `null` if they refer to old or incompatible new objects after transformation. Old fields contain old values if they are still V_0-typed and they contain new values if they are V_1-typed. They can contain old or new values if they are foreign- or unknown-typed (`java.lang.Object`). To prevent additional side-effects between the old and new program, fields of old classes/objects are read-only and old methods are erased.

4.7   Programming Framework

The programmer has to take care of two tasks using the Lusagent IDE as depicted in Fig. 3: firstly, instrument a vanilla application with control-flow transformation code, and secondly, implement OTs on every update to the application.

Control-Flow Instrumentation. The control-flow API has been adopted from Rubah [13]: by replacing the application threads by specific Lusagent threads

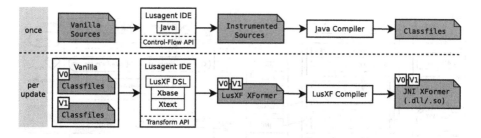

Fig. 3. Lusagent DSU development workflow

and instrumenting the application with *update points* that unwind the stack before update and rebuild it after update, this approach offers to update any code of an application, especially long-running methods. Furthermore, it can be used by the programmer to ensure timely initiation of an update: update points have to be inserted such that all threads visit any of them frequently. Our API can be used to make sleeps, networking and file I/O interruptable by an update.

Object Transformers. To apply a conventional update dynamically, the programmer uses Lusagent's IDE to specify OTs for it in *LusXF*. LusXF is a Java-like language featuring static type-inference and type-checking based on the Xbase [6] language and the Xtext infrastructure. LusXF provides class and object transformations as first-class citizens, allows to specify their execution sequence and implements our programming model. Its implementation covers an Eclipse-based IDE and a standalone compiler which also features validation of OT-specific semantics. Mappings and auto-transformations can be inspected and stubs for OTs of modified and new classes can be generated by Lusagent.

4.8   Updating Runtime

Updating with Lusagent works as follows. The DSU-instrumented application is launched on the JVM using the Lusagent runtime. The runtime replaces the JVM's default classloader by a Lusagent one that manages all *updatable classes*. When an update is performed, a new program version is loaded using a new Lusagent classloader and afterwards control-flow and state is transformed.

As depicted in Fig. 4a, the transformation consists of analysis components to prepare the heap iteration, the heap iteration with automated transformations itself (phase #1), and the subsequent execution of OTs (phase #2). The analyses are independent of platform specifics (neither JVM nor operating system). While phase #2 depends on JNI only, phase #1 operates directly on the internal JVM data-structures (i.e. class, object and heap layouts) to iterate the entire heap efficiently. This part is kept portable using Oracle's Serviceability Agent (SA) interface [15] which holds symbol locations and definitions of data structures in the JVM itself which is usually used by debugging and profiling tools.

The workflow of these components is depicted in Fig. 4b. Given the class-files of V_0 and V_1, the static analyses are performed while V_0 is still running.

(a)   (b)

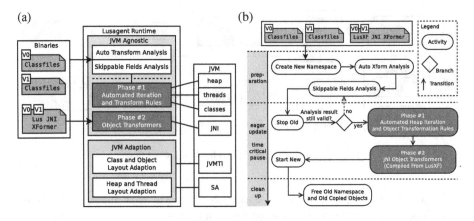

Fig. 4. (a) Lusagent runtime architecture Lusagent eager DSU procedure (b) Lusagent eager DSU procedure

Afterwards, the JVM is stopped, it is validated that no new classes have been loaded since the static analyses have been finished (which would invalidate the analysis results) and the heap iteration is initiated. The heap is partitioned into n equally-sized chunks, each chunk being iterated by an individual thread. Finally, in phase #2, all OTs for the update are executed: to enable this, Lusagent collects all objects OTs have been registered for during phase #1.

5   Case Study: Dynamically Updating Tango Controls

Among other frameworks, Eclipse NeoSCADA and Tango Controls [7] are two actively maintained open-source SCADA frameworks that are at least partially implemented in Java. Eclipse NeoSCADA is based on isolated Java modules using dedicated classloaders which is currently not supported by Lusagent. Instead, we have used Lusagent to add dynamic updating to the JTango[2] library of Tango Controls. Tango Controls' basic architecture consists of sensors and actuators being connected to a central monitoring and control server. Sensors and actuators are entirely proxied by *device servers*. While the central server is exclusively implemented in C++, device servers can either be implemented in C++, Python or Java. JTango is used to implement device servers in Java.

We illustrate the programming efforts necessary to enable dynamic updating of the JTango library in device servers. So far, device servers had to be restarted to update them. As device servers usually do not keep large data structures in main memory, restarts are be possible within a few seconds. They are not instant though, as the Java runtime environment and the JTango boot-up takes several seconds which we have measured on commodity desktop hardware. This procedure is speed up by Lusagent resulting in considerably less disruption: we

---

[2] https://github.com/tango-controls/JTango

have measured only few milliseconds to update device servers which have been continuously reporting sensor values at about 20 Hz to a central server.

5.1   Control-Flow Instrumentation

JTango does not use any own application threads but is exclusively driven by events from the JacORB CORBA [3] library that interconnects it to the Tango Controls server. We have instrumented the request processing threads in recent JacORB releases with Lusagent: v3.6, v3.7 (both released in 2015) and v3.8 (released in 2016). These releases are also used by recent JTango releases.

```
1 public class RequestProcessor extends LusThread /* before: Thread */
2             implements InvocationContext, Configurable {
3     /* ... */
4     public void run() {
5         while (true) {
6             Updater.updatePoint("request-processor"); /* added line */
7             /* ... */ wait(); /* ... */ process(); /* ... */
8         } } }
```

Listing 1: Lusagent Instrumentation in **org**.jacorb.poa.RequestProcessor

We have a single patch for the three JacORB releases. It is depicted in simplified form in Listing 1: to allow each request processor to reach an update point, its standard Java thread has been replaced by a Lusagent thread and an update point has been added into the thread's event-loop. Now, JTango can be updated in-between processing of any two JacORB events. As JTango is not performing long-running operations when processing JacORB events, no code has been added into JTango to interrupt operations and reach update points. JTango itself has not been instrumented: its vanilla releases can be used directly.

5.2   Object Transformers

We have looked at the update code necessary to update 5 subsequent recent minor releases of JTango dynamically: from v9.0.8 to v9.0.11 and v9.1.0 (all released in 2016). Table 1 lists the Lines of Code (LoC) changed between subsequent vanilla releases and lists the LoC of Lusagent OTs we programmed to implement the subsequent releases as dynamic updates. The updates v9.0.9 $\rightarrow$ v9.0.10 and v9.0.10 $\rightarrow$ v9.0.11 are fully covered by Lusagent's automatic transformations. The update v9.0.8 $\rightarrow$ v9.0.9 requires an OT for objects of 2 classes in which a renamed object field and a class field that has become and object field are initialized by copying over the values of their old counterparts. The update v9.0.11 $\rightarrow$ v9.1.0 requires an OT for objects of 3 classes in which newly added object fields are initialized analogously to the new object constructors.

Table 1. Programming efforts with Lusagent for updating JTango

Release		Instrumentation	Vanilla update	OTs
Version	LoC	+/− LoC	+/− LoC	LoC
JTango				
9.0.8	16514	0, 0	10681	12
9.0.9	16532	Same	12899	0
9.0.10	16558	Same	2926	0
9.0.11	16563	Same	166102	18
9.1.0	16628	Same		

6   Evaluation

Besides the previous case study, we have evaluated the *programming efforts* with Lusagent and its *updating performance* on 7 Java server applications: 2 SQL databases (H2 and HSQLDB), the Voldemort key-value-store, CrossFTP, the Moquette MQTT broker, JavaEmailServer and the Glowstone game-server. We measure pauses for updating instances of H2, HSQLDB and Voldemort with in-memory data-stores which have been warmed-up to at least 4 GiB and while benchmarks on them are executed. The pauses of Lusagent consist of synchronizing all control-flows in the DSU runtime and the subsequent heap iteration. For baselining our performance studies, we measure durations of updates with the Rubah [13] DSU system on H2 and Voldemort using equivalent control-flow instrumentations. Furthermore, we measure durations of Garbage Collections (parallel full GC in standard configuration). To illustrate control-flow migration performance with many threads, CrossFTP is stressed by many clients.

6.1   Programming Efforts

Table 2 shows the Lines of Code (LoC) to instrument the applications with Lusagent, the LoC affected by the vanilla updates and the LoC required to implement these vanilla updates by OTs in LusXF. Our experiences confirm that the control-flow instrumentation proposed by Rubah is manageable and a one-time effort. We have extended the instrumentation API by a programming pattern we call *update barriers*: dynamically generated proxies to synchronize external threads with the DSU that cannot be replaced by our LusThreads. This resulted in concise instrumentation solutions for Moquette and HSQLDB.

The first update to Moquette and the last update to HSQLDB are quite complex: the OTs contain many `instanceof` tests to determine the situation in the program state at time-of-update and follow various old fields to access proper values for transformation. Our type-checked language demonstrates its feasibility particularly on these updates as the code is concise and its typing apparent.

Table 2. Programming efforts with Lusagent

Release		Instr.	Van. update	OTs	Release		Instr.	V. update	OTs
Version	LoC	+/– LoC	+/– LoC	LoC	Ver	LoC	+/– LoC	+/– LoC	LoC
H2					*Moquette*				
1.2.121	78738	331, 38			0.7	8468	19, 3		
1.2.122	79185	Same	1184, 610	21	0.8	9691	102, 8	3109, 2629	267
1.2.123	79274	333, 34	2188, 1911	12	0.8.1	9670	11, 1	170, 307	33
HSQLDB					*CrossFTP*				
2.3.0	168130	196, 147			1.07	18082	408, 247		
2.3.1	168212	196, 139	285, 195	4	1.08	18109	Same	97, 46	0
2.3.2	168563	Same	2666, 1871	34	1.09	18174	420, 233	718, 702	33
2.3.3	167638	Same	10526, 11970	201	1.11	18468	Same	615, 189	28
Voldemort					*JavaEmailServer*				
1.5.3	58474	69, 13			1.3.3	2429	262, 85		
1.5.4	58497	Same	82, 24	6	1.3.4	2508	Same	137, 17	0
Glowstone					1.4	2590	Same	134, 7	11
1.8.4	45781	41, 10							

6.2   Pauses for Updating

We have measured the pauses for updating with Rubah and Lusagent on H2, HSQLDB, Voldemort and CrossFTP. The results are listed in Table 3. Both, Lusagent with and without its field skipping technique, outperform parallel full Garbage Collection (GC). On average, the skipping technique improves

Table 3. Pauses (in secs) for updating large memory applications with Rubah and Lusagent. (avg. & std. dev. from 15 samples.)

Update	Mem scale	Lusagent no skip	Lusagent with skip	GC	Eager Rubah	Lazy Rubah
		$\mu \pm \sigma$	$\mu \pm \sigma$	$\mu \pm \sigma$	$\mu \pm \sigma$	$\mu \pm \sigma$
H2						
121 → 122	**64**[a]	3.6 ± 0.04	3.6 ± 0.21	4.6 ± 0.05	21.9 ± 3.89	0.6 ± 0.09
122 → 123	**64**	3.7 ± 0.06	3.6 ± 0.05	4.6 ± 0.04	25.0 ± 0.50	0.7 ± 0.15
HSQLDB						
2.3.0 → 1	**200**[a]	1.5 ± 0.01	1.3 ± 0.01	5.0 ± 0.16	–[b]	–[b]
2.3.1 → 2	**200**	1.5 ± 0.01	1.3 ± 0.01	5.0 ± 0.23	–	–
2.3.2 → 3	**200**	1.8 ± 0.02	1.7 ± 0.02	5.2 ± 0.18	–	–
Voldemort						
v1.5.3 → 4	**M5**[a]	1.0 ± 0.03	0.9 ± 0.02	4.1 ± 0.03	24.6 ± 1.47	0.3 ± 0.03
	M10	1.9 ± 0.02	1.7 ± 0.02	7.9 ± 0.08	80.6 ± 5.52	0.4 ± 0.04
	M15	2.8 ± 0.04	2.5 ± 0.03	14.4 ± 0.48	204.4 ± 12.08	0.4 ± 0.06

[a] *64* is a scale factor for the Dacapo TPC-C benchmark; *200* is a scale factor for the HSQLDB TPC-B benchmark; *M5* is a scale factor for the Voldemort benchmark. All three factors result in processes of >4 GiB unshared memory given by Unique Set Size (USS) on Linux for x64.
[b] We have not yet ported our Object Transformers for HSQLDB to Rubah.

performance by 9.2%. The performance improvements differ significantly between the databases: 1.4% for H2, 11.4% for Voldemort, 15.4% for HSQLDB.

We expect the type hierarchy in the software to be a relevant factor for the performance differences. But as the update pause is dominated by the copying overhead for out-of-place object transformations after heap iteration, this performance improvement during heap iteration becomes less evident with larger updates. We preliminary conclude that our field skipping improves linear heap scanning performance significantly (depending on the type hierarchy) and improves updates significantly that affect only a moderate fraction of heap objects (Fig. 5).

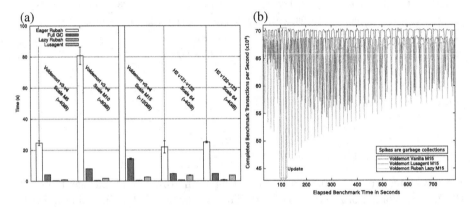

Fig. 5. (a) Update pauses compared to GC. (avg. & std. dev. from 15 samples) (b) Benchmark performance on update. Vanilla application is baseline.

Table 4. Pauses (in secs) for updating many threads with Rubah and Lusagent. (avg. & std. dev. from 30 samples)

Update	Threads	Eager Rubah	Lusagent
	#	$\mu \pm \sigma$	$\mu \pm \sigma$
CrossFTP			
v1.07 → v1.08	64	0.27 ± 0.03	0.18 ± 0.00
	128	0.32 ± 0.05	0.30 ± 0.00
	192	0.38 ± 0.06	0.35 ± 0.00
	256	0.45 ± 0.04	0.43 ± 0.01
v1.08 → v1.09	128	0.27 ± 0.05	0.30 ± 0.00
	256	0.45 ± 0.04	0.43 ± 0.01
v1.09 → v1.11	128	0.27 ± 0.04	0.28 ± 0.00
	256	0.46 ± 0.08	0.42 ± 0.01

Figure 4a also displays the pause durations of the DSUs on H2 and Voldemort for Lusagent and Rubah (parallel eager and lazy). The three Voldemort benchmarks demonstrate that pause times of GC, Lusagent and eager Rubah scale proportionally to memory size. In contrast, lazy Rubah causes a constant pause. Pauses induced by lazy Rubah and Lusagent both outperform full GC.

Table 4 depicts the pauses induced by Rubah and Lusagent on CrossFTP. In this benchmark, memory of the application is only in the range of a several MiB but the DSU instrumentation has to wait for one thread per connected ftp client before updating. Both systems cause similar pauses of <1s which scale by the number of threads. Lusagent exposes a significantly lower variance.

Finally, except for the warmup of the JVM's Just-In-Time Compiler (JIT), Lusagent does not induce short-term overhead after updating, as exemplary depicted in Fig. 4b for the Voldemort benchmark at scale M15.

7   Conclusion

In this work, we have discussed the need for low-disruptive and timely hot-fixing and updating of software components in the Smart Grid infrastructure which is becoming an open system and will be largely standardized for interoperability. Dynamic Software Updating is an approach that tries to enable such updates for highly available software in general. As Smart Grid components are primarily based on software, DSU allows to immediately update them whenever security issues are disclosed that would otherwise put all installations in the system at risk. This particularly becomes an issue if many openly accessible components share the same implementations, e.g. a secure communications library in a distributed system such as the Advanced Metering Infrastructure.

We have presented Lusagent: a system for eager dynamic software updating of Java applications on release-level which has been implemented as a native plugin to industry-grade JVMs. It uses a novel heap iteration algorithm to efficiently update an entire Java application in-memory. It allows to perform hot-fixes, requiring almost no additional programming effort, and it features release-level updates, which can be flexibly programmed using object transformation code.

We have illustrated our updating approach in the context of the Smart Grid in a case study performing 5 subsequent release-level updates on JTango device servers in the Tango Controls SCADA framework. The programming efforts were considerably low: only an event-driven communications library of JTango had to be instrumented to enable dynamic updating of JTango and its device servers.

We have furthermore demonstrated the feasibility of our updating approach by performing 13 release-level DSUs, ranging from small to quite large ones, on 7 server applications. Furthermore, we studied its efficiency in updating 3 database servers with large transient memory and 1 highly multi-threaded file server, showing that update pauses are significantly shorter than the parallel full garbage collections which usually are part of the normal application runtime.

References

1. Ajmani, S., Liskov, B., Shrira, L.: Modular software upgrades for distributed systems. In: Thomas, D. (ed.) ECOOP 2006. LNCS, vol. 4067, pp. 452–476. Springer, Heidelberg (2006). doi:10.1007/11785477_26
2. Brewer, E.A.: Lessons from giant-scale services. IEEE Internet Comput. 5(4), 46–55 (2001)
3. Brose, G.: JacORB: Implementation and Design of a Java ORB, pp. 143–154. Chapman & Hall, Cottbus (1997)
4. Dumitraş, T., Narasimhan, P.: Why do upgrades fail and what can we do about it? In: Bacon, J.M., Cooper, B.F. (eds.) Middleware 2009. LNCS, vol. 5896, pp. 349–372. Springer, Heidelberg (2009). doi:10.1007/978-3-642-10445-9_18
5. Durumeric, Z., Kasten, J., Adrian, D., Halderman, J.A., Bailey, M., Li, F., Weaver, N., Amann, J., Beekman, J., Payer, M., Paxson, V.: The matter of heartbleed. In: Proceedings of the 2014 Conference on Internet Measurement Conference (IMC 2014), pp. 475–488. ACM, New York (2014)
6. Efftinge, S., Eysholdt, M., Köhnlein, J., Zarnekow, S., von Massow, R., Hasselbring, W., Hanus, M.: Xbase: implementing domain-specific languages for Java. In: Proceedings of the 11th International Conference on Generative Programming and Component Engineering (GPCE 2012). ACM, New York (2012)
7. Götz, A., Taurel, E., et al.: TANGO V8-Another turbo charged major release. In: Proceedings of ICALEPCS, San Francisco (2013)
8. Gu, T., Cao, C., Xu, C., Ma, X., Zhang, L., Lu, J.: Javelus: a low disruptive approach to dynamic software updates. In: Proceedings of the 2012 19th Asia-Pacific Software Engineering Conference (APSEC 2012), vol. 01, pp. 527–536. IEEE Computer Society, Washington, DC (2012)
9. Hayden, C.M., Smith, E.K., Hardisty, E.A., Hicks, M., Foster, J.S.: Evaluating dynamic software update safety using systematic testing. IEEE Trans. Softw. Eng. 38(6), 1340–1354 (2012)
10. Hicks, M., Nettles, S.: Dynamic software updating. ACM Trans. Program. Lang. Syst. 27(6), 1049–1096 (2005)
11. Neamtiu, I., Hicks, M., Stoyle, G., Oriol, M.: Practical dynamic software updating for C. In: Proceedings of the 27th ACM SIGPLAN Conference on Programming Language Design and Implementation (PLDI 2006), pp. 72–83. ACM, New York (2006)
12. Nishtala, R., Fugal, H., Grimm, S., Kwiatkowski, M., Lee, H., Li, H.C., McElroy, R., Paleczny, M., Peek, D., Saab, P., Stafford, D., Tung, T., Venkataramani, V.: Scaling memcache at Facebook. In: Proceedings of the 10th USENIX Conference on Networked Systems Design and Implementation (NSDI 2013), pp. 385–398. USENIX Association, Berkeley (2013)
13. Pina, L., Veiga, L., Hicks, M.: Rubah: DSU for Java on a stock JVM. In: Proceedings of the 2014 ACM Conference on Object Oriented Programming Systems Languages & Applications (OOPSLA 2014). ACM, New York (2014)
14. Pukall, M., Kästner, C., Cazzola, W., Götz, S., Grebhahn, A., Schröter, R., Saake, G.: JavAdaptor-flexible runtime updates of Java applications. Softw. Pract. Exp. 43(2), 153–185 (2013)
15. Russell, K., Bak, L.: The hotspotTM serviceability agent: an out-of-process high level debugger for a JavaTM virtual machine. In: Proceedings of the 2001 Symposium on JavaTM Virtual Machine Research and Technology Symposium (JVM 2001), vol. 1, p. 16. USENIX Association, Berkeley (2001)

16. Stoyle, G., Hicks, M., Bierman, G., Sewell, P., Neamtiu, I.: Mutatis mutandis: safe and predictable dynamic software updating. ACM Trans. Program. Lang. Syst. **29**(4), 22 (2007)
17. Subramanian, S., Hicks, M., McKinley, K.S.: Dynamic software updates: a VM-centric approach. In: Proceedings of the 30th ACM SIGPLAN Conference on Programming Language Design and Implementation (PLDI 2009), pp. 1–12. ACM, New York (2009)
18. Würthinger, T., Wimmer, C., Stadler, L.: Unrestricted and safe dynamic code evolution for Java. Sci. Comput. Program. **78**(5), 481–498 (2013)

Performance Evaluation of the Contention-Based Random Access of LTE Under Smart Grid Traffic

Charalampos Kalalas[✉], Francisco Vazquez-Gallego, and Jesus Alonso-Zarate

Centre Tecnològic de Telecomunicacions de Catalunya (CTTC/CERCA),
Av. Carl Friedrich Gauss 7, 08860 Castelldefels, Spain
{ckalalas,francisco.vazquez,jesus.alonso}@cttc.es

Abstract. Power distribution networks are often widely distributed to accommodate electrical power feeds to dense cities while monitoring and control systems typically require extensive information exchange among numerous intelligent electronic devices. Using the existing network infrastructure, cellular technology appears as a key enabler for the support of large-scale metering deployments and wide-area monitoring systems. In this paper, we evaluate the performance of the contention-based random-access mechanism of LTE networks for real-time monitoring and metering applications. In particular, the impact of smart grid traffic is investigated in terms of access delay and outage probability under different network configurations and traffic characteristics. Simulations of realistic network-overload scenarios demonstrate that the random-access channel of LTE/LTE-A is prone to congestion when a high number of smart grid devices attempt for network access, while the bursty nature of monitoring traffic results in even higher performance degradation.

Keywords: LTE · Random-Access Channel · Smart-grid traffic · Metering · Monitoring · Markov-Modulated Poisson Process

1 Introduction

The ongoing modernization of the electrical grid mainly relies on the evolution of the distribution grid into a fully automated and interconnected network. A wide variety of communication technologies and network protocols have been proposed to support advanced distribution-grid operations. Among various communication alternatives, cellular networks based on 3GPP Standards, emerge as a promising solution to enhance the observability and controllability of the distribution network [1]. However, cellular technology was not initially intended for distribution-grid applications and smart grid traffic characteristics are fundamentally different from regular human-type communication. Thus, significant challenges arise for the current structure of cellular networks.

In LTE/LTE-A, the devices use a random-access procedure to request a dedicated communication channel in several cases, e.g., initial network association,

© ICST Institute for Computer Sciences, Social Informatics and Telecommunications Engineering 2017
E.T. Lau et al. (Eds.): SmartGIFT 2017, LNICST 203, pp. 172–181, 2017.
DOI: 10.1007/978-3-319-61813-5_17

transition from idle to connected state, radio-link failure, handover, and uplink synchronization. Cellular networks were designed to support a moderate number of users per base station; thus, the simultaneous channel access attempts of numerous distribution-grid devices render the standard random-access mechanism highly susceptible to congestion, due to the scarce random-access resources compared to the increased demand [2]. Besides the high density of devices requesting channel access, the messages exchanged in monitoring applications are generally event-driven and involve sporadic and time-critical data delivery.

Several methods have been proposed during the recent years to improve the random-access procedure of LTE networks [3–5]. Most of the available solutions are based on initial proposals compiled by the 3GPP, including separation of random-access resources, access class barring (ACB) schemes, and parameter optimization in the medium access control layer [6]. A reliability analysis for smart grid monitoring traffic is performed in [7] based on a developed analytical framework for the ACB scheme. The authors in [8] propose an enhancement of the standard access mechanism by proactively estimating the anticipated network load (alarm reports, periodic measurements) to determine the required random-access opportunities. An adaptive random-access mechanism is introduced in [9] to enable the integration of IEC-61850 communication services in public LTE networks, based on a continuous monitoring of the network loading state by the eNodeB.

Unlike the majority of existing literature where delta traffic or simple Poisson models are used to represent the aggregate smart grid traffic, in this work we leverage the Markov-Modulated Poisson Process (MMPP) framework [10] to capture the bursty behavior of monitoring traffic in event-driven distribution-grid operations. Focusing on two representative scenarios of distribution-grid services, i.e., wide-area monitoring and large-scale metering, we assess the performance of the standard random-access mechanism of LTE for different network configurations and traffic characteristics. We further investigate the impact of the random-access parameters and traffic-load conditions on the access delay and outage probability and several insights can be drawn for the feasibility of the standard random-access procedure when handling massive smart-grid traffic.

The structure of the paper is as follows. Section 2 provides an overview of the random-access mechanism in LTE/LTE-A. Section 3 describes the considered communication scenarios, with LTE applied as the underlying communication technology for wide-area monitoring and metering services. Section 4 provides a performance evaluation of the standard random-access mechanism under smart-grid traffic in network-overload conditions with system-level simulations in ns-3 framework. Our concluding remarks are presented in Sect. 5.

2   The Random-Access Mechanism in LTE Networks

In LTE/LTE-A, the physical Random-Access CHannel (RACH) is used by the devices to request transmission resources or re-establish a connection to the eNodeB [11]. The RACH is formed by a periodic sequence of time-frequency

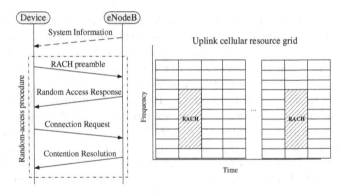

Fig. 1. Overview of the contention-based random-access procedure in LTE/LTE-A. Connection establishment normally involves a four-message handshake between the device and the eNodeB. An access request is completed if the four messages are successfully exchanged.

resources, reserved in the uplink channel for the transmission of access requests. The RACH periodicity is determined by the *RACH configuration index* and may vary from once in every subframe (1 ms) to once every two frames (20 ms). Either a contention-based or a contention-free scheme can be used for the random-access procedure, depending on the purpose [2]. This paper focuses on the challenging contention-based mode, which consists of a four-message handshake between the device and the eNodeB, as shown in Fig. 1. In particular, the following messages are sequentially exchanged between the device and the eNodeB:

1. *RACH preamble.* The first step of the random-access procedure is the transmission of a random-access preamble. Based on the system information broadcast by the eNodeB, each device randomly selects one of the available (up to 64) preamble sequences for contention-based access and transmits it using the RACH. More than one device can possibly choose the same preamble in the same random-access resource, resulting in a preamble collision. In this case, a contention-resolution process is required.

2. *Random-Access Response (RAR).* After receiving the preambles in a specific random-access resource, the eNodeB replies with a RAR message to all the devices with preamble transmission on this resource. In particular, the RAR message includes an identifier of each successfully decoded preamble, timing information for synchronization, a temporary device identifier and an uplink resource grant for devices to transmit a connection request. In case a device receives a RAR without the identifier of the preamble it used, it is signaled, via a backoff indicator attached to the RAR, to wait for a random time until the next preamble transmission attempt. A preamble collision might remain undetected, when devices are located at a similar distance from the eNodeB and their preambles are constructively received. In this case, the contention is resolved in the next step.

3. *Connection Request.* After receiving the RAR, the device transmits a connection-request message conveying the device identifier and the establishment cause, using the resource granted by the eNodeB in the previous step. A retransmission mechanism is enabled to ensure the message delivery. In case of undetected preamble collision in the previous step, more than one device will transmit in the same uplink resource; the eNodeB will not then reply with an acknowledgment and each device will retransmit the message.

4. *Contention Resolution.* The final step of the random-access procedure involves the transmission of a contention-resolution message from the eNodeB to the device. Any contention due to multiple devices attempting channel access using the same random-access resource, is now resolved. The completion of this step renders the random-access attempt successful. Otherwise, if the message is not received by a device within a predefined time window, the random-access procedure is declared as failed and the device needs to restart from the first step until the allowed preamble retransmissions are reached.

As the traffic load and the number of access requests increase, the standard LTE random-access mechanism suffers from congestion due to the high probability of collision in the transmission of the available preambles. Therefore, RACH congestion constitutes a significant challenge in large-scale distribution grid deployments with a high number of communicating entities, as will be described in the following section.

3   Smart Grid Communication Scenarios and Traffic Modeling

As the distribution grid evolves towards more complex loads and decentralized generation, distribution planning may need to account for more dynamic and faster changes to the distribution grid through (*i*) the extensive installation of intelligent electronic devices (IEDs) for *wide-area monitoring* purposes and (*ii*) the large-scale *smart-metering* (AMI) deployments. Two representative communication scenarios in cellular-enabled distribution grids are depicted in Fig. 2. We provide the details in the following.

3.1   Wide-Area Monitoring Systems

Distribution automation deals with system automatic functionalities that involve communication from numerous IEDs installed along the distribution network [12]. The emergence of distributed energy resources results in a growing need for real-time monitoring and quasi-real-time analysis of the grid behavior to enhance the observability and controllability of the distribution network. As illustrated in Fig. 2, in this paper we focus on wide-area monitoring systems, where IEDs -equipped with LTE communication interfaces- transmit monitoring information for situational awareness and supervision of the distribution equipment.

Besides the periodic transmission of monitoring information, we consider a scenario where event-driven IED communication is required to detect out-of-step

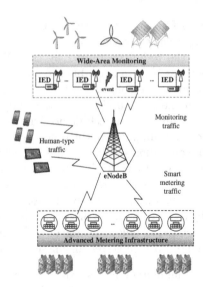

Fig. 2. LTE networks as the underlying communication technology for advanced distribution grid applications, e.g., distribution automation and advanced metering infrastructure.

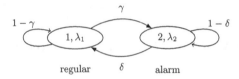

Fig. 3. The state diagram of an IED traffic generation modeled with an MMPP.

conditions (e.g., excessive/increasing phase angle), issue alarms and initiate control actions to rectify the fault and/or isolate the system. In order to capture the bursty characteristics and varying behavior of IED traffic, we may model each IED traffic generation using a two-state Markov Modulated Poisson Process (MMPP) [10]. In particular, the MMPP can be viewed as a superposition of the two Poisson processes with an underlying two-state Markov chain modeling the transition between the processes. As illustrated in Fig. 3, the first state corresponds to the regular IED operation, modeled as a Poisson process with rate λ_1; the second state represents the alarm IED operation where the generation of a traffic burst is also modeled as a Poisson process with rate $\lambda_2 > \lambda_1$, to account for the higher arrival intensity of the alarm traffic.

Let P be the state-transition matrix that incorporates the transition probabilities between the states of the Markov chain. Then,

$$P = \begin{bmatrix} 1 - \gamma & \gamma \\ \delta & 1 - \delta \end{bmatrix}, \tag{1}$$

where γ is associated with the frequency of a burst occurrence and δ is related with the duration of each burst. Let also $\pi = \{\pi_1, \pi_2\}$ be the stationary distribution vector. Then, from the steady-state equations $\pi = \pi P$ and $\pi_1 + \pi_2 = 1$, we derive the stationary distribution π of the chain and the overall rate λ_g of the MMPP as

$$\pi = \left\{ \frac{\delta}{\gamma + \delta}, \frac{\gamma}{\gamma + \delta} \right\} \quad \text{and} \quad \lambda_g = \sum_{i=1}^{2} \lambda_i \pi_i, \tag{2}$$

respectively.

3.2 Advanced Metering Infrastructure Systems

In the case of metering-data delivery, a typical AMI system uses smart meters to communicate information between consumers and power utilities for operating and billing purposes. The enhanced coverage offered by LTE/LTE-A networks allows smart-metering deployments to span over vast areas and remote endpoints to be connected into the same management network. As illustrated in Fig. 2, in this communication scenario, spatially distributed smart meters transmit consumer-meter information from a large number of customer/industrial premises at the utility end for data processing. The AMI systems require infrequent uplink transmissions of small-sized data packets and traffic generation is assumed to follow a Poisson process with an aggregate arrival rate λ_0.

In both communication scenarios, the channel-access attempts of numerous distribution grid devices, i.e., IEDs in wide-area monitoring and smart meters in dense AMI deployments, render the standard access mechanism of LTE highly susceptible to congestion due to the limited random-access opportunities compared to the increased resource demand. Therefore, RACH scalability constitutes a significant challenge especially for the dynamic environment of the future distribution grid where the number of devices joining the network rapidly evolves, i.e., frequent entry/re-entry [12]. In the following, we evaluate the RACH performance under different network settings and smart grid traffic characteristics.

4 Performance Evaluation

To evaluate the performance of the LTE random-access scheme for monitoring and metering traffic, we consider realistic network-overload scenarios in ns-3 discrete-event simulator where each traffic type is solely present in the system. The standard RACH implementation initially developed in [2] is extended with the traffic modules of Sect. 3 and the integration with LTE radio protocol stack is performed as in [9,13]. In the simulation setup, numerous IEDs or smart meters generate traffic within the eNodeB coverage area and contend for channel access. Starting from a medium-load scenario, new devices appear in the system according to a Poisson process with arrival intensities based on the traffic modeling described in Sect. 3. The MMPP parameters are selected to closely

Table 1. Simulation parameters

Parameter	Value
Preambles for contention-based access	54
RACH configuration index[a] CI	{3, 9}
Backoff indicator[a]	20 ms
Preamble duration	1 ms
Max. allowed preamble transmissions[a]	10
RAR window size[a]	5 ms
Contention resolution timer[a]	24 ms
Arrival rates λ_0, λ_1, λ_2 (in attempts/ms)	$\{10^{-3}, 2 \cdot 10^{-3}, 0.5\}$
Traffic model transition probabilities γ, δ	{0.5, 0.3}

[a]Standard values available in [6,11]

match the traffic behavior of IEC-61850 automation services [13]. As the simultaneous channel attempts progressively drive the system to overload, the RACH performance is evaluated under different network configurations and traffic characteristics when the system operates close to its capacity limits.

Two performance indicators have been used to assess the RACH performance, namely: (*i*) average access delay, defined as the time elapsed between the first preamble transmission until the contention-resolution message reception from the eNodeB, and (*ii*) outage probability, defined as the probability that a device reaches the maximum number of transmission attempts and is still unable to complete the random-access process. Table 1 summarizes the basic parameters used in our simulations.

The impact of RACH configuration index (CI) on the average access delay and outage probability is illustrated in Fig. 4, for both monitoring (IED) and metering (SM) traffic. In particular, as shown in Fig. 4a, the average access delay experienced per IED/smart meter increases with increasing monitoring/metering traffic load since contention becomes heavier. A greater value of CI corresponds to a more frequent recurrence of random-access opportunities per time frame; i.e., the index CI = 3 corresponds to one random-access slot per frame whereas for CI = 9 each frame has three random-access slots. Thus, when CI is configured to a higher value, we observe that the average access delay is reduced. In addition, as shown in Fig. 4b, the outage probability experienced per IED/smart meter also decreases with a greater CI. In both figures, the average access delay and outage probability are higher for monitoring traffic compared to the metering traffic, due to the bursty traffic nature of IEDs and the higher arrival rates.

The impact of the number of available preambles for contention-based access on the average access delay and outage probability is illustrated in Fig. 5 for both types of smart grid traffic and a high number of attempting devices. In use cases where the RACH resources are shared with the conventional LTE users, a dedicated set of preambles needs to be allocated to smart grid traffic given the aimed quality-of-service requirements. In particular, as shown in Figs. 5a and b

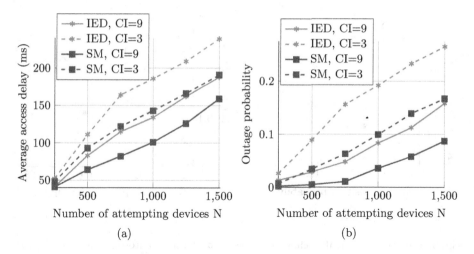

Fig. 4. Impact of the RACH configuration index (CI) on (a) average access delay and (b) outage probability for monitoring (IED) and metering (SM) traffic with increasing number of attempting devices.

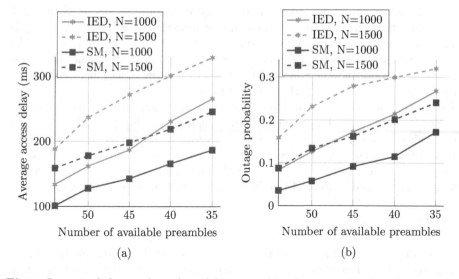

Fig. 5. Impact of the number of available preambles for contention-based access on (a) average access delay and (b) outage probability for monitoring (IED) and metering (SM) traffic in network-overload conditions.

respectively, the average access delay and outage probability experienced per IED/smart meter increase as the number of dedicated preambles decreases due to the lack of adequate random-access opportunities. As it can be observed, the performance degradation is higher for the monitoring traffic compared to the metering traffic, due to the more aggressive arrival rate of monitoring messages.

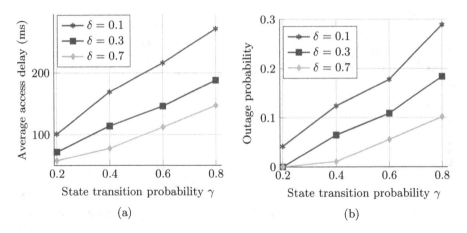

Fig. 6. Impact of the traffic characteristics γ, δ of the monitoring IEDs on the (a) average access delay and (b) outage probability in network-overload conditions.

In the case of monitoring traffic, the impact of the traffic characteristics γ, δ on the average access delay and outage probability is depicted in Fig. 6 for a high number (i.e., 1000) of attempting devices. As defined in Fig. 3, γ is associated with the frequency of a burst occurrence and δ is related with the burst time duration. In Fig. 6a, it can be observed that as the frequency of a burst increases, or equivalently γ increases, the average access delay increases due to the higher attempt rate in the alarm state which leads to a surge of channel access attempts. Similarly, due to the heavier contention, the outage probability in Fig. 6b increases with increasing γ since it is more possible for an IED to reach the limit of the allowed preamble retransmissions without a successful attempt. In addition, as the length of each burst increases, or equivalently δ decreases, the average access latency and outage probability increase since the IEDs remain longer in the alarm state and RACH becomes more prone to congestion.

5   Conclusions

In this paper, we conduct a performance evaluation of the contention-based random access in LTE networks under monitoring and metering traffic for emerging distribution-grid applications. We investigate the impact of different network configurations and smart grid traffic characteristics on the standard random-access procedure of LTE and LTE-A. Our feasibility study aims to reveal the performance limitations and signaling bottlenecks of the RACH when a high number of smart grid entities attempt for channel access in a highly-synchronized manner. The simulation results of realistic network-overload scenarios illustrate that the standard LTE mechanism becomes highly susceptible to congestion while the bursty nature of monitoring traffic results in even higher performance degradation. Radical enhancements are thus required for the efficient accommodation of a high density of smart grid devices in future cellular networks.

Acknowledgment. This work has been funded by projects ADVANTAGE under Grant 607774, P2P-SmarTest (646469), CellFive (TEC2014-60130-P) and the Catalan Government (2014-SGR-1551).

References

1. Kalalas, C., Thrybom, L., Alonso-Zarate, J.: Cellular communications for smart grid neighborhood area networks: a survey. IEEE Access **4**(1), 1469–1493 (2016)
2. Laya, A., Alonso, L., Alonso-Zarate, J.: Is the random access channel of LTE and LTE-A suitable for M2M communications? A survey of alternatives. IEEE Commun. Surv. Tutor. **16**(1), 4–16 (2014)
3. Lee, K.D., Kim, S., Yi, B.: Throughput comparison of random access methods for M2M service over LTE networks. In: IEEE Globecom Workshops (GC Wkshps), pp. 373–377. IEEE Press, Houston (2011)
4. Cheng J.P., Lee C.h., Lin T.M.: Prioritized random access with dynamic access barring for RAN overload in 3GPP LTE-A networks. In: IEEE Globecom Workshops (GC Wkshps), pp. 368–372. IEEE Press, Houston (2011)
5. Wei, C.-H., Cheng, R.-G., Al-Taee, F.: Dynamic radio resource allocation for group paging supporting smart meter communications. In: IEEE 3rd International Conference on Smart Grid Communications (SmartGridComm), pp. 659–663. IEEE Press, Tainan City (2012)
6. 3GPP TR 37.868 v11.0.0: Study on RAN improvements for machine-type communications (2011)
7. Kalalas, C., Alonso-Zarate, J.: Reliability analysis of the random access channel of LTE with access class barring for smart grid monitoring traffic. In: IEEE International Conference on Communications Workshops (ICC), pp. 1–6. IEEE Press, Paris (2017)
8. Madueño, G.C., Pratas, N.K., Stefanović, Č., Popovski, P.: Massive M2M access with reliability guarantees in LTE systems. In: IEEE International Conference on Communications (ICC), pp. 2997–3002. IEEE Press, London (2015)
9. Kalalas, C., Vazquez-Gallego, F., Alonso-Zarate, J.: Handling mission-critical communication in smart grid distribution automation services through LTE. In: IEEE International Conference on Smart Grid Communications (SmartGridComm), pp. 399–404. IEEE Press, Sydney (2016)
10. Heffes, H., Lucantoni, D.: A Markov modulated characterization of packetized voice and data traffic and related statistical multiplexer performance. IEEE J. Sel. Areas Commun. **4**(6), 856–868 (1986)
11. 3GPP TS 36.211 V10.4.0: Evolved Universal Terrestrial Radio Access (E-UTRA); Physical Channels and Modulation (2011)
12. Zhabelova, G., Vyatkin, V.: Multiagent smart grid automation architecture based on IEC 61850/61499 intelligent logical nodes. IEEE Trans. Ind. Electron. **59**, 2351–2362 (2012)
13. Kalalas, C., Gkatzikis, L., Fischione, C., Ljungberg, P., Alonso-Zarate, J.: Enabling IEC 61850 communication services over public LTE infrastructure. In: IEEE International Conference on Communications (ICC), pp. 1–6. IEEE Press, Kuala Lumpur (2016)

Mobile Secure Communications in Smart Grid Control

Giovanna Dondossola and Roberta Terruggia[✉]

Transmission and Distribution Technologies Department,
Ricerca sul Sistema Energetico, Milan, Italy
{giovanna.dondossola,roberta.terruggia}@rse-web.it

Abstract. This paper analyses the communication required to connect the Distributed Energy Resources with power grid substations securely. The IEC 61850 standard communications enhanced with IEC 62351 security standard are evaluated by implementing the information exchanges related to voltage control in an experimental test bed deploying cellular M2M access networks. Particularly the end-to-end security is implemented using peer authentication and packet encryption in compliance with the IEC 62351-3 standard profile. Based on the network traces obtained from the test bed, the security overhead and the impact of cellular networks on transmission delay are measured by protocol specific performance indicators and the results are discussed in the paper.

Keywords: Cellular networks · Cyber security · Distributed energy resources · Standard communications · Voltage control

1 Introduction

The probability of security threats to critical infrastructures of smart grids has been increasing with the deployment of advanced automation and communication technologies, specifically considering the connection of DER (Distributed Energy Resources) from third parties with the power grid substations located in the DSO (Distribution System Operator) domain. Given the high severity of possible communication malfunctions, stringent time and security requirements have to be meet by DER control communications, with a major focus on *deterministic transmission delays* of monitoring and control data exchanges, *high availability* of always on communication links, *no losses* of application messages, *authenticity and integrity* of sending and receiving data streams. The achievement of such challenging requirements using standard communications for interoperability purposes and telecommunication services based on new generation cellular M2M technologies for economic convenience is an ambitious objective for the roll out of full smart grids. Of great importance for the technological evolution of smart grids is the setup of experimental platforms for the performance evaluation of the entire communication architecture and the definition of measurable performance indicators as part of the service level agreement with the telecommunication provider. The experimental activity described in the paper is exactly meant to address such an urgent need.

© ICST Institute for Computer Sciences, Social Informatics and Telecommunications Engineering 2017
E.T. Lau et al. (Eds.): SmartGIFT 2017, LNICST 203, pp. 182–191, 2017.
DOI: 10.1007/978-3-319-61813-5_18

In this paper the focus is on the security of the communications among the DERs and DSO substations.

Section 2 introduces the related work on SCADA (Supervision Control And Data Acquisition) systems and communications between Substations and DERs, the communication standard IEC 61850 and the security standard IEC 62351, and the cellular access network. Section 3 details the reference voltage control use case and explains the setup and configuration of an experimental test bed implementing the IEC 62351-3 compliant security enhancement of the use case communications over the mobile M2M network. The evaluated metrics and results are compared and discussed in Sect. 4, followed by the conclusions and future works in Sect. 5.

2 Background

The traditional SCADA systems need to be enhanced in order to allow the Smart Grid control. More in specific SCADA infrastructures require to support the management and operation of the MV grids in DSO control centres and substations in this new landscape. To integrate with active DERs connected to MV bars and feeders, the architectures of current SCADA systems have to be upgraded with new control functions and related information exchanges. In [1] an ICT architecture is described detailing the information flows required by the voltage and power optimization algorithm as defined in [2].

2.1 IEC 61850 – MMS

IEC 61850 defines standardized data models, communication services and protocol profiles for the information exchanges in substations based on both state of the art communication technology and powerful object modelling. The approach of IEC 61850 is based on the separation between the object models virtualizing real devices and their components and the requirements on the underlying communication protocols, in order to be technology independent and hence "future-proof". The object models are defined in terms of standardized types and services. Real devices and functions are modelled by Logical Nodes composed by standardized data objects. Logical Nodes are grouped into Logical Devices which model the behavior of Intelligent Electronic Devices (IED). The abstract definitions provided by IEC 61850-7 are independent of specific protocol stacks, implementations and operating systems. IEC 61850-8-1 [3] specifies how to implement the services and algorithms defined in IEC 61850-7 by using the MMS (Manufacturing Message Specification) [4] and other protocols. Object models modeling DER systems are defined in IEC 61850-7-420 [5] which is under development as a DER specific part of IEC 61850 standards.

2.2 IEC 62351

The scope of the IEC 62351 series is information security for power system control operations. Its primary objective is to undertake the development of standards for security of the communication protocols defined by IEC Technical Committee 57 for the information exchanges in power systems. According to the security standard IEC 62351-3 [6], the SCADA and telecontrol protocols that make use of TCP/IP as message transport layer have to be protected by specific TLS (Transport Layer Security) configurations applicable to the telecontrol environment. Specifically securing the MMS traffic via IEC 62351-4 and IEC 62351-6 is done on the application and the transport level. Message authentication is performed at the application level by carrying authentication information in the protocol data units. Authentication information comprises a X.509 encoded certificate, a time stamp and the digitally signed time value. For security on the transport layer IEC 62351 refer to TLS [7]. The document specifies the use of port 3782 for secure communications instead of standard port 102. It also specifies a set of mandatory and recommended cipher suites (the allowed combination of authentication, integrity protection and encryption algorithms) and states requirements to the certificates to be used in conjunction with TLS. These requirements comprise for instance dedicated certificate context, application of signatures, and the definition of certificate revocation procedures.

2.3 Cellular M2M Networks

Due to the different penetration of the communication technologies in the geographical regions where DER sites are located, the control functionalities shall work with heterogeneous DER networks (e.g., wired, wireless). The communication can be carried by different cellular technologies, in particular the new generation of cellular networks uses technologies, like LTE and LTE-Advanced, which theoretically meet the most stringent requirements for higher data rates and lower latencies of the most demanding smart grid applications [8].

3 Experiment Setup

This section presents the implementation in a laboratory environment of a platform for the analysis of the communications needed by the Medium Voltage Control function.

3.1 Use Case – Voltage Control in Active Grids

The connection of DERs to medium voltage grids can influence the state of the power grid, affecting the capacity of the DSO to comply with the terms contracted with the TSO (Transmission System Operator) and can have an impact on the quality of service of their neighbor grids. In order to maintain stable voltages in the distribution grids a Voltage Control (VC) function has been designed [2] to monitor the grid status acquiring field measurements and to compute optimized set points for the available flexible assets such as DERs, flexible loads and power equipment deployed in HV/MV substations. The VC function is performed by a controller that is a node of a HV/MV substation control network. In order to compute an optimized voltage profile, the algorithm needs to communicate both with components inside the DSO area, and with systems outside the DSO domain. In particular DERs and flexible loads communicate with the controller via the DER/Flexible loads communication network, possibly deploying heterogeneous communication technologies. The system level outlay of the voltage control function is shown in Fig. 1. Its detailed specification can be found in the Annex B of [1].

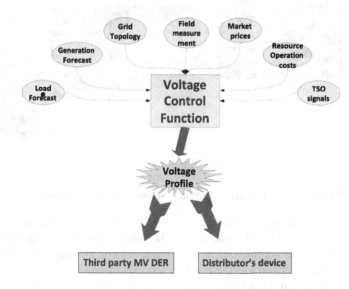

Fig. 1. Voltage control function

3.2 Test Bed Layout

A test platform has been set up in RSE PCS-ResTest Lab (Power Control Systems – Resilience Testing Laboratory) [11] for running cyber security experiments over realistic VC scenarios in the operation of active grids. Figure 2 illustrates the simplified view of the physical setup deployed for the experimental analysis [12]. At the logical level the test bed consists of a set of software building blocks including in particular for the focus of this paper:

- **HV/MV substation network:** each substation includes automation, communication, SCADA and Operator HMI functions. At each substation the behavior of the electrical process is simulated by a Field Simulator application that cyclically reads and updates a virtual I/O interface. The substation hosts the client module managing substation-DER communications.
- **DER sites:** 4 large DERs sites connected to the HV/MV substation through the server module.
- **DER control networks:** connecting each DSO substation with multiple third party DER sites located in different geographical areas deploying heterogeneous communication technologies.

Grid and ICT Control Centres

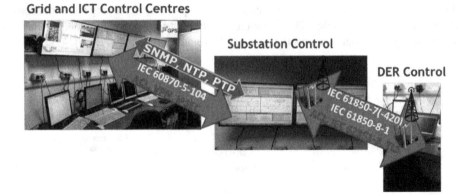

Fig. 2. Test bed layout

3.3 M2M (Machine to Machine) Cellular Network Configuration

In order to evaluate the performance of cellular M2M network technologies (e.g., LTE/ 4G, 3G and 2G) that enable the connection of DER sites with the DSO substations, one DER site in our test bed is connected to the substation through a wired Ethernet VLAN (Virtual Local Area Network) as the baseline test, and three DER sites (located in the RSE test facility and in other places in the Milan area) are connected via a cellular network. Data from substation and DER move in and out being routed through the M2M LTE network, by proper LTE SIM cards inside 4G routers configured with private static IP addresses. Both the primary substation and the DER rely on their own Ethernet based LAN, and connect to the mobile access network via LTE routers, through a GRE (Generic Routing Encapsulation) tunnel configured on both sides.

3.4 Client and Server Test Application Based on IEC 61850

MMS information exchange between DERs and substations, related to the VC scenarios, is provided by a test client-server application: the server application is associated to the DER site while the client resides on the substation SCADA. The client establishes an MMS session with the server, requests the transmission of the IED's profile (as specified by IEC61850), then enables a report control block provided by the server requiring the transmission of periodical information reports. The number of reports to be sent by the server and the interval between the emission of two consecutive reports are configurable. Report transmission causes the information flow from the server towards the client. To generate the information flow in the other direction, from the client towards the server the test client can be instructed by the user, to send setpoints on a periodic basis. Also in this case the period is configurable. The client-server application is implemented on top of the API provided by the libIEC61850 library [9]. In turn the library implements the most important parts of IEC 61850 on top of the MMS mapping, providing the MMS services needed by IEC 61850.

3.5   Security Features According to IEC 62351-3

Security features as specified by IEC 62351-3 have been integrated into the communication protocol by enabling TLS encryption and authentication as stated in the security standards for TCP/IP based protocols, specifically MMS. The implementation of the TLS protocol is based on OpenSSL [10].

As mentioned before the MMS protocol stack is implemented by libIEC61850. This library provides a Hardware/OS Abstraction Layer (HAL) to hide the dependencies from the underlying platform. Currently this layer consists of thread, socket and time abstractions. To support TLS enabled sockets, a TLS HAL implementation for POSIX (Linux) is added to the library, which is shown in Fig. 3. The TLS HAL module works as a wrapper offering the library's standard socket API to the upper layers but providing TLS authentication and encryption services. The TLS extension is transparent to the upper layers of the MMS application: the adoption of TLS protection for MMS traffic does not cause any change to the application. To establish a TLS session on top of a TCP connection, the TLS HAL uses the OpenSSL library, which is a free (BSD-style license) C implementation of SSL/TLS based on Eric Young's SSLeay package. Server side listens on secure port (3782) and supports basic authentication, encryption and message authentication according to TLS v1.2 [7].

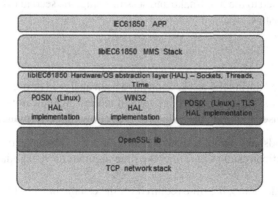

Fig. 3. libIEC61850 MMS stack and IEC 62351-3 implementation

3.6   Test Cases

The medium voltage control test bed focusses on the core control and communication components for the voltage control use case. Also the components supporting ICT maintenance and monitoring functions are integrated in the test bed. Up to now, the tests carried out on our test bed as described in the above sections, can be grouped into two comparable test classes verifying the behavior of communication under the following security measures:

- **Plain Security:** tests verifying the VC communications with basic security measures, i.e. access control to communication gateways. These tests aim at checking the plain communications among DSO substations and DER sites. Both Ethernet and cellular

technologies are tested to be compared with each other according to several performance criteria.

- **Standard Security:** tests verifying the VC communications with enhanced security
  measures as suggested by IEC 62351 Part 4 in T-Profile (currently including TLS
  profile recommended by IEC 62351-3).

4 Methods and Results

In order to stress the various aspects of the protocols involved, two scenarios have been
setup:

- **Short tests:** repeated runs (i.e. 10 runs) of relatively short test (50 reports sent from
  MMS server and setpoints sent from MMS client);
- **Long tests:** a single run of MMS where thousand (i.e. 2000/50000) of reports and
  setpoints are emitted by the MMS server and setpoints by the MMS client respectively;

These different scenarios are used in order to obtain relevant estimation of the metrics
described in the next subsection. The first scenario is used to evaluate the mean time of
the indicators related to the handshake and session setup, the second one provides report
and setpoints statistics.

4.1 Metrics

The traces achieved during the test session have been analyzed through a customer built
tool that it is able to extract and calculate several interesting indicators. In particular the
trace analyser is used to obtain the values of the following performance indicators:

- TCP/TLS Handshake Time: handshake duration for TCP connection/TLS session.
- TLS renegotiation/resumption Time: the time required for renegotiation/resumption
  operations.
- MMS handshake Time: the time required for the establishment of the MMS session.
- MMS Profile Exchange Time: the exchange duration of the MMS profile between
  client and server.
- RTT (Round Trip Time)-Report: the time interval between the output of a report and
  the reception of the corresponding TCP acknowledgment by the MMS server.
- RTT-Setpoint: the time interval between the output of a setpoint request and the
  reception of the corresponding TCP acknowledgment by the MMS client.
- Inter-Report Time or Inter-Setpoint Time: the time interval between each two
  consecutive reports or setpoints, respectively.
- Number of TCP Retransmissions for a report or a setpoint.

The Standard Security test trace analysis required a way to perform the deep packet
inspection. This is an issue currently under discussion within the IEC TC 57 WG 15
committee and until now a standard solution doesn't exist. In our tool the problem has

been worked around and messages are decrypted knowing the server private key and the data exchange during the TLS session handshake.

4.2 Results and Discussion

Table 1 lists the average values for time metrics, e.g. TCP/TLS handshake time, MMS profile exchange time or RTT-Report etc., for the test scenarios. The values are extracted from the two test groups. Short tests provide the best approximation for the metrics considering handshake and session/profile exchange because in these tests we have different runs. Long tests have been used to estimate Renegotiation time, RTT-Setpoint and RTT-Report thanks to the thousands of reports and setpoints included in the test. The packet size has a strong impact on the time value of the indicators. In particular the profile size influence the handshake times. The profile size is 2914 byte, the report packet size is 230 (259 with TLS)

Table 1. Metrics for test scenarios

Test case	Network	TCP handshake time	TLS handshake time	TLS renegotiation time	MMS handshake time	MMS prof. exc. time	Total handshake time	RTT-report	RTT-setpoint	Retras mission
Plain security	ETH	0.000986	–	–	0.002477	0.103992	0.107455	0.001153	0.001411	0
	4G	0.04966	–	–	0.115076	0.308075	0.472811	0.12716	0.107341	3
Standard security	ETH	0.001159	0.047849	0.044036	0.002729	0.103911	0.155647	0.001157	0.001704	0
	4G	0.054625	0.132415	0.176210	0.076725	0.343444	0.607209	0.101212	0.107154	1.87
	3G	0.390826	1.229483	0.431360	0.54844	2.451566	4.620315	0.506906	0.498593	2.887
	2G	2.003555	5.64858	4.568160	3.694058	11.99704	23.34323	2.293466	2.293621	8.06

TLS Performance

The overhead brought by TLS on the different metrics can be easily taken from Table 1 considering the Ethernet network as base case. The results show that the inclusion of the TLS causes the increase of the time for each single communication phase, and introduces an extra time of 0.047849 s for the TLS handshake. We can conclude that the total time for the initial handshake and session phases is 0.107455 s without TLS and 0.155647 s including TLS security which means an overhead of 0.048192 s corresponding to a increment of 44.84% of the total time. Considering only the MMS Handshake and Profile Exchange Time indicators the impact of TLS is not so consistent. Also considering the RTT-Report and RTT-Setpoint indicators it is possible to note that the impact on the time is irrelevant (0.000004 s and 0.000293 s). Similar results may be inferred analyzing the trace from the 4G cellular test. Here it is important to consider the bias due to the unpredictability typical of the mobile networks for the presence of variable background traffic.

Cellular Technology Performance

The aim of this subsection is to compare the baseline technology (Ethernet) performance with the ones obtained considering different type of cellular access network. We focus on Standard Security scenarios, but an Ethernet vs 4G comparison considering Plain Security is also performed.

The magnitude of the total handshake time (see Fig. 4 and Table 1) in Ethernet test is of 100 ms, considering the 4G/LTE technology we have a value of 500/600 ms, but if we change the cellular technology we scale up of one order of magnitude with 3G (4600 ms) and of two orders with 2G (23300 ms). The values in Fig. 4 refer the mean value over the three DER sites for each of the run in the Short Tests. Considering 2G not all the DER values are available for all the run (means of the * symbol in the legend). The cellular results are deeply influenced by the TCP retransmissions occurring during the tests over the mobile network.

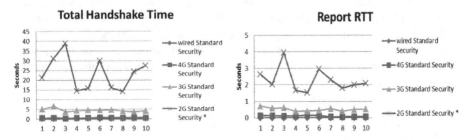

Fig. 4. Total handshake time   **Fig. 5.** Report RTT

If we focus on RTT values (see Fig. 5 and Table 1), we see that the gap between 4G and 3G is less evident (100 ms with 4G and 500 ms with 3G). The main step is between the Ethernet solution (1 ms) and 4G (100 ms) and between 3G (500 ms) and 2G (2290 ms). In Fig. 5 the means over the three DERs for each run is plotted. Also in this case for 2G test not all the DER values are available for all the run (marked with * symbol). From the test results it is clear that the 2G technology does not meet the availability and delay requirements of the VC application (neither those of the DER protection applications most probably sharing the same communication link). The 4G radio transmission seems to be provide acceptable performances. In case the 4G mobile coverage is not able to guarantee the service due to the DER site geographical position or the mobile network condition is degraded, the 3G technology can be a valid backup solution. Another important aspect to take into account for the right interpretation of the test results is the dependency of the evaluated indicators on the cellular network topology and condition: the size of the mobile cell, the relative position of the DER site within the mobile cell, the background traffic changing with the daytime and the weekday are all key parameters that influence the QoS results. We have to underline that the 4G/3G/2G network equipped for this test bed is a prototypal solution, to be improved also using the trial results here gathered to build a more satisfying implementation in order to meet theoretical RTT values of less than 20 ms.

5   Outcome and Future Work

This paper presented the implementation of a test bed to perform experiments on MMS communications according to IEC 61850 data models, among DSO substation and DER sites, over heterogeneous networks and end-to-end security through TLS encryption and authentication conforming to IEC 62351-3. Using the test traces obtained, the overhead of TLS and the impact on communication times of the cellular (in particular LTE) network are analyzed and discussed. These results represent a crucial step in order to allow the evolution of the security standards and to analyze the applicability of the different cellular technologies to critical smart grid applications. Because of the strongly experimental nature of the adopted M2M platform, the results obtained must be consolidated by running further tests under different network conditions. In the test bed setup used for these analyses, the features of TLS session resumption has been implemented within the MMS application but not quantitatively evaluated. Moreover, as a third test case with ICT fault or malicious attack has been implemented in the testbed, the application reconnection and the TLS session resumption after a network fault or attack could be investigated in the future.

Acknowledgement. This work has been supported by the European FP7 project SmartC2Net (under grant agreement no. 318023). Further information is available at www.smartc2net.eu.

References

1. SmartC2Net European Project, Deliverable D1.1: SmartC2Net Use Cases, Preliminary Architecture and Business Drivers, September 2014. http://www.smartc2net.eu
2. Moneta, D., Mora, P., Belotti, M., Carlini, C.: Integrating larger RES share in distribution networks: advanced voltage control and its application on real MV networks. In: Integration of Renewables into the Distribution Grid, CIRED 2012 Workshop, Lisbon, May 2012
3. International Standard IEC 61850-8-1 Ed. 2: Communication Networks and Systems in Substations - Part 8-1: Specific Communication Service Mapping (SCSM) - Mappings to MMS (ISO 9506-1 and ISO 9506-2) and to ISO/IEC 8802-3, June 2011
4. ISO/IEC 8650-1 Information technology – Open Systems Interconnection – Connection-oriented protocol for the Association Control Service Element: Protocol specification, ISO (1996)
5. International Standard IEC 61850-7-420 Ed. 1: Communication networks and systems for power utility automation – Part 7-420: basic communication structure – distributed energy resources logical nodes, March 2009
6. International Standard IEC 62351-3 Ed. 1: Power systems management and associated information exchange - data and communication security – Part 3: communication network and system security – profiles including TCP/IP, International Standard, October 2014
7. Network Working Group TLS Version 1.2: The Transport Layer Security (TLS) Protocol, RFC 5246, August 2008
8. Latency and Bandwidth Analysis of LTE for a Smart Grid – Xu. http://kth.diva-portal.org/smash/get/diva2:565509/FULLTEXT01.pdf
9. libIEC61850 – open source library for IEC 61850. http://libiec61850.com/libiec61850/
10. OpenSSL: The Open Source Toolkit for SSL/TLS. https://www.openssl.org/
11. http://www.rse-web.it/laboratori/laboratorio/60
12. SmartC2Net European Project, Deliverable D6.3: Final results from laboratory tests, November 2015. http://www.smartc2net.eu

Congestion Probability Balanced Electric Vehicle Charging Strategy in Smart Grid

Qiang Tang[1,2(✉)], Kun Yang[3], Yuan-sheng Luo[1,2], and Yu-yan Liu[4]

[1] Hunan Provincial Key Laboratory of Intelligent Processing of Big Data
on Transportation, Changsha University of Science and Technology,
Changsha, China
tangqiangcsust@163.com
[2] School of Computer and Communication Engineering, Changsha University
of Science and Technology, Changsha, China
[3] School of Computer Science and Electronic Engineering,
University of Essex, Colchester, UK
kunyang@essex.ac.uk
[4] School of Economics and Managent, Changsha University of Science
and Technology, Changsha, China

Abstract. In this paper, a coordinated charging strategy CCCS (Charging Congestion probability based Charging Strategy) is proposed, which considers the congestion probabilities of the charging stations (CSs), the charging costs of the electric vehicles (EVs), the distance between EV and charging station and EV users' satisfactions. The coordinated charging issue is formulated as a convex optimization problem, which can be solved to get the distributed charging algorithms, based on which the communication system is further proposed. In order to illustrate the performance, we put forward three benchmarks. In the simulation, we combine the power grid i.e. MATPOWER and the charging module together to build the simulation platform. Simulation results show that CCCS performs well in terms of balancing the congestion probabilities, reducing charging costs, and mitigating the impacts on the power grid voltage.

Keywords: Congestion probability · Charging cost · Voltage level · Electric vehicle · Smart grid

1 Introduction

In recent years, EV charging strategy is an important issue in smart grid [1]. The EV charging strategy mainly contains two categories: centralized charging strategy and decentralized charging strategy [2].

In the centralized category, a lot of EVs' information is collected by a central unit, which considers many constraints to make the comprehensive charging decisions. A.S. Masoum et al. [3] proposed an online fuzzy coordination algorithm (OL-FCA) for the EV charging, which aims at reducing the total cost of energy generation and associated grid losses. In [4], a novel method for EV charging was put forward, which considers the power grid constrains, the voltage as well as the power to avoid the distribution grid

© ICST Institute for Computer Sciences, Social Informatics and Telecommunications Engineering 2017
E.T. Lau et al. (Eds.): SmartGIFT 2017, LNICST 203, pp. 192–201, 2017.
DOI: 10.1007/978-3-319-61813-5_19

congestion while satisfying the charging requirements. A GVs (gridable vehicles) concept was defined by Ahmed Yousuf Saber et al. [5], who also proposed an optimization EV charging algorithm combining the V2G (vehicle-to-grid) technology to reduce the cost and emissions of UC (unit commitment). In order to minimize the grid operation cost while considering the EVs' random charging behaviours, the stochastic security-constrained unit commitment model is adopted [6]. In [7], the coordinated charging of minimize distribution system losses is studied. A two-stage strategy is proposed in [8]. In the strategy, the electricity price and demand at first by the control center, and then the control center purchases the energy from the market, and dispatches it to each EVs.

The centralized strategies have the ability to solve the optimization problems precisely, but they need a lot of computing resources to process the massive EV charging request. In order to mitigate the computational burden for large-scale EV charging, the decentralized charging strategies become more and more popular in recent years. In the decentralized charging strategy, each participant has the ability to compute the optimal decision and communicate with other participants. Every participant's decision will be finally stable, and the whole EV charging strategy will be in an equilibrium state.

In [9], a non-cooperative Stackelberg game is used for the EV charging. In the game, smart gird is a leader which provides the price at first, and the EVs are followers who decide their charging strategies according to the price. In [10], a non-cooperative game is adopted to formulate the parking-lot EV charging problem. In order to solve the coupled constraint problem, the Rosen-Nash normalized equilibrium is utilized in the game model. Julian de Hoog et al. [11] took advantages of a market mechanism to allocate the charging capacity to ensure the network stability. For the purpose of processing the large population and dynamic EV arrivals, the authors in [12] proposed a local scheduling scheme, which divides the EVs into different groups and the charging decision is determined based on the group information. In [13], in order to minimize the charging cost, Yijia Cao et al. put forward an optimized charging model, which considered the SOC curve and TOU price. In regarding with the security problems, Chao-Kai Wen et al. in [14] proposed a distributed charging strategy, which only requires the EV demand rather than the private information for protecting the users privacy.

A lot of research work is mainly related with the charging cost, security, price curve and distributed generation et al. In [15], the authors believed that the congestion management is an important issue in smart grid. They summarized that the congestion management is used to manage and control the charging EVs, so as to minimize queue at the charging station. According to their survey, only two papers are related with they defined congestion management. The two papers are about finding the minimum congestion travel routings. Islam Safak Bayram also studied the congestion management problem in [16], where they brought forward a control mechanism to avoid congestion at busy charging station, but the authors did not consider the congestion probabilities balance among different charging stations.

In this paper, we propose a distributed charging strategy CCCS, which focuses on balancing the congestion probabilities among different charging stations, and meanwhile the charging costs, traveling distances to the charging station as well as the users' satisfactions are all considered. The rest of this paper is organized as follows. Section 2 introduces the system model as well as the charging algorithm of CCCS. In Sect. 3, the performance of CCCS is evaluated. Conclusions and future work are presented in Sect. 4.

2   Mathematical Model of CCCS

2.1   Utility Function of Charging Station

Every charging station has the maximum charging power *Pmax*, which is deter-mined by the following equation:

$$P_j^{max} = P_k^{max} - P_k^{basic} \tag{1}$$

Where P_k^{max} the is the maximum allowed power of the electricity bus k, which the charging station j connects to. The P_k^{basic} is the basic load consumed by other entities, such as buildings, equipment, et al. In this paper, we assume each CS connects to only one bus node.

Each charging station also has different charging piles in different time slots, which is defined as follows:

$$N_j^{pile} = \frac{P_j^{max}}{P^{charging}} \tag{2}$$

Where $P^{charging}$ is the charging power of EV, and we assume it is a constant. In order to express conveniently, we omit the annotations of time slot on every variable.

Because of the finite charging piles in each charging station, we further define a congestion probability to represent the charging congestion:

$$C\,on_j = \begin{cases} \frac{N_j - N_j^{pile}}{N_j}, & \text{if } N_j > N_j^{pile} \\ 0, & \text{if } N_j \le N_j^{pile} \end{cases} \tag{3}$$

Where N_j is the number of EVs that willing to charge at the charging station j. In order to introduce the proportion of the available charging piles in charging station j, we define the following indicator:

$$Ava_j = \begin{cases} \frac{N_j^{pile} - N_j}{N_j^{pile}}, & \text{if } N_j^{pile} > N_j \\ 0, & \text{if } N_j^{pile} \le N_j \end{cases} \tag{4}$$

The utility function of charging station j is defined as:

$$U(L_j) = p_j L_j - a(L_j)^2 - bL_j - c \tag{5}$$

Where L_j is the charging load of charging station j, and p_j is the charging price. Besides a, b, and c are constants for all the charging stations in this paper. P_jL_j denotes the income of charging, and $a(L_j)^2 + bL_j + c$ denotes the cost for generating L_j electricity quantity of power grid. Equation (5) can be proved as a convex function.

2.2 Utility Function of Electric Vehicle

Every EV i has a coordinate (cx_i, cy_i), destination coordinate (cx_i^{des}, cy_i^{des}) and distance d_i^j to charging station j whose coordinate is $(cx_j, cy_i) \cdot d_i^j$ is:

$$d_i^j = \sqrt{(cx_i - cx_j)^2 + (cx_i - cx_j)^2} \tag{6}$$

The convex utility function is defined as:

$$U(x_i) = \alpha_j(r \ln(\omega x_i) - p_j x_i - p^{last} d_i^j \beta + C) \tag{7}$$

Where r, ω and β are constants, and β is the constant coefficient of converting the distance 1 km into the electricity quantity 1 MWh. p^{last} is the charging price of the latest time slot, and we assume it is a constant for simplicity. p_j is the charging price of this time slot of charging station j, and its initial value is p^{last} C is a big positive constant for ensuring the value of $U(x_i)$ is positive. α_j is a probability related factor, which is defined as follows:

$$\alpha_j = (m + Ava_j)(m - Con_j) \tag{8}$$

Where m is a constant. In the actual environment, the electricity charging quantity of EV is limited to a range $[x_i^{min}, x_i^{max}]$, the boundary values of which are defined as follows:

$$x_i^{min} = \begin{cases} \beta d_j^{des} & \text{if } \beta d_j^{des} < (0.8 - SOC_i)Cap_i, \\ (0.8 - SOC_i)Cap_i, & \text{else} \end{cases} \tag{9}$$

$$x_i^{max} = (0.8 - SOC_i)Cap_i \tag{10}$$

$$d_j^{des} = \sqrt{(cx_j - cx_i^{des})^2 + (cy_j - cy_i^{des})^2} \tag{11}$$

Where SOC_i the is the state of charge (SOC) of EV i, which belongs to the interval (0, 1). In order to avoid the overcharge, we set the maximum SOC is 0.8. Cap_i is the battery capacity of EV i, which is a constant for all EVs. d_j^{des} is the distance between charging station j and the destination of the EV i.

2.3   Optimization Problem

We define the following optimization model for the maximum social utility:

$$maximize \sum_{j=1}^{M} \left(U(L_j) + \sum_{i=1}^{N_j} U(x_i) \right) \tag{12}$$

$$s.t. \, L_j = \sum_{i=1}^{N_j} x_i$$

Where M is the charging station number. The solution of problem (12) is also the solution of the follow problem:

$$maximize \left(U(L_j) + \sum_{i=1}^{N_j} U(x_i) \right) \tag{13}$$

$$s.t. \, L_j = \sum_{i=1}^{N_j} x_i$$

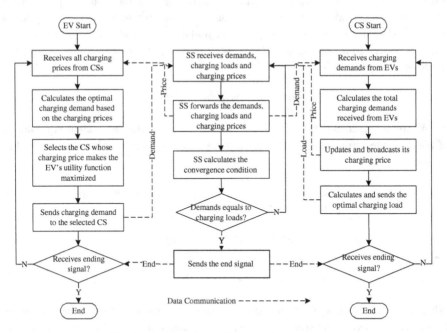

Fig. 1. The flowchart of communication system

Problem (13) can be solved by the convex theory, and after using the dual decomposition to the dual problem of the (13)'s Lagrangian function [17] the sub-optimization strategies can be obtained for both EV and CS. Based on the strategies of EV and CS, we further propose a coordinated charging communication system, shown in Fig. 1. As for the ending signal, we define the following inequality to represent the ending condition:

$$convergence = \frac{\sqrt{\sum_{j=1}^{M}\left(L_j^* - \sum_{i=1}^{N_j} x_i^*\right)^2}}{\sum_{j=1}^{M}\sum_{i=1}^{N_j} x_i^*} < \sigma \tag{14}$$

Where $\sqrt{\sum_{j=1}^{M}\left(L_j^* - \sum_{i=1}^{N_j} x_i^*\right)^2}$ means the standard deviation between the optimal

charging demands of EVs and charging loads of CSs. $\sum_{j=1}^{M}\sum_{i=1}^{N_j} x_i^*$ means all the optimal

charging demands. σ is a very small positive value.

3 Simulation

3.1 Environment Setting

In the simulation, we have developed a platform, which combines the MATPOWER [18] and the charging module together. We use the MATPOWER to calculate the power flow for the node voltage verification. The charging module is developed based on the Java environment.

The basic load is obtained from [19], and we have adjusted the load data in proportion manner to adapt the simulation scenes. The basic load is divided into several parts and dispatched to every charging station. The EVs are randomly distributed in a square area with the side length as 100,000 m. There are 20 charging stations randomly located in this area. We assume each charging station connects to only one electricity bus node. The IEEE 30-bus power grid is used for simulation, and its parameter values are the same as that in [18]. The maximum allowed power of each bus node is defined as the same values in MATPOWER case30 testing file. The necessary parameters' values are assigned in Table 1.

3.2 Comparison Strategies

We define three benchmarks: CCS (Congestion based Charging Strategy), DCS (Distance based Charging Strategy) and COSTCS (COST based Charging Strategy).

In the CCS, the utility function of CS is the same as that of CCCS. But the utility function of EV is different:

$$U(x_i) = \alpha_j \tag{15}$$

Table 1. Parameter settings

Parameter name	Assigned value	Remarks
Area side length	100,000 m	–
CS Number (M)	20	–
EV Number	2000	–
$p^{charging}$	0.048 MW	Fast charging power (ref [16])
a	0.01	–
b	0.8	–
c	0.5	–
r	2.0	–
ω	25.0	–
β	0.0002	1 km consumes 0.0002MWh (ref [1])
m	5.0	–
C	10000	Big enough positive value
Cap_i	0.024 MWh	The same value for EVs (ref [1])
p^{last}	2.0	Initial price for every CS
σ	0.002	For ending iteration process

According to (15), the x_i^* is an arbitrary value, and we fix it as x_i^{min}. In the DCS, the utility function of EV is:

$$U(x_i) = -d_i^j/1000 + C \tag{16}$$

The value of x_i^* is also fixed as x_i^{min}. In the COSTCS, the utility function of EV is:

$$U(x_i) = -p_j x_i - p^{last} d_i^j \beta + C \tag{17}$$

Because it is a linear function, the x_i^* is also fixed as x_i^{min}.

3.3 Charging Congestion Probability and Charging Cost

In this sub section, we simulate the four algorithms in one time slot. The parameters values are shown in Table 1. The charging congestion probability and average charging cost are simulated, and the results are shown in Fig. 2.

In Fig. 2(a), because the curves of the CCCS and CCS are the most flatten, the charging congestion probabilities of CSs are almost equal to each other. So, CCCS and CCS have the best performance in terms of charging congestion probability. Meanwhile, the DCS and COSTCS do not have the ability to balance the charging congestion probability among charging stations. The main reason is that DCS and COSTCS do not consider the charging congestion probability in their utility functions of EV.

In Fig. 2(b), the COSTCS has the best performance of the average charging cost, which is because the COSTCS only considers the charging cost in its utility function.

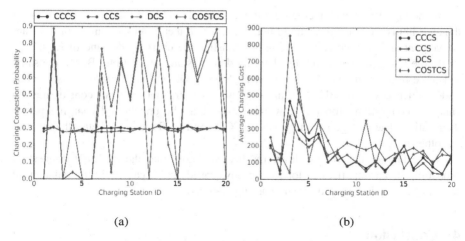

Fig. 2. The charging congestion probability and average charging cost of different CSs

The CCS has the worst performance in terms of the average charging cost, because it only considers the charging congestion probability. Both the CCCS and DCS have the moderate performance as they have partly considered the charging cost in their utility functions.

3.4   Convergence and Bus Node Voltage

In this sub section, the parameters are the same as that of 4.3. Simulation results are shown in Fig. 3. The Bus node minimum voltage level is set as 0.95. When the Bus voltage is simulated, we let all the charging demands from EVs are injected into the power grid at the same time.

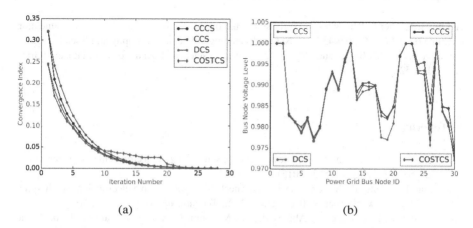

Fig. 3. The convergence performance and influences to the power grid voltage

In the Fig. 3(a), the convergence index is defined in (14). As shown in Fig. 3(a), all the algorithms are convergent in 30 iterations, which means all the four algorithms are convergent and each charging station has satisfied the charging demand of EVs.

In the Fig. 3(b), we let all the charging demands are injected into Bus at the same time. We find that the voltage levels of DCS and COSTCS are very low at some bus node, which is because the EVs in these charging strategies are not considering the charging congestion probability, which results into the unbalanced charging power distribution. The voltage performances of CCCS and CCS are much better than that of the other two.

According to the voltage level results, we know that the charging congestion probability is an important factor for the power grid, and it can avoid the unbalanced charging demand among different charging stations.

4   Conclusion

In this paper, we propose an EV charging strategy CCCS, which considers the charging congestion probability, charging cost, distance and users' satisfactions in the utility function. The charging station utility and EV utility are combined together to formulate a social welfare maximizing convex problem. Simulation results show that the CCCS performs well in terms of balancing the charging congestion probabilities among charging stations and reducing charging costs. Most importantly, this paper presents that the charging congestion probability is an important factor to balance the charging demand among different charging stations.

In the future, we will focus on the uncertainly to the EV charging strategy, such as the distributed resources integration. Besides, the implement of the EV charging algorithms is also an important issue, where each participant executes distributed algorithm, and how to make them execute algorithms in synchronous manner is essential. Besides, there are many other factors should be considered, such as the transportation conditions, communication data loss etc.

Acknowledgement. This work is partly supported by the National Natural Science Foundation of China (Grant No. 61303043), and National Planning Office of Philosophy and Social of China (Grant No. 15CGL018), and Provincial Natural Science Foundation of Hunan (Grant No. 13JJ4052).

References

1. Mukherjee, J.C., Gupta, A.: A review of charge scheduling of electric vehicles in smart grid. IEEE Syst. J. **9**, 1541–1553 (2015)
2. Wang, R., Wang, P., Xiao, G.: Two-stage mechanism for massive electric vehicle charging involving renewable energy. IEEE Trans. Veh. Technol. **65**, 4159–4171 (2016)
3. Masoum, A.S., Deilami, S., Abu-Siada, A., Masoum, M.A.S.: Fuzzy approach for online coordination of plug-in electric vehicle charging in smart grid. IEEE Trans. Sustain. Energ. **6**, 1112–1121 (2015)

4. Sundström, O., Binding, C.: Flexible charging optimization for electric vehicles considering distribution grid constraints. IEEE Transactions on Smart Grid **3**, 26–37 (2012)
5. Saber, A.Y., Venayagamoorthy, G.K.: Resource scheduling under uncertainty in a smart grid with renewables and plug-in vehicles. IEEE Syst. J. **6**, 103–109 (2012)
6. Khodayar, M.E., Wu, L., Shahidehpour, M.: Hourly coordination of electric vehicle operation and volatile wind power generation in SCUC. IEEE Trans. Smart Grid **3**, 1271–1279 (2012)
7. Sortomme, E., Hindi, M.M., MacPherson, S.D.J., Venkata, S.S.: Coordinated charging of plug-in hybrid electric vehicles to minimize distribution system losses. IEEE Trans. Smart Grid **2**, 198–205 (2011)
8. Wu, D., Aliprantis, D., Ying, L.: Load scheduling and dispatch for aggregators of plug-in electric vehicles. IEEE Trans. Smart Grid **3**, 368–376 (2012)
9. Tushar, W., Saad, W., Poor, H.V., Smith, D.B.: Economics of electric vehicle charging: a game theoretic approach. IEEE Trans. Smart Grid **3**, 1767–1778 (2012)
10. Zhang, L., Li, Y.: A game-theoretic approach to optimal scheduling of parking- lot electric vehicle charging. IEEE Trans. Veh. Technol. **65**, 4068–4078 (2016)
11. Hoog, J.D., Alpcan, T., Brazil, M., Thomas, D.A., Mareels, I.: A market mechanism for electric vehicle charging under network constraints. IEEE Trans. Smart Grid **7**, 827–836 (2016)
12. He, Y., Venkatesh, B., Guan, L.: Optimal scheduling for charging and discharging of electric vehicles. IEEE Trans. Smart Grid **3**, 1095–1105 (2012)
13. Cao, Y., Tang, S., Li, C., Zhang, P., Tan, Y., Zhang, Z., Li, J.: An optimized EV charging model considering TOU price and SOC curve. IEEE Trans. Smart Grid **3**, 388–393 (2012)
14. Wen, C.-K., Chen, J.-C., Teng, J.-H., Ting, P.: Decentralized plug-in electric vehicle charging selection algorithm in power systems. IEEE Trans. Smart Grid **3**, 1779–1789 (2012)
15. Rigas, E.S., Ramchurn, S.D., Bassiliades, N.: Managing electric vehicles in the s- mart grid using artificial intelligence: a survey. IEEE Trans. Intell. Transp. Syst. **16**, 1619–1635 (2015)
16. Bayram, I.S., Michailidis, G., Devetsikiotis, M.: Unsplittable load balancing in a network of charging stations under QoS guarantees. IEEE Trans. Smart Grid **6**, 1292–1302 (2015)
17. Samadi, P., Mohsenian-Rad, A.-H., Schober, R., Wong, V.W.S., Jatskevich, J.: Optimal real-time pricing algorithm based on utility maximization for smart grid. In: First IEEE International Conference on Smart Grid Communications, pp. 415–420. IEEE Press, New York (2010)
18. Zimmerman, R.D., Murillo-Snchez, C.E., Thomas, R.J.: MATPOWER: steady-state operations, planning and analysis tools for power systems research and education. IEEE Trans. Power Syst. **26**, 12–19 (2011)
19. Australian Energy Market Operator (AEMO). http://www.aemo.com.au/

IRENE Workshop

A Tool for Evolutionary Threat Analysis of Smart Grids

Tommaso Zoppi[✉], Andrea Ceccarelli, and Marco Mori

University of Florence, Viale Morgagni 65, Florence, Italy
{tommaso.zoppi,andrea.ceccarelli,ma.mori}@unifi.it

Abstract. Cyber-security is becoming more and more relevant with the advent of large-scale systems made of independent and autonomous constituent systems that interoperate to achieve complex goals. Providing security in such cyber-physical systems means, among other features, identifying threats generated by novel detrimental behaviors. This paper presents a tool based on a methodology that is intended to support city evolution and energy planning with a focus on threats due to novel and existing interconnections among different components. More in detail, we report a tool demonstration which shows the application of a tool devised to (i) deal with security threats arising due to evolutions in a Smart City - intended as a complex cyber-physical system -, and (ii) consequently perform threat analysis.

Keywords: Threat analysis · Smart Grids · Evolution · IRENE

1 Threat Analysis for Planned Evolution

Most of the approaches supporting the achievement of safety and security requirements are based on threat analysis processes that are mostly intended for static scenarios, with limited inherent solutions to support the planned evolution of infrastructures and especially of Smart Cities. Tackling evolution of Smart Cities as main challenge, in [3, 4] a threat analysis methodology was identified that lists the occurring threats through an incremental approach. Concisely, the methodology is based on both observing changes in the Smart City topology and performing a threat analysis on detected changes. The focus is on: (i) new threats that can arise from the addition of new components (either buildings or connections), and (ii) threats that are no longer affecting the Smart City due to some topology changes. This methodology is intended to support city evolution and energy planning with a focus on threats due to interconnections among different components of the grid.

The methodology was developed within the project IRENE [7, 2], which is focused on collaborative city planning for resilient energy management. The project investigates the interplay and coordination of social, economic and technical components to improve robustness of the urban electricity network.

Starting from the methodology we presented in [3] in the context of the IRENE project, this paper is intended to complement the live demonstration of the threat analysis tool that will be performed at the workshop IRENE @ SmartGift 2017.

© ICST Institute for Computer Sciences, Social Informatics and Telecommunications Engineering 2017
E.T. Lau et al. (Eds.): SmartGIFT 2017, LNICST 203, pp. 205–211, 2017.
DOI: 10.1007/978-3-319-61813-5_20

2   Background: Evolutionary Threat Analysis (ETA)

In order to provide safety and security requirements for Smart Grids, it is essential to analyze the interdependencies regulating the flow of information among constituent systems. Their interactions and interdependencies may generate cascading effects, which represent possible security threats and damages. To avoid such situations, the transient threat analysis should be supported by new approaches that are able to deal with cascading contingency chains revealing the effect of evolving the grid.

The evolutionary threat analysis described in [3, 4] adopts the guidelines defined from NIST in the SP 800-30 [1] regarding both the approach to follow and the main steps to perform and validate the risk assessment process. In particular, it follows an *asset-oriented* approach as defined in the NIST standard, by identifying threat events depending on critical assets of the grids, i.e., the internal behavior of a component (e.g., a hospital) and their possible interactions. It supports an incremental threat identification process that is carried out after the grid evolution. Starting from the identification of impacts or consequences of the addition/removal of assets, the approach identifies the threats and/or the vulnerabilities that can arise due to this scenario's evolution. Consequently, the mitigation strategies to apply/remove are identified according to the traceability of their threats. The methodology is not reported here for brevity; please refer to [3, 4] for more details.

3   Background: Tool Design, Implementation and Configurations

The methodology in [3, 4] has been implemented in a tool.

Design Choices.   According to the purpose of the IRENE project, the tool is intended to support city planners when they have to plan – or to assess – an evolution of the existing grid that contributes to provide smart services in the near future. Anyway, evolving the grid leads to modifications that can introduce new threats or vulnerabilities (e.g., a substation that is fundamental for critical grid components) as well as architectural changes that need to be supported by the whole grid (e.g., energy rebalancing due to a failure in a connection or a generic component).

Moreover, considering threats happening in a scenario as a formal relation between two components (i.e., threats and scenarios) allows viewing the results of the threat analysis as a Formal Concept Analysis (FCA) structure [8]. This view established hierarchical relations between scenarios depending on threats.

Implementation Choices.   We describe here our implementation choices.

- *Language.* We choose *Java* as tool platform since it is not OS-dependent and other tools in the IRENE [7] toolset were developed with the same language. This will help the future integration of the single tools to build a unique toolset.
- *Interface and I/O.* The tool has not a graphical interface since it should be used in cooperation with other tools that offer a graphical user interface. However, the tool can be considered as a standalone resource that has its inputs and outputs into text

files. This allows a simple integration with other tools that can read and write the input and output files to tune the preferences of the threat analysis tool according to their actual needs.

- *Performance.* The complexity of the threat analysis implemented in this tool is not so relevant to require deep performance analysis. However, during the CPU-intensive phase – while threats for each evolution step are listed – the tool executes the most expensive tasks in dedicated threads, to not lock the main thread responsible to collect the outcomes of the created threads. This will increase the performances of the tool in workstations where several (physical or virtual) CPUs are available. The management of such threads is left to the *Java* scheduler that runs a preemptive priority-based scheduling algorithm.

Complexity. The tool performs satisfactorily with the scenario's inputs, given that it is polynomial with respect to the inputs. Consequently, we expect to have an acceptable scalability with larger scale Smart Grids.

Code characteristics. The implemented code was checked to obtain quality metrics in order to give an overview on its complexity and on how it is written, that we partially report in Table 1 Moreover, we refactored the code to eliminate the code flaws identified by *FindBugs* [5]. *FindBugs* was tuned to identify the following bug categories: security flaws, bad practices, dodgy code, and multi-threading correctness.

Table 1. Quality metrics values for the ETA source code

Metric			Results		
Code	Name	Detail	Average	St. Dev	Max
WMC	Weighted methods per class	Type	18.571	14.783	52
NOM	Number of methods	Type	6.571	7.178	29
MLOC	Method lines of code	Method	8.229	9.164	39

4   Tool Demo: Define Inputs, Outputs, Execution

We exercise the tool on a simple evolving Smart City (Smart Grid) scenario. We consider as possible ways to evolve the grid i) a simple change of the topology (e.g., the addition of a wire), and ii) a set of evolutionary features that lead to changes in the grid functionalities (see [3, 4]).

Inputs. The tool requires the following inputs: (i) a list of threats, (ii) a list of threat categories, (iii) a list of mitigations, (iv) a list of grid components, and (v) a (set of) scenario including a grid topology. More in detail, the *list of threats* and *threat categories* define the threat model, or rather the threats that the user is investigating for the specific study (e.g., cyber-security, environmental, etc.). The *mitigations* are a set of strategies that can be instantiated and implemented on a specific grid to mitigate or avoid the detrimental effects of the happening of the threats. This information is therefore used to analyze the *grid scenario* the user wants to analyze, which can be either a brand new one or an evolution of a previously analyzed grid scenario. In both cases, the grid scenario is defined as a grid topology that is composed by the components in the *components list*, complemented with assumptions about the city scenario under investigation (e.g., seismic zone, prone to terrorism, etc.).

Outputs. The output of the tool is provided both in terms of a list of identified threats and a Formal Concept Analysis (FCA) file. In particular, it consists in a set of files listing the threats identified in each input scenario along with the mitigations that can be applied accordingly. The relations between evolutions of the same scenario are highlighted through the usage of the FCA output, which helps defining a hierarchy for the involved grid scenarios. The hierarchy is based on the threats that can arise in each scenario: a grid scenario is an ancestor of another one if it is interested by a subset of threats that occur in the child scenario.

Dependencies. The tool is written in Java 8. However, a compatible version is available for Java 7. Moreover, one of the outputs of the tool is a *.cex* file containing the result of the FCA. This needs to be opened by dedicated tools such as *ConExp* [6], which allow visualizing the FCA through the support of the *Colibri-Java* API.

Running the Tool. The tool is an executable *.jar* that can be run via command line on *Windows*, *OSX* and *UNIX* systems invoking the *Java Virtual Machine* with "java –jar <pathname>/WP2_ThreatAnalysis.jar". The tool is compiled with the current standard version of *Java* (*Java* 8); therefore, it cannot be run on systems where *Java* is not installed or if *Java* 7 or previous versions are installed.

5   Tool Demo: Results from Execution

Here we report the results of an execution of the tool using the scenario in Fig. 1, and the threats, mitigations and evolutionary steps described in [3, 4]. First, inputs are read. In the example, the tool shows that 38 threats, 19 mitigations and 120 possible novel interdependencies were loaded.

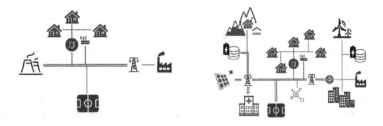

Fig. 1. Evolution steps from [3]: 0_InitialScenario (left) and 5_BuildingIndustrialDistrict (right)

Then, all the considered evolving scenarios are loaded and each of them is analyzed incrementally. In the example, 8 evolutions of the initial grid are considered: an initial definition of the grid (*"0_initialScenario"*) and 8 temporal evolutions, leading the grid being exposed to 494 threats (414 structural threats and 80 threats due to novel inter-dependencies) in its final state.

In Table 2 we can observe a summary of the threat analysis executed on the scenarios mentioned above. In the first scenario all the components - and, consequently, the threats - are new, while other steps add or remove components from the previous scenario. The threats related to the scenarios changes accordingly: considering *"5_BuildingIndus-trialDistrict"* we can observe that 2 components are added and 4 are removed, totalizing 384 structural threats and 81 threats due to novel interdependencies. We observed that 8% of this threats are new with respect to the previous *"4_InseringStorages"* scenario due to the addition of 2 components, while 17% of threats that affected the *"4_Inser-ingStorages"* where eliminated due to the removal of 4 components.

Table 2. Threat analysis summary

Scenario	Components				Threat statistics (%)			
	Prev	Add	Del	Tot	Structural	Dependencies	Add	Del
0_InitialScenario	0	15	0	15	91	9	100	0
1_DiscoveringResources	15	4	0	19	88	12	26	0
2_GrowingNumberOfPeople	19	6	0	25	86	14	28	0
3_AddingKeyBuildings	25	4	2	27	85	15	14	6
4_InseringStorages	27	6	0	33	81	19	24	0
5_BuildingIndustrialDistrict	33	2	4	31	83	17	8	17
6_InsertionSCADA	31	2	2	31	83	17	8	9
7_InstallingMicroGrids	31	0	0	31	83	17	0	0
8_ImprovingDecarbonisation	31	2	0	33	84	16	6	0

Figure 2 shows the graphical interface to specify/import the input threats of each scenario and the results of the FCA. The latter consists in a graph where large nodes are evolution steps (i.e., scenarios), represented according to a hierarchical view. In particular, we can see how scenarios 6 and 7 are represented in the same point since they are threatened by the same items. The only change here is the substitution of the Basic Data Centre (BDC) component with a SCADA that is not threatened by any additional item. Lastly, we can observe that a hierarchy is established between two or more scenarios if the evolution step only adds threats (as for scenarios 0, 1, 2); in other cases we may have both to consider additional threats and to discard others thus changing the base threats set (as for scenarios *"4_InseringStorages"* and *"5_BuildingIndustrialDistrict"* previously discussed).

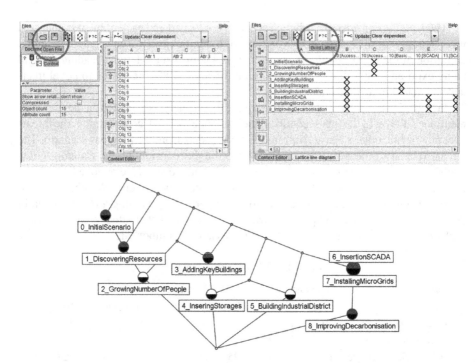

Fig. 2. Steps to build a graphical lattice with *ConExp* FCA tool: loading file, showing components, and depicting the hierarchical relationships among scenarios

6   Concluding Remarks

Tackling evolution of Smart Cities as main challenge, within the IRENE project we identified a threat analysis methodology that was implemented into a tool. *This paper described the tool above, complementing the live demonstration of the threat analysis tool that will be performed at the workshop IRENE @ SmartGift 2017.* Concisely, the novelty of the tool we presented relies in (i) identifying new threats that can arise from the addition of new components, (ii) build formal threats-scenarios and scenario-scenario relationships, and (iii) propose suitable high-level mitigations.

We lastly underline that the usefulness of the tool – which is assessed based on feedbacks of users as presented in [9] - are strictly related to the set of threats and mitigations that are chosen. For example, depending on the targeted scenario, a list of threats containing more threats due to physical attacks can be more representative than the IRENE list, which is mainly based on threats to cybersecurity.

Acknowledgments. This work has been partially supported by the projects JPI Urban Europe IRENE, FP7-ICT-2013-10-610535 AMADEOS and FP7-IRSES DEVASSES.

References

1. Grid, NIST Smart. Guide for Conducting Risk Assessments. Special Publication 800-30, September 2012
2. Jung, O., et al.: Towards a collaborative framework to improve urban grid resilience. In: 2016 IEEE International Energy Conference (ENERGYCON), Leuven, pp. 1–6 (2016)
3. IRENE, D2.1 – Threat Identification and Ranking (2015). http://ireneproject.eu/public-deliverables/
4. Mori, M., Ceccarelli, A., Zoppi, T., Bondavalli, A.: On the impact of emergent properties on SoS security. In: 2016 11th System of Systems Engineering Conference (SoSE), Kongsberg, pp. 1–6 (2016)
5. Ayewah, N., et al.: Using FindBugs on production software. In: Companion to the 22nd ACM SIGPLAN Conference on Object-Oriented Programming Systems and Applications Companion (2007)
6. ConExp. https://code.google.com/archive/p/colibri-java
7. IRENE project, Improving the Robustness of Urban Electricity Networks. http://ireneproject.eu/
8. Ganter, B., Wille, R., Wille, R.: Formal Concept Analysis. Springer, Heidelberg (1999)
9. Alexandr, V., et al.: Towards security requirements: iconicity as a feature of an informal modeling language. In: 3rd International Workshop on Requirements Engineering for Self-Adaptive and Cyber Physical Systems (RESACS) (2017, to appear)

A Tool that Uses Demand Side Management for Planning the Grid Response to Outages

Sandford Bessler[✉], Daniel Hovie, and Oliver Jung

Austrian Institute of Technology (AIT), Donau-City 1, 1220 Vienna, Austria
sandford.bessler@ait.ac.at

Abstract. This work addresses the electric grid planning process in general and the outage response in particular. Using the advance control architecture of microgrids, we show that by planning for demand reduction in the microgrids, certain outages can be mitigated, without the need of additional local generation or islanding. We describe the load models, their outage behavior and present the results in a case study.

Keywords: Grid planning · Grid outage response · Energy flexibility · Demand management · Microgrid control · CEMS controller

1 Introduction

The reliability of power supply is increasingly threatened both by natural disasters like floods, storms, earthquake, and by cyber attacks on the power grid.

The energy system stakeholders, such as city planners, facing budget constraints, need to decide which parts of the grid are (a) most vulnerable to various attacks and natural disasters and (b) most critical from a societal, economical, or functional point of view. In order to analyse the response to an outage they first need a simulation environment in which different buildings can be plugged in as electrical loads, generators, storage, etc. One first step in this direction is presented in the work conducted in the JPI Urban Europe project IRENE[1].

IRENE has developed a methodology for the city planners and other stakeholders to address systematically the threats on the grid operation and to find ways to prevent a part of them (especially the cyber attacks). In case an outage is inevitable, as in the case of a natural disaster, one way would be to provide power supply backup for certain islands, another approach would supply only the critical demand, or a combination of the two. In Fig. 1 the general planning process and the tools developed in IRENE are mentioned.

In this work we propose a demand reduction approach in order to deal with a certain type of outages due to power interruption. This planning approach is supported by the Microgrid Evaluation Tool (MGE) that is described in the following by means of a use case study and simulation results.

---

[1] This work was partially supported by the JPI Urban Europe initiative through the IRENE project.

© ICST Institute for Computer Sciences, Social Informatics and Telecommunications Engineering 2017
E.T. Lau et al. (Eds.): SmartGIFT 2017, LNICST 203, pp. 212–222, 2017.
DOI: 10.1007/978-3-319-61813-5_21

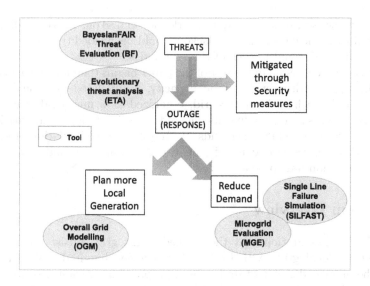

Fig. 1. IRENE planning process and tool overview

2   Types of Outage and Outage Response

A number of previous works describe the anatomy of power outages in the grid, stressing the cascading effect of outages leading to blackouts [11,12]. A well-known method is to simulate single-line contingencies, i.e. the outage of one of transmissions or main distribution power lines.

Not all the outages manifest themselves by transmission line interruption; power plants, substations and SCADA systems may also be damaged or attacked. At the edges of the grid, so called Microgrids [1] have the capability to disconnect from the main grid (islanding). Planning a microgrid against total loss of power includes adding dispatchable local generation. Once the outage is detected, the microgrid goes in islanding mode and the generators ramp up their power. A detailed grid resilience study in the New York state [9] estimated that the costs of migration to a microgrid with islanding capability, including backup generators (during an outage) become higher than the benefits. However, conclude the authors, if the microgrid participates in demand response program, such that the peak demand is reduced, then less generation capacity is needed and the microgrid solution becomes economically feasible.

Several threats including natural disasters like floods, storms, earthquake, and cyber attacks, frequently result in the disconnection of a power line. This leads to a drop in the supply, not necessarily to a total loss of power. The single power line failure simulation is a known method to check the resilience of a grid. Following a link removal from the grid topology, the single line failure simulation tool (SILFAST) recalculates the power flows and provides information about the node voltages and line currents. Lines that exceed the nominal current (are overloaded) would trigger the circuit protection after some time and trip (disconnect), causing other lines to be overloaded and so on. This cascading effect observed during the emerging of a blackout could be avoided through immediate reduction of the demand in each of the grid nodes.

The use case discussed in the rest of the paper begins therefore with an outage caused by a partial drop in the supply capacity, as simulated with the developed SILFAST tool. Each node of the grid, organized as a microgrid, receives the outage alert and is able to reduce its demand. The simulation on microgrid level determines the new reduced demands. By repeating the simulation of different outages with the reduced demands, we can determine the nodes where local backup generation has to be added.

3   System Overview

We make the assumption that the studied smart grid consists of microgrids at its edge - local grids with loads between a few hundred kW and several MW. The microgrid architecture has been proposed in previous research due to its advanced control mechanisms for local generators (DER), to its flexibility, reliability and islanding capability [1,3,5].

Few works have studied, however, the impact of Demand Side Management on the microgrid operation during long lasting outages. Using the classification in [3] we adopted a secondary control centralized architecture, in which the time horizon is in the range of a few hours, that is, significantly larger than for primary control systems.

The control system in Fig. 2 covers only the microgrid level and consists of the microgrid (MG) controller and a number of customer energy management controllers (CEMS) associated to each of the buildings in the microgrid.

In the current approach controllers use flexibility information, demand management and scheduling to cope with the changes in the power supply caused by an outage [4]. The flexibility concept applies to those loads which are tolerant (in certain limits) to an increase, decrease or shift in time, such as a thermostat controlled cooling, a battery charging, etc. The idea is to let other systems, energy providers, aggregators know (and pay for) this information. Demand Side Management (DSM) includes mechanisms based on flexibility, price information, or direct load control, that allow external actors to modify the demand of a consumer.

For the realisation of the control loop, the Model Predictive Control (MPC) technique [2,6] is used, meaning that the power consumption (and generation) is predicted for a certain time horizon (e.g. six hours), however the actuation is performed only for the next period. The MPC mechanism is combined with the periodical exchange of flexibility information between controllers, see Fig. 2. Energy flexibility models exist in this system for HVAC (heating, ventilation, air conditioning), electric vehicle charging and battery storage. Each CEMS controller aggregates the flexibility of its assets and reports the resulted profile (during the time horizon) together with the planned consumption profile. The latter is the result of an optimization step, taking into consideration local goals,

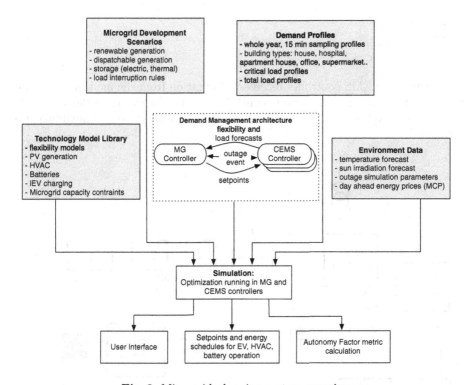

Fig. 2. Microgrid planning system overview

the desired load value from the MG controller perspective (called setpoint) and constraints from local assets.

The MG controller reads the latest flexibility and consumption plans from the CEMS and computes updated setpoints (for the whole time horizon). In case the CEMS proposed consumption is too high, the setpoint following objective in the CEMS optimization has the effect that some flexible loads are reduced (within their flexibility limits). For details, see [10].

3.1 Power and Energy Flexibility

Demand Side Management can be performed either through direct load control or through price signals. Direct load control needs however more information about each load flexibility, besides historical load profiles. For energy storage devices such as EV charging, home batteries, profile data is anyway not available. Therefore, we have developed models that predict the consumption and calculate the flexibility information. Power flexibility (minimum and maximum power in each time period) and energy flexibility (minimum and maximum) models are provided for the following appliance types: (see [7,10]).

- HVAC
- EV charging
- (home) battery

In Fig. 3 the EMS controller receives information from the models and static load profiles. As a result, various control variables for the local flexible loads are updated, and new values for PV generation, consumption and flexibility are estimated.

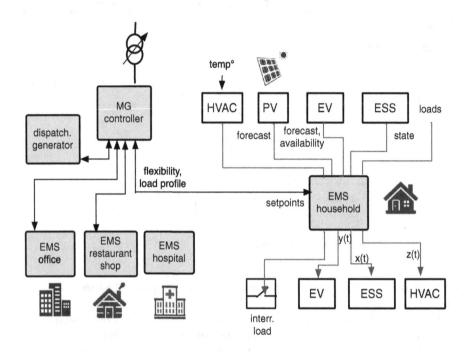

Fig. 3. Building model with its inputs and outputs

3.2 Demand Characterization

For the purpose of planning the consumption of a microgrid, both in normal operation and in outage mode, load profiles are the main source of information.

The EIA (Energy Information Administration) provides high qualitative annual consumption data on a hourly basis, for various climatic regions in the US. The Chicago area has been selected, as it seems to be the most similar to northern Europe.

Fortunately, the consumption data of residential and commercial buildings in [8] has been de-aggregated in the categories ventilation, cooling, heating, lights and equipment. To these categories we added model-based loads such as EV charging, home battery storage, as well as PV generation. The cooling/heating consumption has been modeled separately in order to exploit the flexibility due to heat storage. We used a simplified thermodynamic model of the building and thermostat based control. The HVAC models have been then calibrated to match the yearly consumption in the profiles.

The critical demand has to be defined for each building type in advance, and consists of loads and appliances that have to operate during an outage. The rest is interruptible load and will be discontinued during the outage. Here are some example (not all the appliances below have been modeled).

- partial lighting in houses, commercial places, industrial
- local controllers (e.g. CEMS), microgrid controller
- wireline communications (ICT infrastructure for control, internet) and WLAN, cellular nodes and antennas,
- cash dispensers and their communication infrastructure
- refrigerators in food stores, pharmacies, hospitals, storage houses.
- water pumps for district/town
- gasoline pumps in gas stations
- lifts and automatic doors in house blocks and commercial
- special buildings: hospital, pharmacy, police and fire stations
- gas-based space and water heating (needs electronics to operate).

Interruptible loads are by definition disconnected during an outage. Examples of interruptible loads in the household are: loads in the kitchen, entertainment, washing machine, vacuum cleaner, air conditioning, EV charging. In the EIA dataset and also throughout Europe, (depending on building type and climate region), space and water heating is often done with natural gas. Therefore, the visible electricity consumption during the summer due to air conditioning is higher than in winter.

In Fig. 4 the obtained critical consumption and the total consumption are depicted for a house and a small office. In case of the house P_{in} is the total consumption, obtained by adding to the critical load (fan, light and equipment) the HVAC, EV charging and PV generation: $P_{in} = P_{critical} + P_{HVAC} + P_{EV} + P_{PV}$.

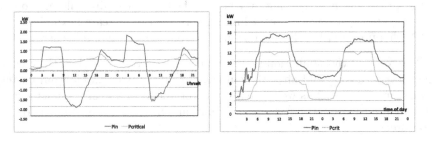

Fig. 4. Consumption profile examples: residential house (left), and small office (right)

Table 1. Summary of building characteristics

Building type	Size [sqm]	Critical: fan (f), ICT (i), light (l)	Interruptible:	PV kWp
Residential flats	3100	f, i, l	HVAC, EV	
Small office	511	f, i, l	HVAC	8
Residential house	250	f, i, l, battery	HVAC, EV	5
Supermarket	4180	refrig., f, i, j		
Clinic	3804	f, i, l, HVAC		
Battery 100 kWh		x		

4 Microgrid Evaluation Tool Operating Modes

The MGE Tool is an event based simulation of the interacting CEMS controllers and the MG controller. Each HVAC, EV, and battery load model in a building produces at each iteration an updated load prediction and flexibility information which is combined with the "static" load profile. The CEMS optimization updates the local control actions. On the MG controller side, the optimization of the load "distribution" consists of the setpoint update for each building controller.

Once an outage event is received by the controllers in the microgrid, each CEMS controller activates certain rules concerning the critical/interruptible load classification. The rules can be restrictive or more relaxed, depending on the energy balance, i.e. the amount of dispatchable generation available and the societal needs in the different building types. In Table 1 columns 3 and 4 indicate the load types defined as critical and as interruptible.

- economic, price dependent criteria are disabled in the CEMS optimization, the load profiles still must follow the setpoints and keep the strict balance between supply and demand, as mentioned in [1].
- shedding the PV generation is not allowed, the PV output is maximized.
- interruptible loads are disconnected.
- the air conditioning/heating may be switched off in certain buildings to save energy. In any case thermostat limits are relaxed to increase flexibility.
- EV charging is either disabled or may use only local renewable energy.

The result of the simulation is the detailed load profile of each of the components before, during and after the outage. Generation (renewable) and battery storage are considered as well. Finally, the total load profile of the microgrid is computed during a particular outage situation, outage duration, time and date of occurence.

5 Case Study

In this section we use a benchmark grid, the IEEE 14-node test topology in Fig. 5. The original capacity of 280 MW has been scaled down, and each of the

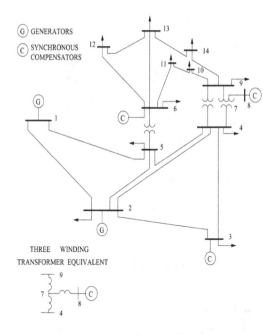

G GENERATORS

C SYNCHRONOUS COMPENSATORS

THREE WINDING
TRANSFORMER EQUIVALENT

Node	Type	Pgen	Qgen	P$_{LOAD}$	P$_{REDUCED}$
1	3	2.32	0.0	0.00	0.000
2	2	0.40	0.0	0.217	**0.160**
3	2	0.00	0.0	0.942	**0.550**
4	0	0.00	0.0	0.478	**0.250**
5	0	0.00	0.0	0.076	0.076
6	2	0.00	0.0	0.112	0.112
7	0	0.00	0.0	0.00	0.000
8	2	0.00	0.0	0.00	0.000
9	0	0.00	0.00	0.295	**0.200**
10	0	0.00	0.00	0.090	0.090
11	0	0.00	0.00	0.035	0.035
12	0	0.00	0.00	0.061	0.061
13	0	0.00	0.00	0.135	0.135
14	0	0.00	0.00	0.149	0.149

Fig. 5. Left: Selected overall grid topology. Right: Loads in the adapted 14-Node test grid

Failed line	Overloaded lines (regular bus loads) current [kA]	Overloaded lines (at reduced load)
No failure	1-2:3.5	
1-2	1-5: 5.6, 4-5: 2.8, 5-6: 2.1	1-5: 3.5
1-5	1-2:5.4	
2-3	1-5:2.2, 3-4:2.4, 5-6:2.1	
2-4	1-5:2.2, 2-3:2.1	
2-5	1-5:2.2	
3-4	2-3:2.3	
4-5	5-6:2.2	
4-7		
4-9	5-6:2.4	5-6: 2.26
5-6	4-5:2.4	
6-11		
6-12		
6-13		
7-8		
7-9		
9-10		
9-14		
10-11		
12-13		
13-14		

Fig. 6. Results of SILFAST - the contingency test

nodes can be populated with a microgrid, such that the loads correspond to P_{load} values in Fig. 5.

As mentioned in Sect. 2, running the single line failure tool (SILFAST) is used to perform contingency tests [13]. It simulates a grid capacity reduction, because the load remains the same but the capacity is reduced due to outage of

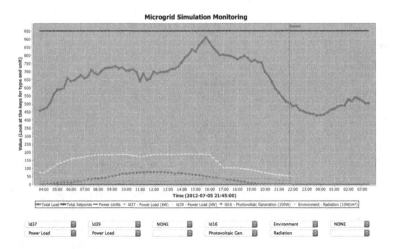

Fig. 7. Node3, Microgrid net consumption, normal simulation

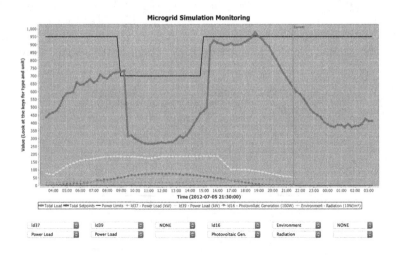

Fig. 8. Node3, Microgrid net consumption, outage simulation (6 h)

one distribution line. As a result, several other lines are overloaded as we can see in column two of Fig. 6.

It is assumed that the microgrids, which consist in our case of a set of buildings, are associated to the respective nodes. In Fig. 5 the total nominal load of the nodes is shown. For the demand reduction we selected the largest nodes 2, 3, 4 and 9. The other nodes do not reduce their load during an outage.

The MGE Tool is being used to determine the reduced load. Figure 7 shows the total load of Node 3 in normal operation mode and in case of an outage between 9 am to 3 pm, see Fig. 8. The user interface allows to select single CEMS or components (EV, PV generation, battery) to be displayed during the run. On the right of actual simulation time, the predicted load values are updated each iteration, and corrected so that they do not exceed the setpoint values.

With the obtained reduced load values, the single line failure simulation is run again. The results can be seen in of Fig. 6. In the 3rd column, most overload situations disappeared, only two overloaded lines 1–5 and 5–6 remain, a situation which could be improved for example by adding local generation at node 5.

6 Concluding Remarks and Further Work

In this work we addressed the outage response of a microgrid entity, from an energy management perspective. The approach is generic: it provides a framework for configuring different type of consumer (buildings) with a number of flexible loads: thermal and electric storage, renewable generation, in addition to a precise classification of interruptible and critical loads in every building.

The developed simulation tool makes use of course of a particular demand side management algorithm (described in detail in [10]), which could however be replaced with another one.

The simulation result depends heavily on the consumption profiles and the distinction between critical and interruptible consumption that has to be made for each scenario. To the critical loads we count ICT systems which include the controller, the internet connection and various wireline and wireless communication systems. Although entertainment equipment is not necessarily critical, a functioning internet radio and TV are crucial in emergency situations. Additional outage rules can been configured in the model, in case for instance air conditioning or EV charging should be enabled during an outage.

Dispatchable generation can be planned complementarily or in combination with DSM. More case studies have to be made in order to determine the feasibility and costs of DSM in comparison with backup generation.

Using Demand Side Management together with rules for critical load identification for planning an outage response is helpful only if such a scheme can work similarly in practice and if it is economically viable. The CEMS and MG controllers are real software components working on historical profile data. The problem in a real setting is the delay between the outage event and the load reduction, see Fig. 8. Currently, this delay is due to the sampling time (15 min) and needs to be reduced substantially in a practical realisation of the proposed scheme.

Concerning the implementation costs, DSM comes with a higher costs both for planning and for the operation of control and communication systems in the microgrids. Moreover, in order to control the critical and the interruptible loads, changes in the electric wiring in each building have to be performed. However, alternative solutions could be much more expensive [9].

References

1. Lopes, J.A.P., Vasiljevska, J., Ferreira, R., Moreira, C., Madureira, A.: Advanced architectures and control concepts for more microgrids (2009)
2. Parisio, A., Rikos, E., Glielmo, L.: A model predictive control approach to microgrid operation optimization. IEEE Trans. Contr. Syst. Technol. **22**(5), 1813–1827 (2014)
3. Olivares, D.E., Mehrizi-Sani, A., Etemadi, A.H., Canizares, C., Iravani, R., Kazerani, M., Hajimiragha, A.H., Gomis-Bellmunt, O., Saeedifard, M., Palma-Behnke, R., Jimenez-Estevez, G., Hatziargyriou, N.D.: Trends in microgrid control. IEEE Trans. Smart Grid **5**(4), 1905–1919 (2014)
4. Lopes, J.P., Hatziargyriou, N., Mutale, J., Djapic, P., Jenkins, N.: Integrating distributed generation into electric power systems: a review of drivers, challenges and opportunities. Electr. Power Syst. Res. **77**(9), 1189–1203 (2007)
5. Katiraei, F., Iravani, M.R., Lehn, P.W.: Microgrid autonomous operation during and subsequent to islanding process. IEEE Trans. Power Delivery **20**(1), 248–257 (2005)
6. Chen, C., Wang, J., Heo, Y., Kishore, S.: MPC-based appliance scheduling for residential building energy management controller. IEEE Trans. Smart Grid **4**(3), 1401–1410 (2013)
7. Bessler, S., Drenjanac, D., Hasenleithner, E., Ahmed-Khan, S., Silva, N.: Using flexibility information for energy demand optimization in the low voltage grid. In: SmartGreens Conference, Lisbon, Portugal (2015)
8. US Energy Information Administration, CBECS. http://www.eia.gov/consump tion/commercial/data/2012/
9. Cuomo, A.M., et al.: Microgrids for critical facility resiliency in New York state. Final report, New York State Energy Research and Development Authority (2014)
10. Bessler, S., Jung, O.: Energy management in microgrids with flexible and interruptible loads. In: Innovative Smart Grid Technologies Conference (ISGT), pp. 1–6. IEEE Power & Energy Society, IEEE, September 2016
11. Albasrawi, M.N., Jarus, N., Joshi, K.A., Sarvestani, S.S.: Analysis of reliability and resilience for smart grids. In: 2014 IEEE 38th Annual Computer Software and Applications Conference (COMPSAC), pp. 529–534. IEEE, July 2014
12. Estebsari, A., Pons, E., Huang, T., Bompard, E.: Techno-economic impacts of automatic undervoltage load shedding under emergency. Electr. Power Syst. Res. **131**, 168–177 (2016)
13. Ejebe, G.C., Wollenberg, B.F.: Automatic contingency selection. IEEE Trans. Power Apparatus Syst. **PAS-98**(1), 97–109 (1979)

An Overall Grid Modelling Tool for Modelling Smart Grids

Eng Tseng Lau$^{(\boxtimes)}$, Kok Keong Chai, and Yue Chen

Queen Mary University of London, Mile End Road, London E1 4NS, UK
{e.t.lau,michael.chai,yue.chen}@qmul.ac.uk

Abstract. The strategic positioning of new grid components may enhance the resiliency of a city to electricity outages, thus improve the quality of life that meets residents' needs. However, the cost and resilience associated to the grid are the two conflicting goals. This paper presents a user-interface-based Overall Grid Modelling (OGM) tool that allows city-level stakeholders to manipulate and control the tool for grid planning purposes. The OGM tool provides stakeholders the demonstration of cost and resilience needed to analyse the impact of altering the grid components, and through the normal and islanded operation (the penetration of microgrid).

Keywords: Grid planning · Grid resilience · Overall grid modelling tool · Smart grid

1 Introduction

An initial comprehensive holistic approach of a supply, demand and load balancing optimisation module was developed for grid distribution planning purposes [1]. The optimisation model allows the full integration of the wholesale electricity market price, distributed generators (renewable and non-renewable), battery storages, and the inclusion of outage events. The optimisation model is based on a cost minimisation function with the determination of economic balancing the output of generation units (economic dispatch and unit commitment). The outage event is included to evaluate the capability of the grid to sustain the outage through the isolation from the main grid and operation in islanded mode, or by isolating grid portions and dropping the load (normal grid-connected operation for unaffected grid nodes). The ability to sustain the islanded operation allows the resilience evaluation of the urban grid.

Even though numbers of tools exist to model grids as summarised in [2], they lack important features to enable an interactive analysis, especially the graphical user interfaces that allows stakeholders to manipulate and control the grid. Besides, having user interface enables the interactions with less experienced stakeholders. Therefore, an Overall Grid Modelling (OGM) tool is developed. The OGM tool is based on the integrated methodology and policy developed from the earlier IRENE deliverable [1,3]. The tool development is based on the

© ICST Institute for Computer Sciences, Social Informatics and Telecommunications Engineering 2017
E.T. Lau et al. (Eds.): SmartGIFT 2017, LNICST 203, pp. 223–232, 2017.
DOI: 10.1007/978-3-319-61813-5_22

agile process, where the processes of specification, design, implementation and testing are concurrent, and as an iterative approach. The tool is developed in a series of increments where the user (stakeholder) will evaluate each increment and make proposals for later increments. The OGM tool aims to account the effects of grid planning that may benefit the city, for instance, through the introduction of renewable energy sources. The OGM tool enables the interactive feature that allows the decision makers (city-level stakeholders) to manipulate/control the OGM tool and varieties of analysis results across the grid are illustrated whenever a modification within the grid component is applied.

Overall, the OGM tool was developed for project IRENE [4,5], which accounts the collaborative city planning within multiple city-level stakeholders for resilient energy management. Project IRENE determines the better alternatives to mitigate vulnerabilities of urban electricity grids by utilizing the decentralized generation and smart control. This is to ensure availability of power supply for critical infrastructures are prioritized to enable minimal viable operation during large scale power outages or shortages.

This paper presents the context of the OGM methodology developed in [6] and further demonstrates the OGM tool at the IRENE workshop as part of the 2nd EAI International Conference on Smart Grid Inspired Future Technologies (SmartGIFT 2017).

The organisation of the paper is as follows. Section 2 presents the design of the OGM tool. Section 3 demonstrates the OGM tool user interface. Section 4 presents example analysis of grid simulations using the OGM tool. Section 5 concludes.

2 Design of the OGM Tool

The earlier developed optimisation module [1] automatically optimises the load during grid-connected or islanded operation. The optimisation problem is typically the economic dispatch in the combination of unit commitment problem comprising the distributed generators and energy storages. Both problems are associated with the amount of electrical power production problems.

With the implementation of the optimisation module into the OGM tool, the users are able to manipulate/control the tool and to calculate changes whenever a new case/scenario is applied (for instance, adding or remove an alternate generation sources). The tool does not only supports the simulation of electricity continuity planning from the technical perspective, but also ensures the cost concerned through the interventions for benefits of business planning [7].

The user interface of the OGM is developed using IntelliJ IDEA, the Java IDE software. For the numerical optimisation algorithm in Java, the dual-simplex algorithm is applied for such Linear Programming problem of the grid optimisation. The lp solve 5.5.2.3 [8] is applied as the library file for Java that is called to perform the numerical optimisation for the OGM tool.

Figure 1 shows the workflow of the OGM system. The system starts by allowing users to define the components inside the grid (selection of consumer and

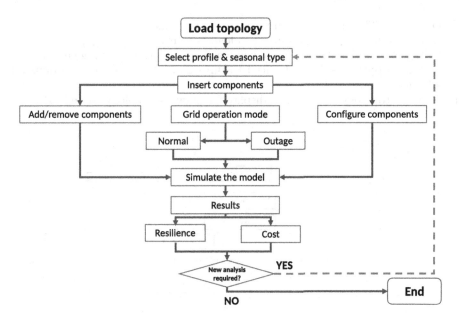

Fig. 1. The workflow of the OGM system.

seasonal profiles, addition, configuration and removal of grid components), and applying the grid operation mode (normal or outage simulation). The grid components are those associated with the electricity network system (consumers, generation sources, point of coupling nodes (transformers)). Once the input settings are accomplished, the optimisation algorithm is performed/simulated. A new output simulation window will report on cost of savings based on optimised generation costs, the resilience metric of the network during the islanded operation. If new analysis is required, the user can navigate to the input window to reconfigure the grid components easily.

3   The OGM Tool Interface

The user interface of the tool at the first instance is shown in Fig. 2. Figure 2 shows the clear user interface input window as before the user loads the network topology and configures the component specifications. Based on Fig. 2, the input user interface of the OGM tool consists of:

a. Status window - The status window explaining the progress of the overall simulation configured by the user;
b. Seasonal profile - The toggle selection of summer or winter seasonal demand profile;
c. Demand profile - The toggle selection of demand profile either the demand data adopted from the public domain, or the reduced-demand profile demand management capability;

d. Optimise - The action button to perform the numerical simulation;
e. Load system - The action button to load the network topology;
f. Outage simulation - The outage window for simulation of outage events;
g. Advanced options - The advanced features and additional input options for advanced users;
h. Network topology - The input display for network topology to be loaded.

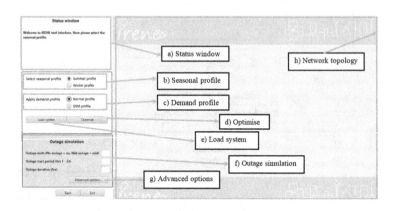

Fig. 2. The user interface input window of the OGM tool.

3.1   The Grid Topology and the Component Settings

In the input window, the user will select the type of seasonal and demand profile as before loading the network/grid topology. As outlined in [1], the IEEE 14-bus tree is used as the fundamental representation of grid architectural topology. The network topology presenting the integration of the grid and microgrid-connected is necessary. Such topology is implemented in this case as the main user interface for grid modelling and simulation, where the user can manipulate the whole integration of the grid (without altering the nodes/buses as constructed).

The IEEE 14-bus tree network topology is loaded as shown in Fig. 3, where the topology consists of low-level microgrid connections, mid-level lines and a high-voltage line.

The next step involves the step of adding grid components (the generating and consuming components) and configuring the components. Figure 4 demonstrates an example of adding the 'Household' profile component into the input model. Figure 5 illustrates the configuration settings for the consumers, and generation for generators, renewables and energy storages. Specification settings for consumers and generations are provided by default and the user can apply the additional specifications provided for further simulations. Those settings can be modified if the user wishes to supply additional information of the generation settings that ensures the scalability of the modelled grid architecture (for instance, the generating capacity is sufficient to supply the overall demand when new components are added).

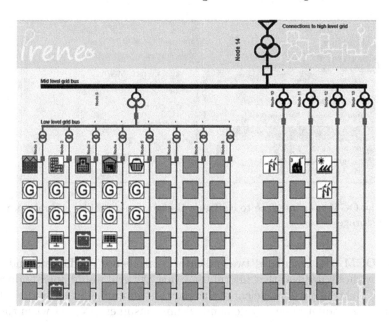

Fig. 3. OGM input user interface of the IEEE network topology. (Color figure online)

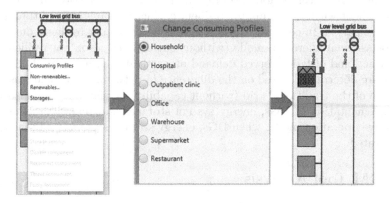

Fig. 4. The OGM user interface in adding a component.

3.2 Outage Simulation

In default configuration, if no outage is introduced in the input model, the OGM tool will apply the normal mode of simulation without outage. For the case of single node of failure/branch or a complete failure in a grid (N-1 compliance), the configuration is adjusted as illustrated in Fig. 3, where the outage is introduced in Node 2 by opening up the circuit breaker (green colour block is changed to red colour) in Node 2. The outage period and duration are set in the input outage simulation window (Fig. 2).

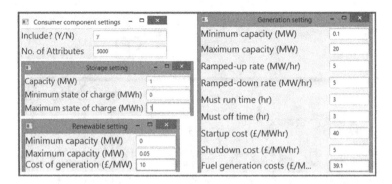

Fig. 5. The OGM user interface to configure the consumer profile, generation, renewable and storage settings.

The OGM tool calculates two indicators - resilience coefficients and costs (with or without savings) that inform users how the grid would operate during a blackout. The resilience coefficient in this paper is computed based on the extents in which the amount of energy demand within consumers are met when there is an outage in the grid [9]. The resilient coefficient is determined as the mean fraction of the demand served for the outage node divided by the overall demand. A grid is resilient when the computed resilient coefficient is maintained throughout the outage period. In contrast, the grid is considered as 'not resilient' during the business-as-usual operation mode (without outage) and also, 'not resilient' due to the fractional of failed served demand at particular outage period. The cost savings are determined based on the difference in between the business-as-usual operation of the traditional grid (without capability of islanding, and also without implementation of DGs, energy system storages and renewables), and the alternative operation mode, when DGs, energy storage systems and renewables are activated.

4   OGM Tool Analysis

This section explains the OGM tool analysis that performs the simulation for each indicated scenarios. The network topology of Fig. 3 is considered. Such topology has been applied in various IRENE's gaming simulation exercises and stakeholder workshops [10]. From Fig. 3, Nodes 1–5 consist the small-scale generations (back-up generations, PV panels and battery storages) and the loads (households, offices, hospitals, warehouses and supermarkets), while Nodes 10–14 consist of the mid-scale generation sources. Finally, Node 14 is the connection to the rest of the grids. The distribution of load profiles in this case is not intended to include the profiles of commercial services (e.g. hospitals, offices) and domestic households within the same bus. However, the variety of commercial services within a same node is still possible. Additionally, most of the commercial services are connected with their own substation due to the huge amount of loads required.

Two types of grid operations are simulated the normal and outage operation. The normal operation is accomplished when no outage occurs. However, the so-called 'economic-islanding' is operating in the normal mode where the small-scale generations automatically discharges energy within the microgrid level when the overall electricity market price is high. In this case the entire microgrid level is isolated from the mid and high level grid and self-capability of islanding operation is performed. The outage operation, in contrast, is triggered when there is an outage occurs within the low level nodes, or the complete grid outage. Two different operation modes are chosen in order to examine the resilience of the city in sustaining the normal and outage effects on the changes of the supply towards the demand profile across individual consumer and the overall demand, as well as the changes in the monetary savings and resilient coefficient in the grid level city.

4.1 Case 1 - Normal operation

In this case, assuming no failure occurs, the normal mode of operation is applied. The distributions of the overall demand, the cost savings and battery storage load are presented in Fig. 6. Cost savings are achieved (£964.05 within 24 h of simulated time) particularly for 'economic-islanding' normal mode of grid operations. The resilience coefficients are all zeros. This is because the grid resilience is not considered during the normal mode of operation (without any outage events). The battery storage also shows the capability of discharging (generating) energy to the consumers at time of high electricity price, and recharge at low-peak electricity price. The simulation, however, excludes the addition of installation and maintenance costs of individual generators.

4.2 Case 2 - Outage operation

In this example, outage event is triggered in Node 2 as configured in Fig. 3, at 0900 in the morning, with six hours of outage duration. The 'economic-islanding' capability is disabled in the case of outage events. Figure 7 shows the result of the outage simulation of the overall demand and its deviated demand during the outage, the plot of cost savings, the battery load, and the resilient coefficient. It can be seen that in order to compensate the deviation of outage loads, £1386.65 additional costs are required. The amount of cost saving is highly dependent on the distribution of consuming and generating components configured by users, the state of operation within small-scale generations, and the outage durations. The amount of cost saving in this case is the optimised amount of cost that reduces the cost of damages during the outages. In this case all loads are served during the outage events. Therefore, computed resilience coefficients are maintained in this case.

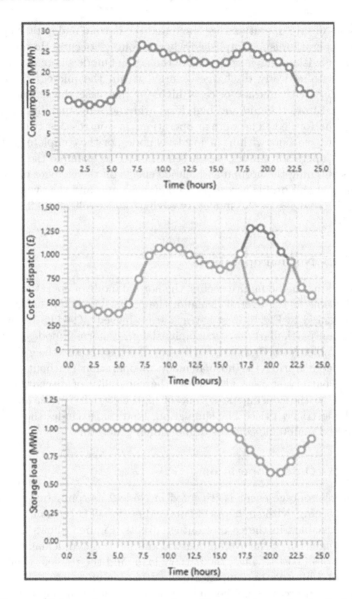

Fig. 6. The overall demand, monetary costs and battery storage load calculated for the grid during the normal operation: top panel - overall grid demand; middle panel - plot of monetary savings in relation to the business-as-usual (red plot) and the optimised solution (orange plot); bottom panel - battery storage load. (Color figure online)

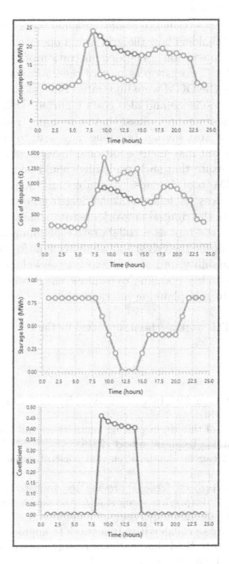

Fig. 7. The overall demand, monetary costs, battery storage load and resilience coefficient calculated for the grid during the outage operation: first panel - the overall grid demand without outage (red plot) and the outage demand (orange plot); second panel - plot of monetary savings in relation to the business-as-usual (red plot) and the optimised solution (orange plot); third panel - battery storage load; bottom panel - the distribution of resilience coefficient (Color figure online).

5   Conclusion

This paper presents a user-interface-based OGM tool that allows city-level stakeholders to manipulate/control the tool for grid planning purposes. The OGM tool calculates two indicators - resilience coefficients and costs (with or without savings) that inform stakeholders how the grid would operate at different situations (normal and islanded operation). The demonstration of the OGM tool will be performed at the IRENE workshop as part of the 2nd SmartGIFT 2017.

Types of inputs to the OGM were illustrated that allow stakeholders to evaluate the overall grid resilience and also costs incurred. Different cases (normal and islanded operations) were presented that showed the trade-off in between the resilient coefficient and cost savings (e.g. one may wish to achieve the resilience of electricity network but may incur additional investments). The OGM tool is therefore needed to ensure that such trade-offs should be minimised.

Overall, the OGM tool intends to enable an interactive analysis with user-interface experiences for fellow stakeholders from diverse background (for instance, city planners, distributed network operators and grid system operator) to be available to use the tool as a collaborative planning for a city-level grid. The target future work for the OGM tool shall account for the meshed-network analysis, the grid scalability and a complete business-planning model in addition to electricity continuity planning to examine the detailed monetary costs of different approaches in grid planning interactively.

Acknowledgment. This work has been supported by the JPI Urban Europe IRENE.

References

1. IRENE. D3.1–system architecture design, supply demand model and simulation. Technical report (2016)
2. IRENE. D5.1–state-of-the art in gaming simulations and stakeholder workshops for method evaluation. Technical report (2016)
3. IRENE. D2.2–root causes identification and societal impact analysis. Technical report (2016)
4. JPI Urban Europe project. Irene improving the robustness of urban electricity network (2014–2017). http://ireneproject.eu/. Accessed 6 Dec 2016
5. Jung, O., Bessler, S., Ceccarelli, A., Zoppi, T., Vasenev, A., Montoya, L., Clarke, T., Chappell, K.: Towards a collaborative framework to improve urban grid resilience. In: Proceedings of 2016 IEEE International Energy Conference (ENERGYCON), 4–8 April, pp. 1–6. IEEE (2016)
6. IRENE. D4.1–toolsets of supply demand prediction and threat identifications and security classification. Technical report (2017)
7. International Electrotechnical Commision (IEC). White paper - microgrids for disaster preparedness and recovery with electricity continuity and systems. Technical report, IEC WP Microgrids, Switzerland (2014)
8. lp_solve. Introduction to lp_solve 5.5.2.5 (2015). http://www.lpsolve.sourceforge.net/5.5/. Accessed 19 Oct 2016
9. Bollinger, L.A.: Fostering climate resilient electricity infrastructure (2015). http://repository.tudelft.nl/islandora/object/uuid:d45aea59-a449-46ad-ace1-3254529c05f4/datastream/OBJ/download. Accessed 6 Dec 2016
10. IRENE. D5.2–evaluation method design, evaluation of irene methods, collaboration framework and modelling tool. Technical report (2017)

A Modeling Framework to Support Resilient Evolution Planning of Smart Grids

Tommaso Zoppi[1](✉), Sandford Bessler[2], Andrea Ceccarelli[1],
Edward Lambert[3], Eng Tseng Lau[4], and Alexandr Vasenev[5]

[1] University of Florence, Viale Morgagni 65, Florence, Italy
{tommaso.zoppi,andrea.ceccarelli}@unifi.it
[2] Austrian Institute of Technology, Donau-City-Straße 1, 1220 Vienna, Austria
sandford.bessler@ait.ac.at
[3] EthosVO Ltd., Beech Road, Merstham, Surrey RH1 3AE, UK
edward.lambert@ethosvo.org
[4] Queen Mary University of London, Mile End, London E14 NS, UK
e.t.lau@qmul.ac.uk
[5] University of Twente, Drienerlolaan 5, 7522 NB Enschede, The Netherlands
a.vasenev@utwente.nl

Abstract. Cyber security is becoming more and more relevant with the advent of large-scale systems made of independent and autonomous constituent systems that interoperate to achieve complex goals. To ensure security of cyber-physical systems, it is important to analyze identified threats and their possible consequences. In case of smart grids as an example of a complex system, threats can result in power outages that damage the continuous supply of energy that is required from critical infrastructures. Therefore, city planners must take into account security requirements when organizing the power grid, including demand-side management techniques able to mitigate the adverse effects of outages, ultimately improving grid resilience. This paper presents a modeling framework developed within the IRENE project that brings together methodologies, policies and a toolset to evaluate and measure the resilience of the targeted smart grid. This will support stakeholders and city planners in their activities, specifically the resilient evolution planning of Smart Grids.

Keywords: Threat analysis · Smart grids · Evolution · Resilience · City Planning · Power flow equations · Demand side management · IRENE

1 Planning for Resilience

This paper describes the modelling framework that was developed within the IRENE project [18]. This framework aggregates methodologies, policies and the toolset to evaluate the resilience of the targeted smart grid. The framework will be used to investigate threats in the smart grid and to implement the identified solutions. Based on the smart grid topology, possible outages and risk analyses, the framework provides a way to support city planners in their decisions. The usage of the modeling framework is then regulated by [19], which traces the bounds of the interaction among different users e.g., generic stakeholders, DNOs, city planners, regulators.

© ICST Institute for Computer Sciences, Social Informatics and Telecommunications Engineering 2017
E.T. Lau et al. (Eds.): SmartGIFT 2017, LNICST 203, pp. 233–242, 2017.
DOI: 10.1007/978-3-319-61813-5_23

The framework includes tools performing an extensive threat analysis that leads to the identification of possible root causes of outages (kill chains, [13]), which are then simulated to estimate the capabilities of the grid to supply its components also when an outage happens. Further, different mitigation methods are integrated into the framework to enable users to evaluate the efficiency of fault and attack mitigation measures, the energy resilience outcomes, and the impact on critical infrastructures.

More in detail, this paper summarizes all the tools developed within the IRENE project [18] and devises a strategy and a workflow to integrate them in a unique framework. This gives a final output that summarizes the results of the single tools, ultimately providing resilience metrics of the investigated smart grid that are built taking into account all the technical contributions of IRENE. The document focuses on: (i) the integration of disconnected tools within the IRENE modeling framework by providing a workflow for the consequent usage of such tools, and (ii) the validation of such integration, using a case study in which we executed the tools according to the workflow above.

The document is structured as follows. Section 2 summarizes all the inputs of the modeling framework, while Sect. 3 defines the tools that were developed within the project. For each tool, we report a description of its functioning and its interfaces. In Sect. 4, we define the workflow that integrates all the single tools supporting the open modeling framework, which is finally executed in Sect. 5 by applying the workflow on a simple smart grid scenario based on the IEEE 14 node grid topology.

2   Inputs of the Modeling Framework

In this section, we report the main inputs that the user must provide to exercise the modeling framework. More in detail, this inputs are needed for the execution of the tools constituting the toolset that, together with the workflow (see Sect. 4) and some policies, defines the framework mentioned above.

Portfolio of Grid Changes (GC). In general, the IRENE project aims at investigating a specific (smart) grid scenario S. The grid scenario is mainly composed by a grid topology and assumptions about the city where the grid is installed. Scenarios can be updated based on long-term planning that relies on the knowledge of experienced city planners and other city-level stakeholders. At the same time, local and punctual intervention can be performed to improve the grid efficiency or to fix address some issues. Therefore, updates can be planned and implemented due to:

- Long-term planning of evolutions, defined by city planners in agreement with the relevant stakeholders. Municipalities may decide to invest money to make the energy distribution more resilient and efficient. Further, they may decide to modify governance e.g., opening the market to new DSOs, or promoting the *prosumers* (both producer and consumer) model;
- the inclusion of specific mitigation strategies to improve robustness and security in an existing part of the grid;

- the addition or removal of electric components to improve specific metrics related to the grid (e.g., a new direct power line between two buildings, new breaker, redundant hardware to improve fault tolerance).

List of Grid Components (CL). The list of components is based on the lists identified in [1, 2]. Moreover, novel components were identified in the process of the project, to guarantee a specific and realistic architectural description [4], supported by available datasets. The additional components consist mainly of commercial building types that allow a more realistic modelling of urban consumption. The characteristics of these buildings are described in [8].

Consumption Profiles (CP). According to the origin of the consumption data, we mainly distinguish between (i) *commercial* buildings, and (ii) *residential* buildings. Both the MGE and OGM tools (see Sect. 3) use the reference building models from the US Department of Energy (DoE). The dataset called "Commercial and Residential Hourly Load Profiles for all TMY3 Locations in the United States" is found under [9]. Since several consumption modules such as cooling, heating, ventilation, ICT etc. are available, new critical and interruptible consumption profiles are created. Flexible loads are added according to the configuration and where possible e.g. cooling, their output is calibrated to fit the profile. The household profile, instead, is taken from the *Elexon Ltd.* database, representing a normal household profile (categorized as *Profile Class 1* in the UK, with 24 h of consumption data [10]. Moreover, an important feature of these profiles is the possibility to aggregate the profiles forecast, which is accomplished through the active-aware-based *Ensemble Kalman Filter* (EnKF), first introduced in [7].

Threat List (TL). The threat list and the attacker profiles are defined in [1, 2]: starting from the NIST [3] guidelines, we built the IRENE list of 38 threats related to cyber-security that is used to define the disaster scenarios [2]. Each threat belongs to a category that is used to classify them depending on their characteristics (e.g., attack conduction, gathering information, accidental and environmental).

Outage Scenarios (OS). The threats that can affect a given grid scenario can be mitigated applying the techniques as presented in [1]. Indeed, (i) such mitigations may not be able to completely prevent the occurrence of the threat or negate its effects, or (ii) the effectiveness and efficacy of the identified mitigations may require further investigation. In fact, at this point, the extent they are able to mitigate the adverse effects of a threat is not analyzed or known a priori.

Specifically focusing on outages, we consider having an *outage scenario*, or rather the consequences of the happening of a threat that negatively impact the grid resulting in one or more outages. The expected duration of this outage is related to the specific source threat and grid scenario we are dealing with. Outage scenarios must be defined by Risk Assessment (RA) experts once the grid scenario is defined. Outage scenarios constitute one of the main dimensions of analysis to evaluate the resilience of the smart grid in presence of such detrimental events.

3   Tools Constituting the Modeling Framework

This section reports the tools that were built within IRENE that, together with methodology and policies, constitute the modeling framework. These tools have been already described in [5, 12–14]. We report a summary here for completeness.

Evolutionary Threat Analysis (ETA Tool). The threat analysis process described in [1] led to the implementation of an evolutionary threat analysis tool. In fact, the threat identification and analysis framework has been implemented into an integrated tool determining the variation of mitigation strategies and the scenario-based distribution analysis [5]. It makes use of the *Colibri-Java FCA API*[1] to analyze the distribution of threats. The tool takes as input the evolution steps defined in terms of evolutionary features and the mapping between threats and their high-level mitigation strategies [1], aiming at providing an actual list of mitigations depending on the current grid scenario, that is obtained merging the evolution steps with the initial grid scenario.

The analysis is evolutionary, meaning that the actual list of threats CT and mitigations is obtained starting from the previous result and considering the new evolution step that e.g., is defined by city planner. Each evolution step is composed of a set of grid changes (e.g., adding/removing a specific component) that can make the set of threats (and consequently mitigations) bigger or smaller. The tool takes the partial set of mitigations and modifies it considering the introduced changes.

Interfaces. (i) ETA: $S \times GC \times TL \rightarrow CT$.

BayesianFair Threat Evaluation (BF Tool). This tool allows numerical threat assessment based on the FAIR factors [12], namely Contact, Vulnerability, Action, and Control Strength. The numerical outputs given by *BayesianFAIR* can help to further rank threats in the same severity SE category (e.g. High or Very High), which is an extension of the FAIR framework [12]. This will be helpful to prioritize threats to assign the constraint security resources, especially in cases many threats are considered in the network [13]. In real scenarios, for each threat, we assume that security experts give input state for every factor. All the Bayesian parameters are obtained from the FAIR tables [16] as guided in the FAIR model and encoded to the tool. Although the parameters are fixed for this particular implementation, they can be updated manually if users want to assess based on different FAIR tables. The assessments of the tools are adjusted to always be in-line with the FAIR assessments.

Interfaces. (i) BF: $CT \times C \times A \times V \times CS \rightarrow SE$.

Single Line Failure Simulation (SILFAST Tool). This tool considers a mid-voltage grid topology in which the buses and branches characteristics are known (given). The loads on the buses are also given and they correspond to entire microgrids or low-voltage radial grids that are considered in detail in the MGE tool below. SILFAST analyses the response of the grid to single line (branch) failure. Line failures are frequent consequences of threats that can be either natural disasters (e.g., fires, floods,

---

[1] https://code.google.com/archive/p/colibri-java.

earthquakes, storms) or cyber-attacks, which could lead to opening line circuit breakers. If a line is disconnected, the power distribution takes place via the remaining lines, and since the loads remains the same, an overload situation is created on some of these lines. If not handled by disconnecting loads or adding generation, the lines will trip after some time creating cascading failures and leading to blackout.

The mechanism to determine this overload is to calculate power flows on the topology created by removing one branch and reporting overloaded links.

Interfaces. (i) SILFAST: S × OS × OL → GS(A).

MicroGrid Evaluation (MGE Tool). *Demand Side Management* (DSM) in micro-grids with flexible loads, distributed generation (DG) and storage has been already addressed previously [6]. However, few works have studied the DSM effect on the microgrid operation during long lasting outages. Using the classification in [6], we focus on a secondary control centralized architecture, in which the time horizon is minutes up to hours, therefore - significantly larger than for primary control systems.

Briefly, the MG controller reads the latest flexibility and consumption plans from the CEMS and computes updated set points (six-hour profiles). In case the proposed load is too high, it sheds certain demands within their flexibility limits. The tool uses certain demand optimization architecture, algorithms and control exchange messages between the MG controller and the building controllers (CEMS). The runs under different configurations produce the energy schedule prior and during the outage. The local control actions for each CEMS are reported, as well as the efficiency of generation, storage and load shifting. A user interface shows the evolution of different house parameters and variables during the simulation. Specific metrics are computed to the energy management performance [14] in a particular grid scenario.

Interfaces. (i) MGE: CP × OS → GS(A) x OL.

Overall Grid Modeling (OGM Tool). A complete holistic approach of a supply, demand and load balancing optimization module is developed for grid distribution planning purposes. The optimization model allows the full integration of the demand forecast, wholesale electricity market price, distributed generators (renewable and non-renewable), energy storage systems, and the perturbation of outage events. The demand forecast and assimilation is performed using the active-aware-based *Ensemble Kalman filter* (EnKF). The outage event is included to evaluate the resilience index RI of the grid, or rather its capability in sustaining the outage by isolating from the main

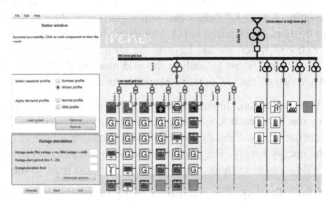

Fig. 1. Interface of the OGM tool

grid and operating in islanded mode, or by isolating grid portions and dropping the load (normal grid-connected operation for unaffected grid nodes). The ability of in sustaining the islanded operation generates a grid state GS, which can be normal GS(N) or anomalous GS(A), and allows the evaluation of the resilience of the urban grid.

The optimization module is performed using the *Matlab* software. The dual-simplex algorithm is applied for *the Linear Programming* (LP) problem of the microgrid optimization. Sensitivity analysis is also performed though the creation of different scenarios in order to evaluate the effectiveness of the grid optimization module. Then, the grid optimization model is implemented into a toolset in [11]. Such model is deployed into graphical user interface (see Fig. 1) using Java environment to allow users to manipulate and control the simulation of the toolset as developed based on the grid optimization model.

Interfaces. (i) OGM: S × CP → GS(N) (No RI without outage), (ii) OGM: S × CP × OS → GS(A), RI, (iii) OGM: S × CP × OS → GS(N), RI.

4   Workflow

We proceed with the description of the *workflow*, or rather the flow of information and actions that the user of the framework can follow to fully take advantage of the IRENE modeling framework. Since the diagram in Fig. 2 is quite complex, we painted with different colors the different phases of the flow. Starting from the upper left corner of the figure, the current grid scenario s is initialized with the grid scenario *is* given as input. Then, the process can start.

(Orange Blocks). We analyze the current grid scenario s looking for all the threats that can be identified using the *ETA* tool. This provides a set CT of current threats that is composed by local threats (LT), which can be mitigated taking actions affecting the single components, and outage threats OT, that instead can directly lead to outages and cannot simply be mitigated locally. The current threats are next estimated using the *BayesianFAIR* (BF) tool, which applies a probabilistic method to estimate a severity *se* of each threat depending on some inputs that are provided by RA experts. This produces a severity set SES that can be used to link each current threat with its estimated severity. All the LT threats can be mitigated according to the links between threats and mitigations summarized in [1]. Moreover, the availability of SES can help city planners to choose which threats have to be mitigated earlier. Once LTs are mitigated, the planner can choose to analyze the grid more in detail, looking at how the grid reacts when one of the OT actually generates an outage.

(Yellow Blocks). In particular, using the set of all the possible outage scenarios OSS we can map each OT to one or more outage scenario COS the current threat can generate e.g., a *Denial of Service* attack targeting a critical node of the grid can block the energy supply. For each of these outage scenarios *cos* we run the MGE and the OGM tools to evaluate the ability of the grid to react to these detrimental events.

(Green Blocks). The green steps in Fig. 2 deal with the evaluation of the response mitigation to an outage. The path to be followed in Fig. 2 depends on the outage type

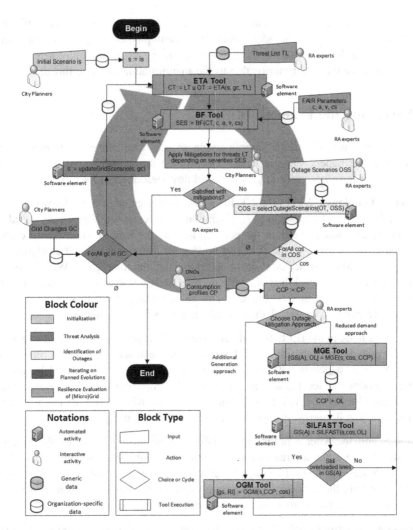

Fig. 2. The workflow constituting the IRENE modeling framework. (Color figure online)

and on the availability of techniques allowing demand side management. The choice is left to the RA expert, who knows the actual techniques installed in the grid and can decide for one path or another. Overall, the usage of reduced demand is preferable since it does not charge additional costs, which are instead required if the RA expert chooses to go for the additional generation path.

(Purple Blocks). Once all the outage scenarios related to s are investigated, we check if some grid changes are provided by the city planner. If he predicts several evolutions for its grid, he builds a non-empty GC set, that triggers a new analysis of the threats and the energy provision considering each grid change gc in GC (see purple boxes in Fig. 2). If GC is empty, or after examining all the changes in the set, the workflow ends. The result is a grid scenario after considering all the grid changes and in which all the mechanisms to mitigate the identified threats are implemented, guaranteeing energy provision to all the components of the grid according to their requirements also in presence of some outage scenarios due to the manifestation of some threats.

5   Exercising the Framework

In this section, we simulate a sample usage of the open modeling framework we described in the paper. More in detail, we provide the evaluation of a sample grid scenario using the tools according to the workflow described in Sect. 4.

Reference Topology. Within IRENE [4] it has been decided to use a known test grid network, the IEEE 14 node grid [17]. Each node represents a different micro-grid. To instantiate a case study, we built the generations and the load distributions of each of the micro-grids involved in the IEEE 14 node grid. Moreover, since the original grid capacity is 230 MW, we scaled it down and populated the microgrids. We assume that the nominal voltage of each bus is 2 kV i.e., a secondary station transformer 2/0.4 kV. Moreover, we assume that (i) the city has an important strategic relevance and is consequently exposed to terrorism, and (ii) the city is in a seismic zone.

Scenario. A node in the IEEE 14 node grid (see [17]) is generally modelled as a whole microgrid associated to an urban neighborhood. For instance, we focused on the total load of Node 3, which is 940 kW and indicates a microgrid constituted by the following components (see [1] for the IRENE grid component list): 1 charging station (with parking lot for 12 EVs), 17 smart houses, 8 small offices, 10 apartment blocks, 1 supermarket, and 1 energy storage i.e., a battery with fixed capacity.

Outage Scenario. After a preliminary analysis using the ETA tool on the grid scenario, we observed that a threat due to possible earthquake (i.e., IRENE threat 33 [1]) damaging Node 3 of the grid i.e., the "Energy storage" component, can cause a 6-hour outage. To clarify the validation process, we will consider this threat as responsible for an outage scenario that is used in the open modeling framework.

Exercising the Framework. We report an overview of the application of the workflow on the specified scenario. The complete description of this evaluation process can be found in [15]. According to the workflow, the first part of the process aims at estimating the exposition to threats of the grid scenario. Overall, the sample grid is exposed to 251 possible threats, roughly 69% structural and 31% that emerge from the interconnections and the relations among different components. In particular, we can observe how the IRENE threat 20 "*Conduct cyber-physical attacks on organizational facilities*" and the IRENE threat 31 "*Incorrect Privilege Settings*" emerge in the higher number of cases in this scenario. For example, cyber-physical attacks can be conducted from a smart home to the offices through the data line that is used by employees to log on organizational services using unsafe connections.

Nevertheless, the grid is in a seismic zone. Consequently, the likelihood of an earthquake is *High*. In this case, the first input state of the FAIR factor (C) is *High* and is the same for all rows in the grid components. However, the remaining input states are different for grid components, depending on the structure and the resistance of the grid components to the disaster. Results show that the Outpatient Clinic has the highest SE due to *High* probability of large-scale damages (i.e., power failure of the lines connected to Outpatient clinic), and the *Low* resistance to the damages (i.e., anti-seismic structure but no installation of backup-generations).

Considering the outage scenario due to the earthquake, power stations and line cables would be destroyed. The MGE tool would use demand management and determine the reduced total load of each microgrid during the outage. With this input data, we can apply the SILFAST test. We perform two series of experiments: one that uses regular loads, and one that take advantage of the output of the MGE tool. Considering the IEEE 14 grid topology, we obtain that using the regular loads roughly half of line failures produce multiple line overloads, ultimately leading to blackout. This adverse effect is mitigated considering reduced loads. In fact, with this loads blackouts can happen only with the failure of two lines: 1–2 and 4–9.

Then, we execute the OGM tool. Due to the earthquake, the microgrid is disconnected from the main grid. Therefore, the islanding mode operates within the microgrid level optimizing the dispatching of generating units. When the outage is solved, the islanding mode is stopped and instantaneous main grid re-connection is achieved activating the normal load. In this case, the specifications and installations of DGs, storage and renewables in the IEEE-14 node grid are adequate in responding to the complete outage. Marginal cost savings are achieved (£66.54) through the optimized generation dispatches, even though the usage of generation units is more expensive in order to balance the demand during the outage. The resilience index RI is based on the demand served during the outage [4] and computed as 1.0. The highest RI is expected due to the complete outage mitigation in this case.

From a decision making perspective, results about threat amount, mitigations, cost savings and resilience may help the city planner to understand economic and security implications of possible evolutions of the targeted power grid. For example, if a city needs a new hospital, the city planner may want to place it in the best location and with the more convenient connections with other buildings. Selecting parallel evolutionary steps where the hospital is placed in different areas of the existing topology can highlight the choice that has a better tradeoff between resilience, cost savings and security.

6 Concluding Remarks

In this paper, we described the modelling framework that was developed within the IRENE project [18]. This framework aggregates methodologies, policies and the toolset to evaluate the resilience of the targeted smart grid. The workflow implementing the methodology defined in the framework was applied to a case-study scenario based on the IEEE 14 node topology. This allowed to demonstrate the effectiveness of the framework and to show some preliminary results.

We highlight that most of the components constituting the framework are tailored for microgrids rather than generic high-voltage or mid-voltage grids. As a future work, these components can be expanded to be suitable also at a non-microgrid level.

Acknowledgments. This work has been partially supported by the Joint Program Initiative (JPI) Urban Europe via the IRENE project.

References

1. IRENE, D2.1 – Threat Identification and Ranking (2015)
2. IRENE, D2.2 – Societal Impact of Attacks and Attack Motivations (2016)
3. NIST, Guide for Conducting Risk Assessments. Special Publication 800-30, September 2012
4. IRENE, D3.1 – System Architecture Design, Supply Demand Model and Simulation (2016)
5. Mori, M., Ceccarelli, A., Zoppi, T., Bondavalli, A.: On the impact of emergent properties on SoS security. In: 11th System of Systems Engineering Conference (SoSE), pp. 1–6. IEEE, June 2016
6. Lopes, J.A.P., Vasiljevska, J., Ferreira, R., Moreira, C., Madureira, A.: Advanced Architectures and Control Concepts for More Microgrids (2009)
7. Evensen, G.: Sequential data assimilation with a nonlinear quasi-geostrophic model using Monte Carlo methods to forecast error statistics. J. Geophys. Res. Oceans **99**(C5), 10143–10162 (1994)
8. US Department of Energy, Commercial reference building models of the national building stock, Technical report NREL/TP-5500-46861, February 2011
9. OpenEI, Hourly Consumption of Commercial Buildings. http://en.openei.org/datasets/files/961/pub/COMMERCIAL_LOAD_DATA_E_PLUS_OUTPUT/USA_IL_Chicago-OHare.Intl.AP.725300_TMY3/
10. Elexon Ltd, average profiling data per Profile Class, Related content. https://www.elexon.co.uk/reference/technical-operations/profiling/
11. IRENE, D4.1 – Toolsets of supply demand prediction and threat identification and classification (2016)
12. Le, A., et al.: Assessing loss event frequencies of smart grid cyber threats: Encoding flexibility into FAIR using Bayesian network approach. In: Proceedings at the First EAI International Conference on Smart Grid Inspired Future (2016)
13. Vasenev, A., Montoya, L., Ceccarelli, A., Le, A., Ionita, D.: Threat navigator: grouping and ranking malicious external threats to current and future urban smart grids. In: Hu, J., Leung, Victor C.M., Yang, K., Zhang, Y., Gao, J., Yang, S. (eds.) Smart Grid Inspired Future Technologies. LNICSSITE, vol. 175, pp. 184–192. Springer, Cham (2017). doi:10.1007/978-3-319-47729-9_19
14. Bessler, S., Jung, O., Hovie D., Energy management in microgrids with flexible and interruptible loads. In: IEEE PES Innovative Smart Grid Technologies Conference (ISGT), Minneapolis, US, 4–9 September 2016
15. IRENE, D4.2 – Open Modeling Framework (2017)
16. Jones, J.: An introduction to factor analysis of information risk (fair). Norwich J. Inf. Assur. **2**(1), 67 (2006)
17. Christie, R.D.: Power Systems Test Case. http://www.ee.washington.edu/research/pstca/
18. IRENE Project. http://ireneproject.eu/
19. Jung, O., Bessler, S., Ceccarelli, A., Zoppi, T., Vasenev, A., Montoya, L., Clarke, T., Chappell, K.: Towards a collaborative framework to improve urban grid resilience. In: IEEE International Energy Conference (ENERGYCON), pp. 1–6. IEEE, April 2016

Outlining an 'Evaluation Continuum': Structuring Evaluation Methodologies for Infrastructure-Related Decision Making Tools

Alexandr Vasenev[(✉)], Lorena Montoya, and Dan Ionita

Services, Cybersecurity and Safety Research Group, University of Twente,
7522 NB Enschede, The Netherlands
{a.vasenev,a.l.montoya,d.ionita}@utwente.nl

Abstract. Validation of tools to support decisions on infrastructures evolutions should account for the context of their future use. Thus, the role of evaluation constructs is very important, because it identifies the operational context of a power grid. This paper reviews relevant evaluation methods that focus on partnership, collaborative planning, tool-supported collaborative planning, and individual decisions. We propose a structure called 'Evaluation Continuum' that embraces the methods. This paper aims to provide readers with a way to account for constructs relevant for validating tools. The outlined 'Evaluation continuum' can be used for planning gaming simulations and stakeholder workshops. It can be also useful for devising questionnaires for such sessions.

Keywords: Evaluation · Validation · Methods · Resilience · Continuum · Infrastructure · Decision making · Collaboration · Smart grid · Management

1 Introduction

With distributed generation changing the power grid, a number of actors, such as transmission and network operators, large consumers, and prosumers, will need to collaboratively manage the grid infrastructure. Specialized software solutions, i.e., tools to assist grid planning and management tasks, should be validated with regards to their purpose: support partnerships, collaborative planning, specific decisions, etc. Validation efforts should therefore account for relevant context factors (i.e., evaluation aspects). Due to the novel nature of this task for the electricity domain, the topic is still under development. Consequently, designing validation sessions can benefit from relevant advances in domains with similar requirements in terms of dependability, and with similar risks, such as the water management domain. Besides facing similar management challenges, water management has been advancing rapidly due to the considerable volume of research on climate change.

This paper first outlines similarities between water- and power-grid management. We then introduce a conceptual framework (the "Evaluation Continuum") that includes constructs that can be useful to validate tools before putting them to practice. Finally,

© ICST Institute for Computer Sciences, Social Informatics and Telecommunications Engineering 2017
E.T. Lau et al. (Eds.): SmartGIFT 2017, LNICST 203, pp. 243–249, 2017.
DOI: 10.1007/978-3-319-61813-5_24

we discuss how this framework can be used for validating tools developed to assist stakeholders to improve the resilience of the power grids.

2 Background

Stakeholder collaboration is vital for improving the resilience of a complex system, such as an urban grid. This was suggested, among others, by the German Federal Office of Civil Protection and Disaster Assistance that analyzed impacts of power outages lasting more than 24 h. The Office stressed the importance of involving infrastructure operators, civil protection authorities and media in disaster response [1]. The US Federal Emergency Management Agency [2] pointed out the need to involve the whole community in enhancing the resilience and security in order to bring stakeholders together, evaluate their needs, get them engaged, and raise awareness.

It is therefore expected that diverse stakeholders should be involved in the modelling and design of critical infrastructure protection [3]. To reach a good understanding of the infrastructure's vulnerability, and potential to improve its resilience, these stakeholders need to collaborate. While this situation is novel for the power grid, significant advances have taken place in the water management domain. Similarities between power and water domains, shown next, allows one to consider applying water management approaches to study tools for managing electricity.

2.1 Similarities Between Power- and Water Domains

The energy and water domains share a number of features. It concerns the critical role of the resources, distributed (renewable) generation, storage for peak and off-peak usage, and the increased use of IT (as listed in [4]).

In addition, similarities in management approaches in both domains can be observed. When necessary, important management and process evaluation aspects from the water resource management could be projected to electricity resource management. This is possible because of their similar goals and characteristics. In particular, when a blackout causes energy to become a scarce resource, water management methods can be considered. Specifically, it was suggested [5] that water resource management particularly concerns the following features:

- Water resources are often managed by the Government. Agencies involved in participation programs may therefore be particularly concerned about the cost-effectiveness of tax payers' resources, and the publics' perception (e.g., through access and representation);
- Water resource management frequently involves multiple interest groups and sponsoring agencies who may be interested in facilitating dialogues focusing on integrating multiple perspectives;
- Water management decisions might be improved by basing them on the maximum information available. Knowledge inclusion might therefore be considered an important characteristic of a good participation process.

These water management features can be projected to electricity management. They are relevant for planning the grid and managing its behavior during (partial) blackouts. The two latter features highlight the need for knowledge inclusion and involvement of multiple actors. The first one particularly emphasizes the need for fair resource distribution, public perception, and the necessity to consider governmental organizations (e.g., the city planning office in the case of urban grids).

2.2 Resilience Management

From the perspective of resilience, power grid management can also be seen as being similar to water resource management. Specifically, according to [6], resilience management has two aims that apply to both domains: (1) Prevent the system from moving to undesired configurations under stresses; (2) Nurture and preserve the elements that enable the system to renew and reorganize itself following a change.

Clearly, governance of common-pool resources invariably involves trade-offs [7]. These trade-offs exist between different stakeholder goals, between risk aversion and productivity, and between satisfying short- or long-term objectives. In power grid one might account for reaching agreements with prosumers [8]. In water management this could mean balancing salt, water and agricultural productivity [7].

Resilience management should build on a shared understanding of the system, resilience goals, and necessary trade-offs. A considerable amount of systemic feedback, cross-scale dynamic interactions, and institutional learning aspects help structuring this process. Walker et al. [6] propose four generic steps which – although intended for water management – are easily applicable to power grid management:

- Step 1: Description of system (processes, ecosystems, structures, and actors);
- Step 2: Exploring external shocks, plausible policies, and exploring vision;
- Step 3: Resilience analysis of 3–5 scenarios obtained after Step 2. This step can result in a return to either Step 1 or Step 2.
- Step 4: Stakeholder evaluation (processes and products). This step can lead to a return to step 1 or provide outputs to policy and management actions.

In sum, given the similarities between features of grid and water management tasks, one can consider applying evaluation constructs across the domains.

3   Evaluation Continuum

This section outlines an 'evaluation continuum' that sketches high level interrelations between methods used to assess (water) infrastructure planning activities, especially those performed with the help of software tools. We propose to see the activities as part of a larger context, consisting of Technology space (T-space) and Interaction space (I-Space) (Fig. 1).

Fig. 1. Evaluation continuum: structuring evaluation constructs

Validation may therefore focus on different aspects relevant to evaluation constructs: collaboration itself, collaborative planning as a process, planning with tools as a part of this process, and tool evaluation. The latter is related to: (1) decision value and (2) perception of decision maker(s). The difference between "tool evaluation" and "planning with tools" concerns the focus of the evaluation activities (see the right part of the Fig. 1 for relevant constructs).

Community collaboration can be evaluated with respect to interactions between participants. This collaboration stays mostly in the interaction domain and is less concerned with specifics of technological solutions. The Partnership Framework developed in Ireland can serve as an example of how one can evaluate this level of interaction [9]. This framework aims at helping individuals and practitioners who are either starting collaboration or need help to strengthen an existing collaboration. The goal of community collaboration is to bring individuals and members of communities, agencies, and organizations together to systematically solve problems that could not be solved by one group alone. Several *Contextual factors* influence and are influenced by the process factors. These factors include connectivity, history of joint work, political climate, policies/laws/regulations, resources, and catalysts. *Process factors* include communication, community development, understanding community, research and evaluation. *The core foundation* is formed by the interrelated Vision, Mission, and Values/Principles. Tools to foster community collaborations in smart grids, similarly to the water domain, might benefit from incorporating views on how actors see the foundation, process, and contextual factors.

A *collaborative planning process* is a process that considers collaborative planning of, e.g., land use and natural areas. Faehnle and Tyrväinen [10] evaluate this process on four dimensions – Knowledge integration, Meaningful involvement, Functioning governance, and Sustainable use of the area (outcomes) – and define several success criteria. These dimensions are important if knowledge from several domains is required, e.g., to identify a suitable location for a large field of solar panels.

Planning with tools concerns evaluation of collaborative systems, when two or more participants attempt to perform a task or solve a problem together using a tool. Compared to the previous framework element, this one concentrates more on how a planning process can be conducted. Systems are evaluated by how well they support various kinds of collaborative work. For this purpose, Cugini et al. [11] describe a 'Collaborative Framework' divided into four levels: requirement, capability, service, and technology. The Technology level is linked to the Service level. The Service level is directed towards the Capability level, which in turn is linked to the Requirement level. The framework can be used in a top-down (requirement level to technology level) or bottom-up fashion. It can be applied, for instance, to study a tool that concerns interactions between grid operators.

Evaluation of *Decision Support Systems (DSS)* – computer-based information systems to support business or organizational decision-making activities – differs from the previous method. Specifically, collaborative planning processes might require using software solutions to model and simulate specific processes and their outcomes. It is not necessary that the tool also promotes collaboration. Therefore, a tool can be evaluated in terms of its ability to support specific decisions. For instance, a tool can concentrate on how incorporating a large water or electricity consumer into the network impacts some system metrics. Three evaluation approaches – a general approach, a three-faceted approach, and a sequential approach – are discussed in [12]. Figure 2 shows the general approach: evaluation criteria influence measurement variables directly and measurement variables relate both to the decision value and to the decision makers' satisfaction. The three-faceted view sees evaluation criteria as a continuum from objective to subjective. Each aspect contains relevant evaluation objects (technical aspects, empirical aspects, and subjective aspects). Objective criteria are related to evaluating technical aspects (e.g., data flow and application control) and empirical aspects (such as cost benefit analysis). Less objective empirical aspects include decision makers' confidence and time taken. Subjective aspects include ease of use, user interface, and understanding.

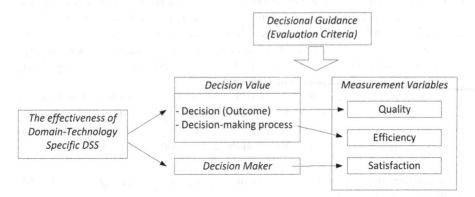

Fig. 2. The general model of DSS evaluation

All the mentioned methods highlight specific features of tools and their use.

4   Discussion on the Utilization of the Evaluation Continuum

The various approaches to evaluation (and their specific constructs) reviewed in the previous section may be useful to design validation efforts, such as stakeholder workshops, focus groups, or serious gaming sessions. In addition, the evaluation frameworks can guide the efforts to devise questions for these sessions. For instance, a workshop organizer could use the outlined Evaluation Continuum to select features and effects of a solution to be investigated. The following process can be envisioned.

First, a construct under study (e.g., resilience) should be defined. For example, one might focus on Engineering resilience, Ecological/ecosystem resilience and social resilience, or Socio-ecological resilience. The resilience plans and strategies can include various activities, such as response-recovery or education-training

Second, constructs (features) relevant to validation efforts need to be specified. For instance, knowledge integration, involvement and other relevant features of the process are to be elaborated. The interfaces between the process and the desired tools should be detailed. Features of the tools might be outlined and metrics assigned to them. Since the evaluation of some features can be complicated, e.g., demand specific domain expertise, indicators and measurement procedures should be specified.

Finally, the organizer might consider system design and systems engineering methods in connection to distinctive characteristics of workshop participants. For instance, less experienced participants of such sessions can provide their view on how a system operates as a whole ('system test' characteristic). More knowledgeable participants could answer questions related to the usability of the solutions. Questions on scalability, specific use cases and limits of applicability can be asked to more experienced practitioners. Specific views on validation constructs are to be collected.

Noteworthy, although similarities between water and grid domains do exist, special features of the grid should be accounted for when devising validation sessions. Electricity is often consumed at the same moment it is produced. Economically viable and efficient storage solutions are not yet in place. Instantly balancing supply and demand is essential. Therefore, decisions on how the grid should operate in normal conditions and under stress should be devised in advance and activated immediately when specific conditions are met. Specifically accounting for these and other features of the grid may result in a variety of framework's instantiations.

In conclusion, the designer of validation efforts (e.g., by means of stakeholder sessions or gaming workshops) could benefit from using the "Evaluation Continuum" constructs. He or she can disambiguate the context and goals of specialized tools, as well as specify measurements to be performed and questions to be asked.

Acknowledgments. This work has been partially supported by the Joint Program Initiative (JPI) Urban Europe via the IRENE project.

References

1. Hiete, M., et al.: Krisenmanagement Stromausfall. Krisenmanagement bei einer großflächigen Unterbrechung der Stromversorgung am Beispiel Baden-Württemberg (2010)
2. Federal Emergency Management Agency: A Whole Community Approach to Emergency Management: Principles, Themes, and Pathways for Action (2011)
3. U.S. Department of Homeland Security, NIPP Supplemental Tool: Executing a Critical Infrastructure Risk Management Approach (2013)
4. Hajebi, S., et al.: Towards a reference model for water smart grid. Int. J. Adv. Eng. Sci. Technol. (IJAEST) 2(3), 310–317 (2013)

5. Carr, G., Blöschl, G., Loucks, D.P.: Evaluating participation in water resource management: a review. Water Resour. Res. **48**(11), W11401 (2012)
6. Walker, B., et al.: Resilience management in social-ecological systems: a working hypothesis for a participatory approach. Conservation Ecol. **6**(1), 14 (2002). http://www.consecol.org/vol6/iss1/art14/. Accessed Jan 2017
7. Janssen, M.A., Anderies, J.M.: Robustness trade-offs in social-ecological systems. Int. J. Commons **1**(1), 43–66 (2007)
8. Verschae, R., Kato, T., Matsuyama, T.: Energy management in prosumer communities: a coordinated approach. Energies **9**(7), 562 (2016)
9. The Institute of Public Health in Ireland: Partnership Framework. www.publichealth.ie/sites/default/files/documents/files/15-PartnershipFramework.pdf. Accessed Jan 2017
10. Faehnle, M., Tyrväinen, L.: A framework for evaluating and designing collaborative planning. Land Use Policy **34**, 332–341 (2013)
11. Cugini, J., et al.: Methodology for evaluation of collaboration systems (1997). zing.ncsl.nist.gov/nist-icv/documents/method.pdf. Accessed Jan 2017
12. Rhee, C., Rao, H.R.: Evaluation of decision support systems. In: Burstein, F., Holsapple, C.W. (eds.) Handbook on Decision Support Systems 2: Variations, pp. 313–327. Springer, Heidelberg (2008)

WCSG Workshop

Optical Fibre-Based Environmental Sensors Utilizing Wireless Smart Grid Platform

Minglong Zhang[1], Kin Kee Chow[2(✉)], and Peter Han Joo Chong[1]

[1] Department of Electrical and Electronic Engineering, Auckland University of Technology,
Auckland, New Zealand
[2] School of Engineering, Manchester Metropolitan University, Manchester, UK
K.Chow@mmu.ac.uk

Abstract. With the advent and development of smart grid in recent years, traditional power grid is undergoing a profound revolution. By utilizing modern wireless technology and sensor, wireless smart grid (WSG) can effectively solve many hard and haunting issues in traditional grid, such as high maintenance costs, poor scalability, low efficiency and stability. In a WSG, data are collected by sensors at first and then transmitted to base station through wireless network. After receiving those data, corresponding actions are executed by control center. We present the integration of optical fibre-based sensor to WSG platform for real-time environmental monitoring. As a proof-of-concept, an optical fibre sensor for refractive index (RI) sensing of fresh water is adopted. The sensing mechanism relies on the reflectance at the fibre interface, where the intensity of the reflected spectra is registered corresponding to the change of the RI of the ambient environment. A sensitivity of 29.3 dB/RIU is achieved for the fabricated fibre sensor within the RI range of 1.33–1.46, and the acquired data is transmitted through wireless smart meters.

Keywords: Smart grid · Wireless sensor networks · Optical fibre sensors · Environmental monitoring

1 Introduction

Current power grid system becomes more and more complicated, as well as out of date in many aspects all over the world. Being lack of modern technology, large conventional power grids suffer from energy loss, overload condition, power quality issues, poor peak load management and time wastage on manual operation. To deal with those problems, many works have been done to upgrade our electrical grid to smart grid. By relying on latest technologies, the goal of smart grid is to provide more reliable distribution, improve fault detection and allow self-healing of the network without the intervention of technicians, create greater efficiencies in monitoring and load adjustments based on peak using times and locations, provide better security to the grid, and to empower the consumer to be able to better manage their usage and costs [1].

Compared with traditional electricity system, smart grids share several characteristics, mainly involving increased use of information and automatic control technology,

© ICST Institute for Computer Sciences, Social Informatics and Telecommunications Engineering 2017
E.T. Lau et al. (Eds.): SmartGIFT 2017, LNICST 203, pp. 253–258, 2017.
DOI: 10.1007/978-3-319-61813-5_25

integration of advanced appliances and consumer devices, dynamic optimization of grid operations and resources, deployment of smart technologies for metering, monitoring and communications concerning grid operations and status. Therefore, a smart grid mainly consists of smart meters, sensors, monitoring system, communication system and data management system [1].

Wireless communication and networking, with its low cost, high flexibility and less complexity, is widely adopted in many smart grids. In a wireless smart grid, data is firstly collected by different types of sensors and then sent to base station through wireless networks. A smart grid sensor, which serves as a detection node, can enable the remote monitoring of equipment such as transformers and power lines. For instance, smart grid sensors can monitor weather conditions and power line temperature, which can then be used to calculate the line's carrying capacity. This process is called dynamic line rating and it enables power companies to improve the efficiency of power transmission lines [2, 3].

In this paper, we propose and demonstrate the integration of optical fibre based sensors with the wireless smart grid platform for real-time remote environmental monitoring. As a proof-of-concept, optical fibre-based refractive index (RI) sensor for fresh water is investigated. Figure 1 shows the overview of wireless smart grid architecture. The sensing probe was fabricated by first fusion splicing a multimode fibre (MMF) segment to a single mode fibre (SMF). The other end of the MMF segment is then cleaved to a certain length to form a joint fibre segment. Carbon nanotubes (CNTs) were then deposited onto the cleaved end face of the MMF segment using an optical deposition procedure [4, 5]. The behavior of the sensing probe to RI perturbations in the external environment was then characterized by a variation in intensity of the spectral features in the output spectrum with little fluctuations in their wavelengths. The deposited CNTs which are known to be a material with unique optical properties, such as a high RI,

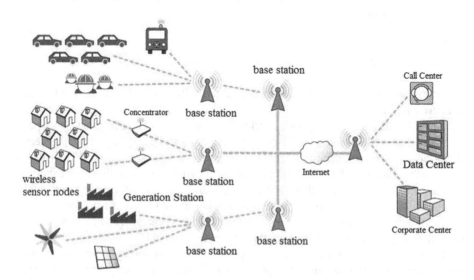

Fig. 1. Overview of wireless smart grid architecture.

enabled the sensing probe to continuously measure a wide range of RIs [6, 7]. The sensing probe also displayed little variation in intensity when it was immersed in a solution of fixed RI over a period of time and can be concluded to exhibit good stability.

2   Fabrication of Sensing Probe

In our experiment, a MMF fibre with core and cladding diameters of 105 μm and 125 μm, respectively, is first fusion spliced to a standard SMF. The MMF is then cleaved to a length of 21 mm from the SMF-MMF splice point to form the SMF-MMF joint fibre segment. To deposit CNTs onto the cleaved MMF end face of the joint fibre segment, a CNT solution is prepared by first dispersing CNT powder into a fixed volume of dimethylformamide (DMF) solution and then sonicating the resulting solution in an ultrasonic water bath for approximately 30 h. Optical deposition of CNTs onto the end face of the MMF is carried out and the structure of the fibre sensor head is illustrated in Fig. 2(a) [4, 5]. Figure 2(b) shows the microscopy image of the MMF end of the joint fibre segment after the deposition of CNTs. As can be seen, CNTs are deposited over the cleaved end face of the MMF. The output spectrum of the joint fibre segment before

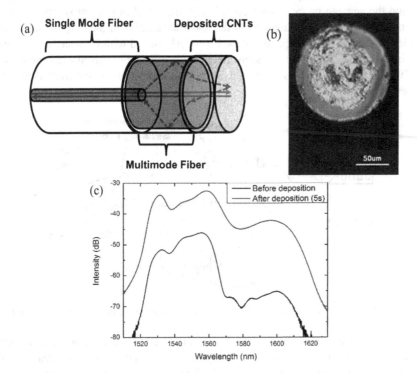

Fig. 2. (a) Schematic illustration of the sensing probe fabricated through depositing carbon nanotubes (CNTs) onto the cleaved multimode fiber end face of the joint fiber segment; (b) microscopy of CNTs deposition onto the MMF end of the joint fiber segment; and (c) the reflected spectrum of the joint fiber segment before and after CNTs deposition.

(dashed line) and after (solid line) the optical deposition process is shown in Fig. 2(c). The increase in intensity of the reflected spectrum is to be expected as the CNTs would vary the amount of reflectance, hence the change of the ambient RI can be registered.

3   Experiment and Discussion

In order to carry out the RI characterization, test solutions of different sugar concentrations and hence different RIs, are used to simulate perturbations in RI of the external environment of the sensing probe. These test solutions are prepared by first dissolving sugar into de-ionized (DI) water until a saturated sucrose solution is obtained. Fixed volumes of the saturated sucrose solution are then drawn out and diluted with different volumes of DI water to obtain the test solutions with different RIs. A commercially available refractometer is used to measure the RI of each test solution. To minimize the cross-coupling effects between RI and temperature, the characterization process is carried out in a thermally stable environment at an ambient temperature of 23.7 ± 0.1 °C. The SMF end of the sensing probe is connected to a broadband source via a circulator as shown in Fig. 3. The back reflected light from the sensing probe is monitored by an optical spectrum analyser (OSA). 1 ml of each of the test solutions is dropped on a glass slide and the sensing probe is then completely immersed in the test solution and the corresponding variation in intensity of the spectral features in the output spectra was recorded on the OSA. The sensing probe is properly rinsed with DI water and allowed to dry in between test solutions. It is ensured that the reflected spectrum when the sensing probe was exposed to air was recovered before the sensing probe was immersed in the next test solution.

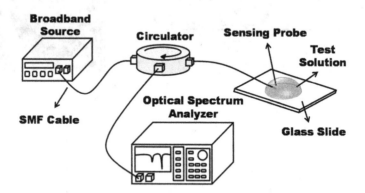

Fig. 3. Experimental setup for the RI measurements with the fabricated sensing probe.

The reflected spectra of the sensor to variations in RI of the ambient environment is shown Fig. 4. It can be seen that the intensity of the reflected spectrum decreased as the RI of the ambient environment increased. The interference dip of the reflected spectrum at 1580 nm was taken as the reference point for RI sensing measurements.

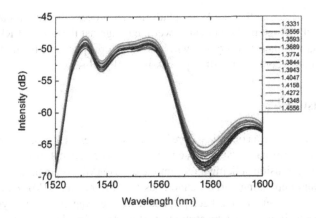

Fig. 4. Output optical spectra of the fibre sensor corresponding to different RI of the ambient environment.

According to the results in Fig. 4, the magnitude of intensity variation is approximately 3.8 dB within the ambient RI range of 1.33 to 1.46, and the sensitivity is calculated to be 29.3 dB/RIU. Considering that the intensity resolution of the OSA is 0.01 dB, the achievable resolution for the sensor can be calculated to be approximately 3.4×10^{-4} RIU. In order to feed the results into the wireless smart grid platform, the OSA in Fig. 3 is then replaced by an optical tunable bandpass filter followed by an optical amplifier and an optical power meter. The optical bandpass filter is centered at the dip of the spectra shown in Fig. 4. Hence, the change in ambient RI can be registered as a change in the output voltage of the optical power meter instead of the intensity of the

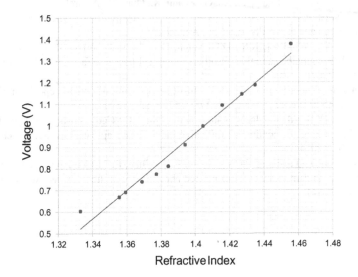

Fig. 5. Plot of the output voltage of the optical power meter corresponding to the various RIs of the external environment.

output optical spectra so that the WSG platform can process the output data. Figure 5 plots the output voltage of the optical power meter against the ambient RI of the fibre sensor. The data is then fed into the wireless smart grid platform for transmission to reach to the control center for further processing and analysing.

4 Conclusion

In summary, an integration of optical fibre based environmental sensor on wireless smart grid (WSG) platform has been proposed. As a proof-of-concept, a RI sensing probe, fabricated through fusion splicing a multimode fibre (MMF) segment to a single mode fibre (SMF) and depositing carbon nanotubes (CNT) onto the MMF end face of the resulting joint fibre segment, has been presented. The sensing probe displayed clear and distinct variations in its output spectrum to perturbations in RI of its external environment. The achievable sensitivity is calculated to be 29.3 dB/RIU for the fabricated fibre sensor within the RI range of 1.33–1.46. The sensing probe also demonstrated good repeatability and stability behaviors as the RI of the external environment varied. The acquired data has been transmitted by the wireless smart meters. Thus, it can allow scalability of the sensing areas.

References

1. Mahmood, A., Javaid, N., Razzaq, S.: A review of wireless communications for smart grid. Renew. Sustain. Energy Rev. **41**, 248–260 (2015)
2. Liu, Y.: Wireless sensor network applications in smart grid: recent trends and challenges. Int. J. Distrib. Sens. Netw. **8**(9), 492819 (2012)
3. Guo, Z., Ye, F., Guo, J., Liang, Y., Xu, G., Zhang, X., Qian, Y.: A wireless sensor network for monitoring smart grid transmission lines. In: 2014 23rd International Conference on Computer Communication and Networks (ICCCN), August 2014
4. Nicholson, J.W., Windeler, R.S., DiGiovanni, D.J.: Optically driven deposition of single-walled carbon-nanotube saturable absorbers on optical fiber end-faces. Opt. Express **15**(15), 9176–9183 (2007)
5. Kashiwagi, K., Yamashita, S., Set, S.Y.: In-situ monitoring of optical deposition of carbon nanotubes onto fiber end. Opt. Express **17**(7), 5711–5715 (2009)
6. Tan, Y.C., Ji, W.B., Mamidala, V., Chow, K.K., Tjin, S.C.: Carbon-nanotube-deposited long period fiber grating for continuous refractive index sensor applications. Sens. Actuators B **196**, 260–264 (2014)
7. Tan, Y.C., Tou, Z.Q., Mamidala, V., Chow, K.K., Chan, C.C.: Continuous refractive index sensing based on carbon-nanotube-deposited photonic crystal fibers. Sens. Actuators B **202**, 1097–1102 (2014)

Scalable Cloud-Based Data Storage Platform for Smart Grid

Hnin Yu Shwe[1]([✉]), Soong Boon Hee[1], and Peter Han Joo Chong[2]

[1] School of Electrical and Electronic Engineering,
Nanyang Technological University, Singapore, Singapore
hninyushwe@ntu.edu.sg
[2] Department of Electrical and Electronic Engineering,
Auckland University of Technology, Auckland, New Zealand

Abstract. Real-time conditional monitoring and instinctive fault diagnosis plays an important role in the smart grid systems. Conventional data storage and management systems are facing the difficulties with the disseminated, heterogeneous and large volume of data. Conventional data management infrastructure utilizes centralized approach which comprises of large-scale server, disk array data storage hardware and relational database management system (RDBMS) for database services. This type of infrastructure may result in poor performance to support the requirement of smart grid applications for very large database with high data request rates at very low latency. Precise, fast, vulnerable and cooperative information system is the basis requirement for the smart grid applications. In this paper, we proposed a distributed data storage and management platform which guarantees high scalability and reliability data storage and management with the huge amount of information in the smart grid application. In order to evaluate and validate our scalable cloud-based data storage platform for smart grid, we deployed our proposed infrastructure in our cyber-physical test-bed which is a facility to test innovative technologies for building efficiency and urban sustainability.

Keywords: Mesh · Cloud · Internet of Things · Data storage · Data management · Smart-grid

1 Introduction

The smart grid is the progression of existing electrical grid, using new technologies such as two-way information communication and computational intelligence in order to optimize the conservation and delivery of power [1]. Transforming the conventional electric delivery system to a smart grid incurs incorporation of real-time monitoring and control, distributed power sources, bi-directional energy flow between the sources and the customers. Integration of intelligent communication and control across the existing electric energy system can maximize the system interoperability and flexibility and minimize the carbon footprint.

© ICST Institute for Computer Sciences, Social Informatics and Telecommunications Engineering 2017
E.T. Lau et al. (Eds.): SmartGIFT 2017, LNICST 203, pp. 259–265, 2017.
DOI: 10.1007/978-3-319-61813-5_26

In the age of IoT, a number of physical and virtual things are interconnected to become smarter, intelligent, informative and enable people to enjoy a better quality of life [2]. Smart grid is one of the application domains of urban IoT in which grid components are considered as IoT objects. Smart grid consists of several components such as smart appliances, smart meters, ecological vehicles, home and office buildings, power plants and renewable energy resources. From IoT perspective, smart grid requires an architecture that supports all information and resources to be accessible from everywhere, obtain relevant grid operational information in efficient time manner, understand data in actual time to allow for further improvements in reliability or power quality [3].

The above illustrated requirements of the smart grid can be achieved by taking advantage of the cloud computing model. Cloud computing practices distributed resources and, as a consequence, it has the profits of greater reliability, flexibility, extensibility and powerful computing capability. To obtain a reliable infrastructure for smart grid, cloud computing solutions and services must be integrated with the conventional scheme. In this work, we proposed a scalable cloud-based data storage platform for smart grid which offers better architecture than conventional centralized scheme to accommodate massive data, analyse data in real time and make rapid decisions to improve reliability and power quality. Considering the key requirements of smart grid architecture and utilizing the modern advanced technologies, the basic idea of this work is to embed control, computational power and monitoring capabilities into the cloud.

The paper is organized as follows. In the next section, we discuss about the other related works in the literature. In Sect. 3, we describe our proposed scalable cloud-based data storage platform for smart grid system followed by its services. Finally, we provide future challenge and conclude our paper.

2   Background

Smart grid is an active field of research, and renewable energy production, real-time monitoring and prognosis health system, remote and local control over communication system play important research areas of interest [4]. The components of smart grid are distributively located in the grid, ranging from residential and office buildings, power sources to utility data and control stations. As described in the introduction, each grid component has the ability to access and exchange data via different communication protocols. Data storage and management system provides facility to store the data in a systematic way and enable the data to extract, compute and analyse either promptly or subsequently. In a conventional system, centralized magmatic hard disk drives are used to store the data.

Smart grids can be assumed as a big data challenge which involves massive amounts of data and analytic. The huge amount of data from smart grid components need to be adequately managed to achieve the maximum reliability and sustainability of the smart grid. Nowadays, cloud computing and cloud database become attractive and many people emphasize on how to obtain profits from cloud technologies in the smart grid environment [5]. A cloud database can either be a virtual or physical database. A virtual cloud database is a database which is installed on a virtual machine instance which can be purchased for a limited time. Alternatively, a physical cloud database is a database as a service in which the service provider installs and maintains the database, and application owners pay according to their usage.

Different approaches towards data center location could be used by a cloud storage provider. In a centralized cloud data storage architecture, the data are being kept in a central data center which is physically located in one geographic location and users can able to access the data via internet connection. Popular cloud data storage provider, such as Dropbox [6], follows the centralized topology and it requires the clients to access the same data center which is located in a specific location [7]. In a distributed cloud data storage architecture, in contrast, the data are being kept in several distributed data centers. The clients can access the different data center which is closest to its location geographically. Eg., Google Drive [8] utilizes the distributed topology and it uses multiple cloud storage data centers which are spread over a geographical area [9, 10].

In addition, cloud data storage can either be public or private. If the infrastructure and services are provided off-site by a third-party provider over the Internet, it is called public cloud. In private cloud, on the other hand, infrastructure and services are maintained on a private network. In spite of both cloud storage services dominate conventional data storage in terms of scalability and performance, the private cloud offers higher level of control and security over public cloud. Additionally, private cloud offers the great ability to customize the storage, computation and networking elements to optimal suit with the requirements of the specific entities.

Integrating the two modern technologies; cloud services and wireless mesh network, in this work, we introduce a cloud-based data storage platform which satisfies the requirements of smart grid applications. Proposed cloud-based data storage platform ensures users to utilize the data storage center more effectively and efficiently in terms of data storage, data accessibility, data analysis, data processing with optimal performance.

3 Proposed System

3.1 Cloud-Based Data Storage System Architecture

High level overview of our proposed cloud-based data storage architecture is presented in Fig. 1. The system is constituted by two-tier network and it mainly supports for multi-level decision making and hierarchical scheduling.

In first-tier, regional wireless mesh access points (APs) are installed in each grid point to form a mesh distributed cloud data storage network. The mesh APs are installed regionally in the grid to distributively store real-time or time-critical data. Central data storage center is considered as second-tier, in which historical and long-term data of the grid system are stored.

In wireless mesh backbone network, all mesh APs are designed with local storage drive to store the data from the grid components and organized as a

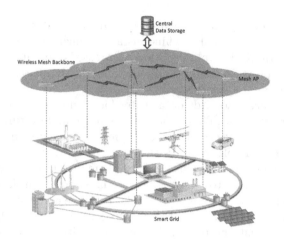

Fig. 1. High level architecture of cloud-based data storage platform.

private cloud distributed data storage network. Every node in the network collaborates for data distribution and data is available throughout the network seamlessly. Gateway node collects raw data from the grid point, store in its local drive and performs first-level data processing or analysis. The proposed cloud-based distributed data storage platform supports large scale data interaction and information exchange among different systems (regions) in the smart grid. Data interaction is available in real-time and, hence, a mesh client can able to retrieve time critical information of the other regions in the grid with near-zero latency. In order to test the performance of our proposed framework, we set up the wireless mesh network by using four-radio dual-band wireless mesh APs. Figure 2 shows the MeshRanger MN4300 AP which is compatible in both outdoor and indoor environment.

Fig. 2. A wireless mesh AP: MeshRanger MN4300.

Cloud platforms are essential to establish a software architecture that meets the requirements of smart grid applications. In the smart grid system, it is very important to constantly monitor and analyse the continuous data streams from multiple sources with near-zero latency. Taking the advantage of cloud architecture over centralized approach, our proposed distributed cloud storage architecture provides the facility to process huge, persistent streams of data in the most efficient way and transparent to the user.

3.2   Data Storing and Processing

One of the facilities of our proposed architecture is to support the user with multi-level decision making and hierarchical scheduling. To achieve this facility, our data storage architecture is composed with two-tier network and it offers data to the users hierarchically. In our data storage architecture, data are generally classified into two types: Type-A and Type-B.

We define time-critical and real-time data as Type-A and which are stored in the first tier, the wireless mesh network. Type-B data comprises historical and long-term data and these data are stored in the second tier, the central data storage. Information exchange can be taken placed among mesh APs over the wireless mesh backbone network. Efficient decision making is supported by providing data access to regional data in each mesh AP. In this way, data can be retrieved in efficient time manner and make the decision locally and perform the control timely, reducing the auxiliary effort to connect the central decision server for every decision making process.

Moreover, our proposed cloud-based data storage architecture takes the power of the cloud and offers it to the users. Proposed system performs first-level data processing with the use of cloud data computing and can execute simple data processing such as data aggregation and data extraction. Another feature of the cloud platform is that the capacity of the network storage can be efficiently and effortlessly scaled up as the system requires. In addition, the proposed architecture offers a semantic platform to make actual information available to each grid component, including connectivity to variety of devices and interoperability of multiple systems.

With the use of proposed cloud data storage platform, the grid operators can obtain the real-time information from the grid and able to understand the current situation of the grid and perform the necessary action to optimize the conservation and delivery of power. By integrating the proposed architecture with decision making service, the proposed platform compromises more value and power to all the users in the smart grid system.

3.3   Services

This section will discuss the services offered by our proposed system.

Database as a Service (DaaS): It supports the grid operators to constantly monitor the performance and condition of the grid and make the control decisions promptly and precisely. Moreover, grid operators are granted to obtain the grid data in real-time in order to immediately detect grid performance issues such as power outages and shortages. Additionally, grid operators can also able to access the long-term grid data to perform trend analyses, prediction, power distribution planning and other necessary arrangements.

Dynamic Cloud Topology: To minimize the resource request time, it supports dynamic cloud topology. The network topology varies dynamically depend upon the user's request.

High Throughput: It offers higher throughput by avoiding network congestion at central data storage. Since the users are able to obtain certain data from the regional mesh APs, it can avoid to access the central stand-alone data center for every process which may prone to heavy traffic congestion and bottlenecks at the central data center.

Data Transparency: Data transparency provides the ability to easily access the data from any point within the grid. Therefore,the users can transparently use the data storage, analyse and exchange the data among the grid components located in the different grid regions.

Low Data Communication Cost: One of the challenging factors of data communication network is data communication cost. Our proposed architecture offers lower data communication cost with the use of distributed data storage network. It minimizes the data communication by providing local data access to the regionally distributed mesh APs.

On-the-go Scaling: Since grid data are increasing rapidly from time to time, scaling plays a key role in the data storage architecture. Our cloud data storage architecture offers the users not to worry about running out of the storage space. The users can scale up the current storage space any-time, easily and seamlessly.

Easy-Access-to-Information: Another advantage of our proposed platform is easy access to the information which are geographically distributed throughout the grid. The users are not necessary to worry about their geographic locations and they can conveniently access the grid information via wireless mesh backbone network.

Massive System: This service is very important for the smart grid which is composed with several different sub-systems. Proposed framework stands as a unified data collector for assorted data types of distinct sub-systems and provides them to work under a consolidated management engine for better achievement.

4 Conclusion

This paper presented a scalable cloud-based data store platform for smart grids. The main objective of this paper is to propose a data storage framework which can handle huge amount of data in smart grid applications. From implementation and testing in our cyber-physical test-bed, we can validate the proposed framework was able to extract, store, process and query the huge amount of grid data with lowest latency. In addition, we reach our target of addressing two main critical issues, data scalability and data efficiency. From the testing in the test-bed, we could see our proposed framework achieves greater data scalability, transparency and efficiency along with an efficient and effective data storage service. We believe this framework can easily scale-up to the deployment of large-scale systems. In near future, we are going to deploy in large-scale and real environment and will improve the system by taken into accounts other performance factors.

Acknowledgement. This research is funded by the Republic of Singapore's National Research Foundation through a grant to the Berkeley Education Alliance for Research in Singapore (BEARS) for the Singapore-Berkeley Building Efficiency and Sustainability in the Tropics (SinBerBEST) Program. BEARS has been established by the University of California, Berkeley as a center for intellectual excellence in research and education in Singapore.

References

1. Zanella, A., Bui, N., Castellani, A., Vangelista, L., Zorzi, M.: Internet of Things for smart cities. IEEE Internet Things J. **1**(1), 22–32 (2014)
2. Miorandi, D., Sicari, S., Pellegrini, F.D., Chlamtac, I.: Internet of Things: vision, applications and research challenges. Ad-Hoc Networks **10**(7), 1497–1516 (2012)
3. Sadiku, M.N.O., Musa, S.M., Momoh, O.D.: Cloud computing: opportunities and challenges. IEEE Potentials **33**(1), 34–36 (2014)
4. Tao, F., Cheng, Y., Xu, L.D., Zhang, L., Li, B.H.: CCIoT-CMfg: cloud computing and Internet of Things-based cloud manufacturing service system. IEEE Trans. Ind. Inf. **10**(2), 1435–1442 (2014)
5. Hu, W., Yang, T., Matthews, J.N.: The good, the bad and the ugly of consumer cloud storage. ACM SIGOPS Oper. Syst. Rev. **44**(3), 110–115 (2010)
6. https://www.dropbox.com/
7. Drago, I., Mellia, M., Munafo, M.M., Sperotto, A., Sadre, R., Pras, A.: Inside dropbox: understanding personal cloud storage services. In: Proceedings of the 2012 ACM Conference on Internet Measurement Conference, Boston, Massachusetts, USA, pp. 481-494 (2012)
8. https://www.google.com/drive/
9. Bocchi, E., Drago, I., Mellia, M.: Personal cloud storage: usage, performance and impact of terminals. In: 2015 IEEE 4th International Conference on Cloud Networking (CloudNet), Niagara Falls, ON, pp. 106-111 (2015)
10. Drago, I., Bocchi, E., Mellia, M., Slatman, H., Pras, A.: Benchmarking personal cloud storage. In: Proceedings of the 2013 Conference on Internet Measurement Conference (IMC 2013), pp. 205-212 (2013)

Author Index

Printed in the United States
By Bookmasters